PRAISE FOR *LIVING AS THE LIVING JESUS*

"Kenneth Wozniak has fruitfully explored the ethical dimension of the letter to the Hebrews. He finds that ethics is grounded in the person and work of Jesus, as in the Gospels. But, whereas the Gospels operate from his earthly lifework, Hebrews also focuses on heavenly aspects, his post-ascension exaltation and eternal nature. Readers will come away with a deeper appreciation of the development of the Letter and its ethical orientation."

—LESLIE C. ALLEN, SENIOR PROFESSOR OF OLD TESTAMENT, FULLER THEOLOGICAL SEMINARY

"Ken Wozniak's *Living as the Living Jesus* motivates one to rethink who Jesus is and explore the implications of this. This book does not give the answers to perplexing ethical questions; rather, it mines the Scripture and proffers a way of thinking about Jesus and life's issues, while in complete dependence on the Lord, that helps one on their journey toward Christlikeness. I wish I had this book years ago."

—PATRICK KRAYER, EXECUTIVE DIRECTOR, INTERSERVEUSA

"Is your Jesus incomplete? I would've said 'no' but Ken Wozniak convinced me otherwise. Utilizing the book of Hebrews, a seasoned background in the discipline of ethics, and a pastoral heart, Wozniak demonstrates that we can only follow Jesus rightly when we understand Jesus well—all of Jesus found in the New Testament and not just the Gospel depictions. Might your Jesus be incomplete? If you said 'yes,' read this book! If you said 'no,' read it any way."

—JON LEMMOND, LEAD PASTOR, TRINITY COVENANT CHURCH, SALEM, OREGON

"As one who seeks to be apprenticed faithfully to Jesus of Nazareth in all matters of life, faith, and ethics, I naturally have looked to the example of his own life and teaching especially as given to us in the Gospels and in the Sermon on the Mount. Ken Wozniak calls for a radical rethinking of and essential enlargement of this approach to ask how the resurrected, exalted, and glorified Jesus of the book of Hebrews can and must be our inspiration, guide, and empowerment for mature Christian life, moral discernment, and ethics. I will be pondering, praying, and seeking to apply this profound insight for a long time."

—CHARLES W. BARKER, CAMPUS STAFF MEMBER, INTERVARSITY CHRISTIAN FELLOWSHIP

Living as the Living Jesus

Living as the Living Jesus

A Broader Jesus Ethic

KENNETH W. M. WOZNIAK

WIPF & STOCK · Eugene, Oregon

LIVING AS THE LIVING JESUS
A Broader Jesus Ethic

Copyright © 2021 Kenneth W. M. Wozniak. All rights reserved. Except for brief quotations in critical publications or reviews, no part of this book may be reproduced in any manner without prior written permission from the publisher. Write: Permissions, Wipf and Stock Publishers, 199 W. 8th Ave., Suite 3, Eugene, OR 97401.

Scripture quotations, unless otherwise indicated, taken from The Holy Bible, *New International Version*®, NIV®.
Copyright © 1973, 1978, 1984, 2011 by Biblica, Inc.®
Used by permission. All rights reserved worldwide.

Wipf & Stock
An Imprint of Wipf and Stock Publishers
199 W. 8th Ave., Suite 3
Eugene, OR 97401

www.wipfandstock.com

PAPERBACK ISBN: 978-1-5326-8051-9
HARDCOVER ISBN: 978-1-5326-8052-6
EBOOK ISBN: 978-1-5326-8053-3

02/01/21

To Jenica and Katrina
Unspeakable treasure,
Constant inspiration,
Unending joy

Contents

List of Tables		ix
Preface		xi
1	Introduction	1
2	The Nature of Ethics and Moral Authority	16
3	Determining a Biblical Hermeneutic for Ethics	34
4	The Historical Jesus of the Gospels and the Moral Realm	70
5	The Living Jesus of Hebrews	113
6	Toward Maturity and Faithfulness	171
7	Conclusion	196
Bibliography		201

List of Tables

Flow of Hebrews 4:14—8:6   7
Integrated Broader Jesus Ethic   195

Preface

THOSE WITH AT LEAST a modicum of understanding of the Christian faith affirm that somehow the Bible is important not only for the individual Christian, but also the Christian community, the church. Beyond that there is little agreement concerning the way the Bible is important, or how it should function. If one were to read Paul's second letter to his protégé Timothy it soon would become clear that the apostle asserted *all* Scripture is important as a guide for one's moral life, and should serve to equip one to do good. This, at least, is a partial yet tangible notion of the Bible's function: to equip one to do good. Yet further contemplation of the function of Scripture on a practical level reveals only parts of the Bible actually receive much actual focus from Christians, while others are effectively ignored.

If the ignored parts of the Bible were to receive equal attention as those that dominate the thinking of many Christians, how would our understanding of faithfulness be altered, and how would the equipping we receive for doing good be different? More pointedly, if the oft-ignored masterpiece letter to the Hebrews carried as much weight as do the Gospels in formulating the commitments of those who claim Jesus is their Lord, how would the outworking of their faith in the society in which they find themselves differ from its current expression?

One may wonder why I chose Hebrews as an example and focus of inquiry, instead of other biblical writings that normally receive little attention. The reason has to do with the significant differences between the Gospel depiction of Jesus compared with the picture in Hebrews of the second member of the trinity. The Gospel narratives show Jesus during his sojourn on earth. They primarily capture the Jesus of history, and couch that depiction within both the social context in which Jesus lived and the broader divine plan to provide salvation for fallen humanity. As historical records they do not even span the entire first century AD. Hebrews, on the other hand, while written in the mid-first century, paints a picture of the second person of the trinity subsequent to his earthly sojourn and continuing until the eschaton. Although in Hebrews certain elements of the human experience of Jesus are captured and explained in ways different and more detailed than depicted in the Gospels, the primary image of Jesus developed in Hebrews is of the present, living, exalted, and enthroned One—the object of Christians' worship when gathered together and the one whom they seek to follow in their daily lives. That being the case, this Jesus—the one pictured in Hebrews—should carry significant influence on the development of notions concerning faithfulness and maturity in the lives of God's people.

This book is not the result of a quick study. Convinced that there could be great gain in understanding Christian maturity by broadening the suite of influencing Scripture to include not only the picture of Jesus in the Gospels but also the one in Hebrews, I began twelve years ago to study Hebrews in earnest. Four years later, sociologist Dr. Ronald Enroth encouraged me to work the fruit of my study into a book. Whereas at the time I dismissed serious consideration of the suggestion, eventually it began to goad me into further efforts, the results of which I have fashioned into the present volume. I am grateful, indeed, to Dr. Enroth for taking the initiative to encourage me.

It will soon become clear that I write from the perspective of a Christian ethicist of orthodox faith. In doing so I embrace the fundamental responsibility of the ethicist not only to speak to and sometimes challenge fellow Christians regarding their moral commitments but, though fallen and fallible myself, also to speak against what I view as the ethical miscalculations that they often affirm all too readily and defend all too vehemently as essentials of orthodoxy. In doing so not only do I anticipate significant opposition, but enthusiastically welcome it as a means to greater faithfulness and maturity for us all.

This is not an issues book, and as such may be a disappointment to some. Yet in my view the wherewithal to engage responsibly with discrete ethical issues is an outgrowth of serious effort spent on prior matters, such as understanding what walking in the way of Jesus entails, seeking a broad knowledge of the nature of Christian faithfulness and maturity, and developing convictions regarding a proper Jesus-driven moral stance within the dominant society. It is in service of these prior matters that this book was written, with the hope that it will be a helpful guide to others who affirm "Jesus is Lord!"

There are many to whom I am indebted for encouragement and guidance. Among them is Mr. Matt Wimer at Wipf and Stock Publishers, who has been a source of invaluable help with and throughout the process. Due to his efforts I have been the beneficiary of an enjoyable publishing experience.

I am deeply grateful to my dear wife and fellow ethicist, Dr. Ann Mulholland Wozniak, not only for her constant support of the effort through the many years from inception to completion, but also for her critical review of the text and innumerable enriching suggestions. In the early stages of the project, communications scholar Dr. Greg Spencer graciously offered advice about the writing process, and has remained an interested supporter. Without his help I would have been lost from the start. Finally, I wish to thank President Gayle Beebe of Westmont College for his wise counsel, enthusiastic support, and continual affirmation of the effort from start to finish. Whereas all of these fellow sojourners have contributed beyond my ability to articulate, I alone bear responsibility for the book's content.

With great joy, then, I offer this volume to others for their enrichment. In the words of nineteenth-century Scottish pastor Rev. Robert Johnstone, LLB, "It only remains to commend to God this humble attempt to expound a portion of His Word. May He forgive its errors and defects and graciously employ it in some measure as an instrument for advancing the cause of truth and righteousness!"[1]

KENNETH W. M. WOZNIAK
Carpinteria, California
November 2020

---

1. Johnstone, *Lectures Exegetical and Practical*, x.

1

Introduction

THE CHRISTIAN LIFE IS not easily defined or described by the vast majority of those who claim "Jesus is Lord." If one were to survey a group of friends about the topic, the likely result would be as many answers as there are friends, with varying levels of specificity and certainty. Some may think they understand the notion completely, and others only to a lesser degree. A small number—those trusting few who are given to a high degree of vulnerability and transparency—may readily admit they don't have much of an understanding of it at all. Yet for those who maintain "Jesus is Lord," that lordship demands they live the Christian life as their Lord requires. If they do not, how can they maintain their claim?

On occasion the Christian who takes seriously the practical side of faith may ruminate on the matter of the Christian life and the way in which one may significantly enhance it, or at least incrementally grow it to a new level. The ruminating may include thoughts about the place of faithfulness, the lordship of Christ, maturity, and various other notions, all of which somehow are part of the overall arena that comprises this nebulous concept of the Christian life.

APPROACHES TO LIVING THE CHRISTIAN LIFE

One school of thought asserts that a more intense or mystical experience is either at the core of the Christian life or its goal, or both. As such, the focus is on the individual's perception that he or she has grown in maturity and faithfulness, or perhaps the witness of another that the individual appears to have grown. Energy is expended in an effort to mimic the experiences to which others give testimony, and experiential variety is perceived as Christian growth.

Another view holds that participation in various activities of a Christian community demonstrates a Christian's level of faithfulness, and constitutes faithfulness in action. Such activities may include worship services, times of meditation, learning opportunities, or other church activities. Yet Christian faith certainly is far more than mere routine participation in a structured church setting, occasional religious reflection, or personal appropriation of Christian content—as Søren Kierkegaard so convincingly argued.[1]

Without doubt there is an essential part of Christianity that entails experience, community participation, and learning. However, the Christian life is much broader than these identifiable religious elements, irrespective of an individual's confidence that through them she or he is living faithfully. The Lordship of Christ may even entail additional elements to a far greater degree than experience, community participation, or individual learning. To be sure, "The Spirit himself testifies with our spirit that we are God's children," (Rom 8:16) and God somehow mysteriously illumines the written word to us as we spend time with it. It is generally agreed by Christians that exercising one's gifts for the benefit of the church community is not optional for the serious believer. Yet these and similar believers' experiences and practices do not exhaust what it means to live the Christian life. Kierkegaard hinted at this when he wrote, "When the believer exists in his faith his existence acquires tremendous content, but not in the sense of paragraph material."[2]

What, then, constitutes ongoing, incremental growth in the Christian life in its most fundamental and practical, yet full-orbed expression? If

---

1. Søren Kierkegaard was repulsed by what he saw throughout nineteenth-century society in his native Copenhagen—a social context in which it was assumed everyone was a Christian by virtue of nominal church participation, and objectification of Christianity was the religious norm. As examples, one place he lamented "one reads a little, thinks a little about Christianity, has once in a while a religious mood—and so one is a believer and a Christian" (*For Self-Examination and Judge for Yourselves!*, 203). In *Training in Christianity* he wrote, "To be a Christian has become a thing of naught, mere tomfoolery, something which everyone is as a matter of course, something one slips into more easily than into the most insignificant trick of dexterity" (Bretall, *Kierkegaard Anthology*, 412). Elsewhere he warned, "people in our age have wanted to become objective with relation to Christianity; the passion by which every man is a Christian has become too small a thing for them, and by becoming objective we all of us have the prospect of becoming . . . a *Privatdocent*" (*Concluding Unscientific Postscript*, 541). Similar concerns were expressed in *Attack upon Christendom*.

2. Kierkegaard, *Concluding Unscientific Postscript*, 340.

someone is maturing in the Christian life, or living a life in which Christ is Lord, what minimally is occurring?

Traditional systematic theologians view the answer as part of the doctrine of sanctification, and thus hope to give guidance through statements such as, "a separation to God, an imputation of Christ as our holiness, purification from moral evil, and conformation to the image of Christ,"[3] or "*that gracious and continuous operation of the Holy Spirit, by which He delivers the justified sinner from the pollution of sin, renews his whole nature in the image of God, and enables him to perform good works*,"[4] or perhaps "that continuous operation of the Holy Spirit, by which the holy disposition imparted in regeneration is maintained and strengthened."[5]

Various forms of these expressions may work themselves into Sunday sermons through less theological language, and popular books often convey the sanctification concept using imagery more recognizable by many believers in Western contexts. While we may affirm the accuracy of the theologians' statements in whatever form we encounter them, at the same time they reflect an ontological mindset that does not give us the practical help we are hoping to get. The answers are not erroneous but from the volitional desire of a believer seeking to be more faithful to God, more mature as a Christian, or more yielded to the lordship of Christ, they fall short of the guidance the believer seeks.

Those who are inclined to look to great thinkers of the past may adopt the view of someone like John Calvin:

> For Calvin, the Christian life finds its source in the intimate spiritual union between Christ and the believing sinner. Through this intimate bond of love and trust, Christian men and women are empowered by the Holy Spirit to put to death their appetites and vanities, submit to God's sovereign will, and make steady progress in holiness.[6]

The personal relationship between the individual believer and God is fundamental and paramount in living the Christian life and maturing in the faith. It is the work of the Holy Spirit in the life of the yielded Christian that results in increasing sanctification. "The Christian life is characterized by self-denial, steady faith, undaunted hope, and unflagging joy—all shaped by the bond of love that believers share with Christ."[7]

3. Thiessen, *Introductory Lectures*, 378.
4. Berkhof, *Systematic Theology*, 532; italics original.
5. Strong, *Systematic Theology*, 869.
6. Manetsch, "John Calvin's Doctrine," 273.
7. Manetsch, "John Calvin's Doctrine," 273. For an excellent detailed review of

As was the case with the expressions of systematic theologians, Calvin's description of the Christian life is not necessarily incorrect. In fact, a great deal of it we may readily affirm. Yet it is just that—a descriptive approach, not a prescriptive one. It does little to inform the reader of what is required of the mature Christian. What is it, then, that she or he can hold on to and pursue every day, all the time, as a guidepost to Christian growth—irrespective of church tradition or lack thereof, tenure as a Christian, educational background, giftedness, political persuasion, vocation, ethnicity, national citizenship, worship style preference, or anything else? Pursuing an answer to that question, at least a nascent answer, is the purpose of this book.

CHRISTIAN MATURITY AND THE EPISTLE TO THE HEBREWS

Whatever one understands of the mature Christian life, a particular passage from the Epistle to the Hebrews presents a significant challenge to the serious believer. We will begin our investigation by considering the rather odd admonition the author of Hebrews has for the letter's recipients at the end of chapter 5 through the beginning of chapter 6, for it speaks directly to the topic we are considering:

> We have much to say about this, but it is hard to make it clear to you because you no longer try to understand. In fact, though by this time you ought to be teachers, you need someone to teach you the elementary truths of God's word all over again. You need milk, not solid food! Anyone who lives on milk, being still an infant, is not acquainted with the teaching about righteousness. But solid food is for the mature, who by constant use have trained themselves to distinguish good from evil. Therefore let us move beyond the elementary teachings about Christ and be taken forward to maturity, not laying again the foundation of repentance from acts that lead to death, and of faith in God, instruction about cleansing rites, the laying on of hands, the resurrection of the dead, and eternal judgment. And God permitting, we will do so.[8]

The goal at this point is not to add more exegetical commentary to the extensive body already available on Hebrews 5–6. A vast array of outstanding scholars has thoroughly exegeted the passage in great detail. However,

---

Calvin's teaching on the Christian life, see the entire article by Manetsch.

8. Heb 5:11—6:3.

reviewing some of their basic conclusions will focus our attention as we launch our investigation of the practical Christian life. To begin, a bit of background on the Epistle to the Hebrews will be of benefit.

One of the aims of the letter's author was to show that the new covenant, which is mediated through the Son, is superior to the old covenant between God and Israel. It is assumed by the author that the reader is familiar with Israel's history and Jewish religious practice. As such, the author felt free to quote from the Old Testament some thirty times. All of the quotations, however, are from the Septuagint, a translation of the Hebrew Old Testament into Greek initially produced in the mid-third century BC. According to Jewish tradition, the Septuagint was the work of seventy Jewish elders in the city of Alexandria, Egypt, and was widely used by Alexandrian Jews. Whereas many theories have been put forth regarding the identity of the author of Hebrews, in the final analysis the third-century church father Origen of Alexandria was correct in asserting only God knows who the author was. Yet it is clear from the text of the letter that the author not only was familiar with the Septuagint, he or she also was thoroughly schooled in Alexandria's Platonic and Stoic philosophy, and was particularly influenced by Alexandria's Jewish philosopher Philo.

In the chronology of the New Testament documents Hebrews was written after the Epistle of James and the Epistles of the apostle Paul, but before the four Gospels and John's Revelation. Thus, the readers of the letter may have been exposed to the Jewish mindset of James' moral treatise and to Pauline thought, but only knew the life of Jesus from oral traditions and perhaps firsthand witnesses. Their understanding of the post-ascension Jesus was not informed by John's vision as recorded in Revelation.

Why is this important for an understanding of the end of Hebrews chapter 5 and the beginning of chapter 6? We will see that the language used by the letter's author, as well as the meaning of certain intentionally chosen terms, is clarified by recognizing the Alexandrian philosophical thought the author employed to issue a basic admonition to the letter's readers. Also, it would be erroneous to seek to understand the language of Hebrews by appealing to language or arguments found in the Gospels, the Revelation, or other New Testament documents that were written subsequent to the writing of Hebrews, and thus were not foundational to the readers' understanding of Christianity. Rather, it is the readers' religious background as Jews and their understanding of the Septuagint that give us insight as we attempt to discern the epistle's message.

Let's return to the passage from Hebrews 5 and 6. Consider that word "mature" used by the author in 5:14. The Greek word is *teleion*, a broad word whose basic meaning is "having attained the end or purpose, complete, perfect."⁹ The Greeks often used the word to connote "totality."¹⁰ When referring to individuals it carries the meaning of "full-grown, mature, adult."¹¹ Contrasted with the immature, or children, the word in the New Testament takes on a particularly ethical tone—a sense also found in Stoic philosophy.¹² Of particular note is the fact that the word occurs in the Alexandrian philosophical thought that influenced the author of Hebrews, where its meaning includes the notions of moral good, ethical decision-making, values, virtues, and moral abilities.¹³

What is emerging is the possibility that the kind of maturity in the mind of the author of Hebrews, influenced by and employing the Alexandrian context in which his or her own intellectual outlook developed, is some form of maturity in the moral realm, rather than mere theological content, religious experience, or community participation. This idea is strengthened by considering two words in the descriptor of maturity that follows immediately in verse 14.

We find in the text that the mature are those who, through some form of ongoing praxis, have developed the ability to distinguish good from evil. The Greek text uses *kalou* and *kakou* for "good" and "evil," respectively. The word for "good" carries the overall sense of something that is inherently beautiful or intrinsically useful. It includes a sense of the noble or the moral good, particularly when coupled with *kakou*.¹⁴ It also carries the sense of moral good when describing an individual's inward disposition. Within Greek philosophical thought the word was central and paramount. If we recall that the author of Hebrews was utilizing the philosophical environment in which she or he was raised, then perhaps Aristotle's understanding of the word—that the good is the result of moral excellence—is part of what the author had in mind. For the Jewish philosopher Philo the word carried a religious significance, and as such referred to moral action that engendered the favor of God. In order to connect this text's admonition to the Jewish audience's mindset, the author appears to have employed Philo's thought, for Old Testament and Jewish ethics understood the word to refer to the moral good.¹⁵ In choosing this word, the author's intent was to call the

---

9. Bauer, *Greek-English Lexicon*, 816.
10. *TDNT*, 8:73.
11. Bauer, *Greek-English Lexicon*, 817.
12. Trench, *Synonyms of the New Testament*, 75–76.
13. *TDNT*, 8:69–70.
14. Bauer, *Greek-English Lexicon*, 401.
15. *TDNT*, 3:537–44.

readers to pursue moral uprightness—not theological content or religious experience—as a demonstration of Christian maturity.

In contrast to moral excellence, the passage's word translated "evil" fundamentally conveys that which is evil, inferior, or against the law,[16] but also includes notions of weakness, lack of ability, incapacity, that which is morally bad, and wickedness.[17] For Philo it is a religious word related to sin, and carries an ethical sense. In the prophets, Psalms, and Proverbs, it is a morally laden term, and the end of such moral evil is death.[18]

Use of these three words clearly was an intentional attempt by the author to focus the readers' attention on the moral realm. The admonition to pursue maturity—the ability to distinguish moral uprightness from moral perversity—is at the core of what the author had in mind. He or she wanted the readers to realize that what minimally is required of them is not more learning, as important as that may be. Nor is experience, be it individual or corporate, to be the focus of their efforts. Rather, the faithful, mature Christian life entails good moral thought, commitment, and action.

To gain a fuller understanding of what this notion of maturity entails, we must include the rest of the passage in our study, from verse 11 of chapter 5 to verse 3 of chapter 6. Immediately after 6:3 there is a section that deals with those who have been exposed to the word of God but rejected it, an exhortation to perseverance, and a reassurance about inheriting God's promises. It, along with verses 5:11—6:3, comprise a section on God's requirements of, and promises to, the mature and faithful. After that, however, is a very long section on Melchizedek, as well as Jesus as a priest in the order of Melchizedek. It is a continuation of another long passage that occurs immediately before the one we are considering—one that also deals with Jesus the great high priest in the order of Melchizedek. The surrounding context and the passage itself, then, is structured like this:

FLOW OF HEBREWS 4:14—8:6			
Hebrews 4:14—5:10	Hebrews 5:11—6:20		Hebrews 7:1—8:6
	God's requirements of and promises to the faithful		
Jesus the great high priest like Melchizedek	5:11—6:3 Description of the mature believer	6:4–20 Risks of faithlessness, perseverance, and God's promises	Melchizedek and Jesus, a high priest like Melchizedek

16. Bauer, *Greek-English Lexicon*, 398.
17. *TDNT*, 3:469.
18. *TDNT*, 3:474–81.

Thus Hebrews 5:11—6:3 is part of a parenthetical section sandwiched between two very long passages that deal with a confusing and difficult subject: the high priests Melchizedek and Jesus. Why is this?

The author wanted to convey to the readers a great deal about the high priesthood, Melchizedek, and Jesus, but found it difficult to do so due to the readers' lack of understanding of the basics of God's word. In 5:12–13, she or he went so far as to indicate that the readers are infants when it comes to perceiving elemental truths, and thus found it necessary to insert 5:14—6:3. The curious thing, at least from what we have learned thus far, is that the inserted portion appears to deal not with additional theological truth, but rather with ethics. Could it be that something having to do with ethics is the necessary foundation for understanding Jesus, Melchizedek, and the high priesthood they share?

One interpreter of Hebrews views the admonition to maturity found in 5:14 as "basically an invitation to imitate Christ,"[19] but then goes on to explain that "Jesus is the pioneer to be followed, not simply a fellow traveler to be imitated. No one else could have blazed the trail. A Christian who faithfully imitates Jesus is like a pianist who plays Mozart well."[20] The way to start doing this is to "move beyond the elementary teachings about Christ," as 6:1 indicates. Those elementary teachings are then outlined in the rest of verses 1 and 2. However, the author did not choose that list of teachings at random; rather, they consist of "the material that would be imparted to someone who was becoming a new member of the Christian community."[21] These are the first teachings a new member would be required to know and affirm as the content she or he would hold in solidarity with the other members of the community.

Why was it that the readers of Hebrews had either remained infants in their understanding of God's word, or regressed into infancy? Perhaps it was because the congregation was in fear for their lives, facing the specter of martyrdom for being Christians.[22] Remember that they were Jews, and likely responded to the threat of martyrdom by trying to remain Christians, but only barely so. "Quite probably they were deliberately holding to a minimalist Christianity that also could pass as a form of Judaism (and thereby avoid persecution)."[23] The result was they were still immature believers, just

---

19. Long, *Hebrews*, 72.
20. Long, *Hebrews*, 72.
21. Long, *Hebrews*, 72.
22. For more on the argument that the readers of Hebrews were facing martyrdom, see Lane, *Hebrews*, 88–89.
23. Hagner, *Encountering the Book of Hebrews*, 86.

as they had been when their Christian faith was in its infancy. 5:14 uses moral language to describe their obligation as Christians, for "The 'adult' is the mature Christian who will recognize the moral claim of God upon his life, even if it exposes him to martyrdom."[24] Since the location and immediate social situation of the recipients is not known for certain, it also is not certain that the threat of imminent martyrdom was the singular reason the readers were tempted to adopt a minimalistic form of Christianity. Yet they already had suffered significantly as a result of becoming Christians, even though they had not yet been forced to shed their blood[25]:

> Remember those earlier days after you had received the light, when you endured in a great conflict full of suffering. Sometimes you were publicly exposed to insult and persecution; at other times you stood side by side with those who were so treated. You suffered along with those in prison and joyfully accepted the confiscation of your property, because you knew that you yourselves had better and lasting possessions.[26]

In light of the suffering they had endured by embracing the Christian faith, "Very probably they were reluctant to sever their last ties with a religion that enjoyed the protection of Roman law and face the risks of irrevocable commitment to the Christian way."[27] Even with the uncertainty about the reason for the readers' ongoing Christian infancy, what is certain is that the author recognized the readers' nascent Christianity, and then realized the passage had to be included as a means to call them to maturity.

There is more, however, to be learned from the passage itself. One textual exegete asserts that the entire end of chapter 5, verses 11–14, "is full of ideas and terms current in the ethical and especially the Stoic philosophy of the day."[28] The first of these occurs in verse 11, and has been translated "you no longer try to understand." Actually it is an ethical term, and conveys the sense of mental sluggishness or dullness, rather than lack of effort.[29] The author of Hebrews is pointing out to the readers that they cannot understand subjects like Jesus' and Melchizedek's high-priestly function because they suffer from insensitivity or imprecise thinking in the moral realm. What this means is not exactly obvious at this point, but it is clear the author's

24. Lane, *Hebrews*, 89.
25. See Heb 12:4.
26. Heb 10:32–34.
27. Bruce, *Epistle to the Hebrews*, xxx.
28. Moffatt, *Critical and Exegetical Commentary*, 69.
29. Moffatt, *Critical and Exegetical Commentary*, 69.

focus from the outset is an ethical one, and the readers' moral acuity is insufficient to grasp it.

In verse 12 the author employed common Greek philosophical phrasing concerning one's obligation—"by this time you ought to be teachers." He or she actually was trying to shame the readers into fulfilling their moral obligation. The argument continues through the imagery of milk and solid food, another metaphor borrowed from Greek ethical philosophy, particularly the Jewish philosopher Philo.[30] At the end of verse 13 we find the phrase, "teaching about righteousness." If the commentator is correct who argues that this is an expression for "*instruction concerning a willingness to experience martyrdom*,"[31] as the reader's prior suffering and resultant regression into minimalist Christianity may suggest, then the phrase is specifically addressing not theological content, but rather the attitude, commitment, volition, and potential conduct of the readers, all of which are moral elements. What is incontrovertible, however, is that the phrase is yet another ethical one which refers to what we would call "moral truth."[32]

We previously considered three words in verse 14: "mature," "good," and "evil," and learned they suggest strongly the kind of maturity the author has in mind is something in the moral realm, rather than those of knowledge or experience. That being the case, we would expect to find more language that references values, commitments, conduct, and the like. Indeed, that is what we discover when looking at the totality of verse 14. Notice the verse indicates the mature are "those who by constant use have trained themselves." That expression, not surprisingly, is yet another from Greek philosophical thought, and is used to describe senses that are conditioned by the development of habits. Aristotle distinguished such habits from either powers or passions[33]—features which are more innate than those which are developed, such as habits. The language referring to senses is borrowed from Stoic philosophy, and carried an ethical tone.[34] Taken together, the key terms describe faculties which, through exercise or practice, have been sensitized and developed in such a way that they function habitually.[35] In the passage upon which we are focusing, such trained faculties enable the possessor to function consistently—even habitually—in a mature manner in the moral realm. F. F. Bruce summarized the author's teaching like this:

30. Moffatt, *Critical and Exegetical Commentary*, 70–71.
31. Lane, *Hebrews*, 89; italics original.
32. Moffatt, *Critical and Exegetical Commentary*, 71.
33. Dods, *Epistle to the Hebrews*, 292.
34. Moffatt, *Critical and Exegetical Commentary*, 72.
35. Bauer, *Greek-English Lexicon*, 24, 275.

"It is ethically mature men,[36] those 'who by reason of use have their senses exercised to discern good and evil', who have built up in the course of experience a principle or standard of righteousness by which they can pass discriminating judgment on moral situations as they arise."[37]

The first three verses of chapter 6 explain how the author proposed to proceed, in light of the teaching at the end of chapter 5. Normally it would be expected that a return to the "milk," or "elementary truths of God's word" would be the course chosen, and progress would be made to bring the readers up to the "solid food" required of the mature. This, however, is not the case. Rather, the author decided to forego such an approach and instead required the readers to jump right to mature functioning in the moral realm as delineated in 5:14.

Notice the author's chosen approach in chapter 6 actually is a *result* of the teaching in chapter 5. Chapter 6 began with the Greek term translated "therefore." It conveys an inferential sense. The author actually was returning to the broader context that gave rise to the parenthetical section starting in 5:11. Recall that the subject matter prior to the section on moral maturity dealt with the high priestly function of Melchizedek and Jesus. It is because of the author's focus on this subject matter that he or she chose to require the readers to focus on maturity in the moral realm immediately, rather than rehearsing anew the "elementary truths." An essential element of such moral maturity involves grasping Jesus' current high priestly function in the order of Melchizedek—something missing from the readers' comprehension of what the Christian life entails. How that is the case is not yet clear, but the author was forcing the readers to jump to it anyway. One commentator paraphrases the author's message to the readers this way: "you must make an effort to enter into this larger appreciation of what Christ means."[38]

What is it, exactly, that the author was so eager to abandon, and why is this? Verses 1 and 2 of chapter 6 identify the six doctrines that comprise the "elementary teaching about Christ:" "repentance from acts that lead to death," "faith in God," "instruction about cleansing rites," "laying on of hands," "resurrection of the dead," and "eternal judgment." These do not initially strike the modern-day Western Christian as elementary. In fact,

---

36. The use of the term "men" by F. F. Bruce reflects the common understanding of his day in his setting in the United Kingdom—that use of such a masculine term is inclusive of both genders. Today authors use gender-neutral terms that actually include both genders. In the case of the quote above, a term such as "individuals," rather than "men," reflects current use, and more accurately reflects the intent of the author of Hebrews.

37. Bruce, *Epistle to the Hebrews*, 109.

38. Moffatt, *Critical and Exegetical Commentary*, 73.

it would be difficult to find many modern believers who can explain such doctrines fully and accurately. Why, then, did the author brand them as "elementary?"

Several scholars who have studied the social and religious context of the letter's Jewish Christian readers suggest what may be the key to understanding why these doctrines are elementary. One comments that "it is remarkable how little in the list is distinctive of Christianity, for practically every item could have its place in a fairly orthodox Jewish community."[39] Another points out the entire list could be affirmed by a non-Christian Jew, and thus the author's Jewish Christian readers had not progressed at all since becoming Christians.[40] It is not surprising, then, that the author saw no reason to spend any effort teaching these doctrines again to the readers, for even though modern-day Christians may be unable to articulate them accurately, in the first century they were not particularly difficult for those raised in Judaism, nor were they distinctively Christian at all. The author's desire was for Christians to mature in their faith, and teaching fundamental doctrines was not the path to achieve Christian maturity.

As a means to help the readers mature, then, the author returned to her or his prior teaching. After the parenthetical section in which maturity is presented as a wholly ethical notion—something the believer achieves only with continual focus on and participation in the moral realm—the author reminded the readers of the fate of those who have been exposed to but reject the word of God, the need for diligence, and the hope of God's promises. There is then a return to a presentation of the postascension Jesus as the readers' forerunner. In some way we do not yet understand, the Jesus depicted in Hebrews is the key to living faithfully in the moral realm, and living the Christian life to which God calls all believers.

In verse 3 of chapter 6 the author acknowledged that the effort to bring his or her readers to maturity requires the enabling of God. Even though such phrases were typical in correspondence of the day,[41] the author's inclusion of it served as a reminder to the readers, as it does for us today, that Christian maturity is not a simple matter, and requires the ongoing enabling of God as the believer's efforts and commitments are focused in the moral realm.

The challenge before us is to pursue an answer to our fundamental question, "What can the believer hold on to and pursue every day, all the time, as a guidepost to Christian growth?" From Hebrews we know that

---

39. Bruce, *Epistle to the Hebrews*, 112.
40. Hagner, *Encountering the Book of Hebrews*, 86.
41. Moffatt, *Critical and Exegetical Commentary*, 76.

the path travels through the moral realm, and in some way involves the living, current, postascension Jesus. What, then, should be the route of our journey?

In looking at verse 14 of chapter 5 we learned that living the Christian life in a mature way requires the habitual use of faculties that have been sensitized and developed through exercise and practice. The result is sound moral judgment. How does this sensitization and development occur? We know disciplined and repeated effort is involved, which suggests the mature believer has at her or his disposal a toolset of some sort that can be employed in a consistent and deliberate manner in the moral realm. Rote adherence to a "code of ethics" or simply doing what one was taught while growing up is not the way to Christian maturity, for such immature approaches are insufficient to render good moral judgment in the vast array of ethical situations the believer will encounter. They may even result in an abdication of moral responsibility in favor of simply "doing what I was told." Instead, working in the moral realm requires the appropriate application and leveraging of a set of honed and sensitized skills and abilities in any ethical situation the mature believer encounters.

THE PATHWAY FORWARD

The rest of the book is structured in such a way as to present the set of tools the mature believer, seeking to live a faithful Christian life, needs in order to reflect the affirmation, "Jesus is Lord." They are not just for the individual, however. When adopted and applied by a Christian community, the result is a community that, as a collective, is mature and faithful to its Lord. Some of the tools have to do with conceptualization, understanding, and awareness; others focus on approach, process, and technique. It needs to be noted and strongly reinforced that repeated use of sensitized skills can be done in nearly an infinite number of ways, and so it would be a mistake to seek a formula for working in the moral realm. Maturity involves individual (or in the case of a community, collective) but consistent judgment, commitment, and action. This is the place for moral courage and creativity, but not moral license.

The second chapter starts building a common understanding of ethics by establishing the nature and scope of the moral realm in which Christian maturity occurs, and probes the nature and objective of ethical thought. The complex and nebulous notion of authority in the moral realm is also explored, concepts promoted by several authorities on the subject are presented, and current commonly accepted authoritative priorities are investigated. Initially it may be assumed that what ethics entails is obvious, but soon it should become clear that understanding the scope of ethics is not quite so simple. Furthermore, as Christians our authority for living in the moral realm needs to be explored, for without a solid understanding of authority our moral foundation will be less than it should be.

Some forty years ago I had occasion to visit the church where I formerly served as associate pastor. One of the dear saints in that congregation, an elderly man who had been part of that community for many years, asked me what I had been involved in since I left that church. When I told him I was working on a PhD in ethics he responded, "How is it possible that there is a PhD in ethics? Just do what the Bible says." That dear saint was quite sincere, but also somewhat naïve. Knowing how to be faithful to the written word of God involves much more than simply "doing what the Bible says." Exploring the subject of the Bible and ethics is the task of chapter 3. It includes an overview of how ethicists have attempted to bridge the gap between the Bible and ethics for our modern society, investigation of the tradition of the Bible as the sole rule not only for belief but also for conduct, a presentation of the difficulties encountered when using the Bible for ethics, and a review of traditional approaches to hermeneutics. After summarizing various ways the Bible can function authoritatively in the moral realm, an appropriate and sufficient Jesus-based biblical hermeneutic for ethics is suggested.

The fourth chapter introduces the Jesus of the Gospels into the subject of ethics, and investigates the question of what place Jesus should have in the Christian's thought and conduct when working in the moral realm. Various historic ways Jesus has been viewed as a moral authority are reviewed, including the views of certain prominent nineteenth-century figures, and Jesus as pictured in the Gospels is developed as a moral authority. A normative view of Jesus' life in his historical and social context is presented, including the role of the Sermon on the Mount, and the significance of the cross and postresurrection period for ethics is investigated.

In the fifth chapter, the picture of Jesus as found in Hebrews is developed. It will be seen that this picture is significantly different from the picture of Jesus that was developed later in the Gospels. The humanity of Jesus is first explored, followed by Jesus' current functions as both the exalted and eternal Son as well as High Priest—the one who is simultaneously like and unlike Melchizedek and superior to all other priests.

In chapter 6, the full picture of Jesus, both the image found in the Gospels and the one found in Hebrews, serves as the basis for formulating a normative ethic by which the mature and faithful can live. The need to embrace the complete Jesus picture when formulating the ethic is demonstrated, and the ethic's constituent components are described. Finally, the broader Jesus ethic, based upon both the historic Jesus of the Gospels and the current, living Jesus of Hebrews, is presented as the appropriate and necessary ethic. By it the faithful can fulfill the expectation of Hebrews that Christian maturity consists in the ability to distinguish good from evil.

The conclusion suggests several learnings from the study that will aid the faithful in their quest to follow in the Jesus way. Practical implications of the learnings help concretize an approach to the broader society that the mature should consider. Finally, some cautions are suggested concerning common ways Christians often accommodate themselves to the surrounding environment in which they live. The hope is that greater maturity and faithfulness will result.

2

The Nature of Ethics and Moral Authority

As a starting point for understanding the call of Hebrews 5, the nature, scope, and limits of the moral realm should be outlined. This will establish a common understanding of ethics as we move through our investigation of the nature of Christian maturity. While circumscribing the arena in which we are working we will soon discover the matter of authority in that arena is a major topic for consideration. With these two subjects, then—the nature of ethics and the notion of moral authority—we will launch our quest to understand how to grow in faithfulness.

ETHICS

During the last half of the twentieth century a noticeable shift occurred within Western society's thinking about ethics and the moral realm, or at least the common understanding of those terms. Our first impression of this shift may be a negative one, for the shift entailed the influence of relativistic thought, contextualization of truth, and the rise of individual expression at the expense of standards for thought and conduct, subjectivism, and the like. Compare this with the understanding of ethics expressed by that old saint from my church that I mentioned in the first chapter, who felt ethics entailed simply doing what the Bible says. His naive and overly simplistic approach implied this was a straightforward matter, for all who would read the Bible certainly would come to the same convictions he had regarding right and wrong, good and bad.

All is not negative with the current situation, however. In fact, the rise in complexity associated with notions of good and bad, right and wrong, morally upright conduct both by the individual and the broader society, virtues, attitudes, and other ethical elements has resulted in greater reflection not only about the nature of the moral realm, but also about how the individual should establish him- or herself as a moral entity. Rather than simply accepting and acquiescing to parental and societal strictures enforced during childhood, or governmental ones during adulthood, individuals to a greater degree are establishing for themselves the convictions and commitments by which they will live, with the commensurate ethical disagreements and debates that find expression throughout the structures of society. Such questioning drives all of us to embrace our responsibility as moral agents, rather than simply to accept what we have been taught without reflection, or what has been legislated. This indeed is a positive change from times past.

This area in which we function as moral agents is, according to the writer of the Epistle to the Hebrews, the sphere of experience in which Christian maturity occurs. It is through developed and honed skills that the mature Christian is able to pass judgment about good and evil. What, however, is this sphere of experience? What distinguishes ethics and the moral realm, and how do they compare with other arenas of human experience? The answers are neither simple nor clear, and there is great disagreement over how to approach these questions. Yet a sampling of thought regarding the nature of ethics will help us form at least a basic sense for this area.

Defining Ethics

In their book, *Readings in Ethics*, editors Gordon H. Clark and T. V. Smith assert that ethics as a distinct discipline dates back to the fifth century BC. They write, "until the later half of the fifth century little systematic attention was paid to ethics."[1] Aristotle is credited with the first systemization of ethics in Western culture when he produced his *Nicomachean Ethics* in the fourth century BC.[2] That work begins with the following sentence: "Every craft and every inquiry, and similarly every action and project, seems to aim at some good; hence the good has been well defined as that at which

---

1. Clark and Smith, *Readings in Ethics*, 9.
2. Albert et al., *Great Traditions in Ethics*, 37.

everything aims."³ Since then the field of ethics has struggled with its own self-understanding. One book on the history of ethics puts it this way: "The initial problem of ethical theory is that of defining the nature of ethics."⁴ It goes on to point out that associating ethics with conditions for human happiness may reflect Aristotle's view of ethics, but not that of, for example, Immanuel Kant. Conversely, to associate ethics with duties would align more closely with Kant's ethics, but would not represent Aristotle's ethics at all.⁵ To express the challenge another way, one source regards the definition of ethics as one of many "unresolved problems of ethical theory," claiming that "Each ethical theorist conceives ethics in his own way."⁶

One such ethical theorist was Henry Sidgwick, a nineteenth-century professor of moral philosophy at the University of Cambridge. An ethical utilitarian, Sidgwick "acknowledging the vagueness of ethics' boundaries, defined the subject as a rational procedure for determining what individual human beings 'ought' to seek to realize by voluntary action."⁷ Notice that Sidgwick not only admits the scope of ethics cannot clearly be defined, he also suggests it minimally has to do with matters of individual obligation. This at least gives us a hint at what characterizes the moral realm, and distinguishes it from other arenas of human experience. The moral realm is that of duty; that which is obligatory. It includes notions of that which is requisite or imperative, responsibility, aspirations, and the like, in the sphere of right and wrong, good and bad.

To help clarify the concept of "ought," it will be helpful to think of "ought" in contradistinction to that which "is." Whereas there are ethicists who contend that in reality the distinction is a false or artificial one—one that does not reflect the true nature of how ethical thinking should be conducted in the real world—nevertheless conceptualizing the distinction has benefit when trying to define the borders of ethics and the moral realm. To that end, consider for a moment the field of systematic theology. How should it be characterized as distinct from the field of ethics? One classic theologian defines theology as "the science of God and of the relations between God and the universe. . . . Theology, therefore, gives account, not only of God, but of those relations between God and the universe in view of which we

---

3. In his excellent book on the history of ethics Alasdair MacIntyre begins his chapter on Aristotle's ethics by citing this passage. Later we will see that MacIntyre asserts a fundamental problem specifically with Christian ethics. See MacIntyre, *Short History of Ethics*, 57.

4. Albert et al., *Great Traditions in Ethics*, 7.

5. Albert et al., *Great Traditions in Ethics*, 8.

6. Albert et al., *Great Traditions in Ethics*, 8.

7. Clark, "Ethics, History Of," 220.

speak of Creation, Providence and Redemption."[8] As such, the theologian's efforts are bound by the world of objective facts. "The aim of theology is the ascertainment of the facts respecting God and the relations between God and the universe, and the exhibition of these facts in their rational unity, as connected parts of a formulated and organic system of truth."[9] A theologian, then, "is the servant and interpreter of the objective truth of God."[10] Facts and objective truth are at the heart of theology according to this theologian, and give definition to the boundaries of the theologian's work. The theologian's world is the world of that which "is." It is not the world of "ought." In contradistinction to theology's world of that which "is," obligation, the requisite, responsibility, values, attitudes, intentions, virtues, conduct, consequences, and the like—in short, the arena of "ought"—circumscribe the sphere of ethics, as opposed to that of theology.

Some attempt to deal with the difficulty not by trying to establish the scope and extent of ethics definitionally, but rather descriptively. The Markkula Center for Applied Ethics at Santa Clara University readily acknowledges, "The meaning of 'ethics' is hard to pin down,"[11] but attempts a descriptive approach by suggesting, "Ethics is based on well-founded standards of right and wrong."[12] It continues by indicating ethics deals with the standards that outline obligatory human conduct, and that ethics "refers to the study and development of one's ethical standards."[13] It is arguable whether development of and adherence to standards form the core and scope of ethics; however, viewing ethics descriptively is a common way to deal with the issue of what ethics actually entails.

Another approach to clarify the nature of ethics descriptively is to circumscribe it by formulating a set of questions with which moral reflection deals. Clark and Smith state simply, "The very first question ever asked was, What things ought I to do? And every moralist since then has to some extent tried to answer. The early moralists occupied themselves chiefly with this one problem."[14] They go on to list questions that have to do with the meaning of moral terms, the means of dealing with virtues when they conflict with each other, and what exactly it is that determines if something

---

8. Strong, *Systematic Theology*, 1.
9. Strong, *Systematic Theology*, 2.
10. Strong, *Systematic Theology*, 2.
11. Velasquez et al., "What is Ethics?," line 10.
12. Velasquez et al., "What is Ethics?," line 1.
13. Velasquez et al., "What is Ethics?," lines 35–36, 43.
14. Clark and Smith, *Readings in Ethics*, 5.

is right or wrong.[15] This last question leads to an investigation of moral authority—a subject we will deal with directly in the next section. Its vital importance is made clear, however, when considering a question like, "is all morality an illusion, foisted on one group of people by another?"[16] A clear conviction concerning the authority for ethics lifts the moral realm out of the mire of illusion.

Christian Ethics

When considering Christian ethics in particular the questions do not get any easier. MacIntyre sums up the matter by stating, "the whole problem of Christian morality is to discover just what it is."[17] He is not alone in his thinking. James McClendon warns, "there is an inherent complexity in Christian moral life not safely to be disregarded by those who want to get the story straight."[18] MacIntyre challenges us even further when he points out the difficulty in simple, direct extrapolation from the New Testament teachings:

> The paradox of Christian ethics is precisely that it has always tried to devise a code for society as a whole from pronouncements which were addressed to individuals or small communities to separate themselves off from the rest of society. This is true both of the ethics of Jesus and of the ethics of St. Paul. Both Jesus and St. Paul preached an ethics devised for a short interim period before God finally inaugurated the Messianic kingdom and history was brought to a conclusion. We cannot, therefore, expect to find in what they say a basis for life in a continuing society.[19]

The degree to which the teaching of Jesus and Paul can function authoritatively in our modern society is certainly arguable, and the extent to which the Christian communities were to separate themselves from their broader society is subject to debate. Yet McIntyre's challenge to the effort to form a code from those teachings is well-taken, and drives us to think beyond the common notion that ethics and the moral realm are limited to lists of principles, standards, or codes. Recall that the Hebrews 5 passage teaches

---

15. Clark and Smith, *Readings in Ethics*, 5–6.
16. Clark and Smith, *Readings in Ethics*, 6.
17. MacIntyre, *Short History of Ethics*, 111.
18. McClendon, *Ethics*, 1:63–64.
19. MacIntyre, *Short History of Ethics*, 115.

that maturity is characterized not by adherence to lists, but rather the constant exercise of developed and honed skills to distinguish good from evil.

In the early 1940s, while developing a major work on ethics, Dietrich Bonhoeffer wrote these intriguing words: "The knowledge of good and evil seems to be the aim of all ethical reflection. The first task of Christian ethics is to invalidate this knowledge."[20] He went on to argue that originally human beings knew only God, and that their acquired knowledge of good and evil was a result of separation from God. In knowing good and evil, then, the individual's stance is one of opposition to God.[21]

Bonhoeffer's thought seems to fly in the face of the Hebrews 5 passage which clearly affirms the ability to pass judgment about good and evil. In fact, that ability is the chief characteristic and evidence of Christian maturity. Bonhoeffer, however, is not suggesting that ethics properly understood is something other than a focus on good and evil. Rather, he is contrasting the ideal human state before the fall—one in which humans did not understand the distinction between good and evil—with the current state in which we find ourselves where good and evil are all-pervasive. "Man[22] knows good and evil, against God, against his origin, godlessly and of his own choice, understanding himself according to his own contrary possibilities..."[23] It is this environment of good and evil—not the ideal of creation but the reality of the fall—that forms the milieu in which ethics takes place. It is, in fact, the moral realm of human experience.

Thus far it may have been assumed the discussion about ethics has the individual as its object. Indeed, on the surface the teaching of Hebrews 5 initially appears to focus on individual Christians. Yet Hebrews was written to a group, not an individual. Similarly, Jesus addressed his landmark Sermon on the Mount to a group of his disciples. Notice at the end of the sermon we are told, "the crowds were amazed at his teaching."[24] Most of Paul's epistles were intended for groups of Christians in various geographic locations rather than individuals. Whereas ethics certainly has personal and individual components, and each person is a distinct and responsible moral agent, our consideration of the nature of ethics and the moral realm would be incomplete if we did not include an element focused on society rather

---

20. Bonhoeffer, *Ethics*, 21.

21. Bonhoeffer, *Ethics*, 21–22.

22. This is yet another case in which an exclusively male term was used by the author to refer to all humankind—a common but unfortunate convention employed at the time Bonhoeffer was writing.

23. Bonhoeffer, *Ethics*, 23–24.

24. Matt 7:28.

than the individual. The work of James McClendon provides us with a good introduction to the corporate nature of ethics.

McClendon agrees with the thinking we have seen from a number of ethicists, that the nature of ethics is not clearly defined: "To describe ethics . . . as a struggle or contest . . . is particularly apt, for moral ground is, almost by definition, contested ground."[25] He has in mind, however, the moral reflection of a local congregation: "we begin by finding the shape of the common life in the body of Christ, which is for Christians partly a matter of self-discovery . . . That is ethics."[26] In the context of the local congregation moral thinking goes far beyond making specific ethical decisions or adherence to principles, and instead envisions the ongoing common life of the members of the congregation, informed and shaped by the narrative they hold in common: the story of Jesus.[27] What is envisioned by reference to a story[28] that informs congregational life is a moral realm that includes the attitudes, commitments, values, priorities, and actions of the local group of Christians as a whole as they live within the society in which they find themselves. As an entity they aspire collectively to be faithful to all that they see in the story, broadly defined. This is known as "narrative ethics." For McClendon, "narrative ethics, which is the regular ethics of every story-informed Christian community, cannot be replaced by a reduced nonnarrative ethics of principles."[29]

In order to add specificity to how the Christian story informs and directs the moral life of the local congregation, McClendon identifies three elements of the moral realm in which the community finds itself. First, he reminds us we are part of the created order, and thus function as participants in God's natural creation. Second, Christians specifically participate

25. McClendon, *Ethics*, 1:48.
26. McClendon, *Ethics*, 1:45.
27. McClendon, *Ethics*, 1:47–48.

28. Use of the term "story" is sometimes viewed as a threat by many who hold to an orthodox view of Scripture, or a veiled assertion that the content of the story is not objectively true. Terms such as "narrative" or "myth" can be similarly stigmatized. On one occasion I presented a paper on the concept of story as a hermeneutical principle in the moral realm to a professional society of theologically conservative scholars. The first question after the presentation was, "Are you saying the Bible is not true?" This question betrayed a clear misunderstanding on the part of the questioner regarding the nature of the presentation. In the context in question terms such as "story," "narrative," and "myth" refer to how the content is being employed by, for example, an ethicist or a congregation, not to the truth of the content. In answer to the questioner I affirmed the objective and historical truth of the content, and sought to point out that the question had nothing to do with the assertions of the presentation; suspicion, however, remained.

29. McClendon, *Ethics*, 1:346.

collectively in the church, which exists as an element of God's social creation. As such they assume specific societal roles and stances within their broader societal context. Third, Christians uniquely participate in God's kingdom, the eschatological realm established by the resurrection of Jesus and directed by his spirit and power.[30] In each of these spheres Christians engage in the broader moral realm, guided by the narrative they affirm as authoritative for their common life.

Much more could be said about the world of collective or community ethics, and more will be explained about the role of narrative in the next chapter. This much, however, should be sufficient to demonstrate that ethics and the moral realm are far more extensive than either the individual or structures of codes, standards, and principles.

The Ethical Task

At this point a sense for the nature, scope, and limits of the moral realm and the work of ethics should be at least somewhat apparent. The intent thus far has not been to provide precision in this arena, but rather to create exposure to moral thinking, including the ambiguities with which those who work in the realm of good and bad deal on a routine basis. To begin to function with at least a modicum of confidence as a moral agent, however, a more specific approach to clarifying the ethical task may be helpful.[31]

William K. Frankena points out that moral thinking happens when the individual is no longer simply following rules (e.g., codes, standards, principles), even if she or he has internalized them to the point of being self-directed. Rather, when the individual begins to think critically about ethics, then she or he has achieved a kind of autonomy as a moral agent.[32] Put simply, "moral philosophy begins when people find their code of prevailing moral rules unsatisfactory."[33] It is not that the rules are necessarily wrong or bad in themselves, but rather they are found to be inadequate for the life situations the individual encounters. As detailed and comprehensive as a code may initially appear, "the actual rules of a society are never very precise,

---

30. McClendon, *Ethics*, 1:66–67.

31. The work of William K. Frankena is an excellent resource in this regard. In particular, see his book in Prentice-Hall's Foundations of Philosophy Series, entitled simply, *Ethics*. Only a small portion of Frankena's thought is referenced here but those who wish to delve more deeply into the nature of ethics will benefit from reading this entire book. See Frankena, *Ethics*.

32. Frankena, *Ethics*, 4.

33. Frankena, *Ethics*, 13.

always admit of exceptions, and may come into conflict with one another."[34] It is the task of the moral agent to struggle with these difficulties, with the hope of yielding a more adequate approach than that which adherence to lists of rules can render. "[M]orality fosters or even calls for the use of reason and for a kind of autonomy on the part of the individual, asking him, when mature and normal, to make his own decisions, though possibly with someone's advice, and even stimulating him to think out the principles or goals in the light of which he is to make his decisions."[35] This autonomy is precisely the objective of the Hebrews 5 passage, that the mature Christian is the one who, through continual use of honed skills, applied within the community context of the local congregation, is able to distinguish good from evil.

We have seen that the ethical enterprise has continued for centuries, and that it reaches far beyond the individual. Frankena, in writing about morality, points out that it refers to "a social enterprise, not just a discovery or invention of the individual for his own guidance. Like one's language, state, or church, it exists before the individual, who is inducted into it and becomes more or less of a participant in it, and it goes on existing after him."[36] His reference to church echoes McClendon's thought, that in the church community the congregation affirms a common narrative that drives its moral outlook and vision of a common life. This is the call the author of Hebrews issues to all who would be faithful to Christ as Lord.

There are at least two ways in which critical thinking in the moral realm functions. One has to do with formulating a structure which is intended to guide conduct and decision-making. The Decalogue functions in this way, when it lists directives such as "You shall not murder. You shall not commit adultery. You shall not steal."[37] Codes of ethics, standards of conduct, and moral principles all function in this way. There are many examples that demonstrate that following these structures is a significant challenge. In fact, a mountain of anecdotal evidence suggests it is not possible for them to be followed perfectly. The history of Israel depicted in the Old Testament is a good example. Failure to follow, however, does not constitute a moral conflict, but rather a moral deficiency. True moral conflict occurs when it is not possible to fulfill all of the stipulations of the structure. Frankena observes, "most moral problems arise in situations where there is a 'conflict of duties,' that is, where one moral principle pulls one way and another pulls the other

---

34. Frankena, *Ethics*, 13.
35. Frankena, *Ethics*, 7.
36. Frankena, *Ethics*, 6.
37. Exod 20:13–15. For the entire Decalogue, see Exod 20:1–17.

way."[38] It is in such situations that the mature Christian, according to the writer of Hebrews, is able to render a proper moral judgment.

The other way in which critical moral thinking functions is to view ethics as a matter of identifying and articulating ideal moral traits. Obligation entails consistently demonstrating those traits in all ethical judgments, attitudes, and conduct. Such traits may include such things as honesty, love, consideration, and justice. Whatever the traits may be that apply to the Christian community in which the Christian finds him- or herself, maturity entails consistently and continually showing them in all moral situations, perhaps irrespective of the consequences. It is likely those traits are identified through appeal to the community's moral authority (the subject of the next section).

What can we affirm, then, about ethics and the moral agent? Ethics and the moral sphere is the arena of human experience in which Christian maturity occurs. Defining that sphere, however, is far from easy, and has been a fundamental area of discussion since before the time of Christ. Some feel the question will never be finally answered and resolve that each ethicist develops his or her own concept of the moral sphere. Yet there is common ground among many who work in the world of ethics. For example, the notion of duty and that which is obligatory are generally held to be moral notions. The world of "ought" is part of the ethical world, and can be distinguished from the world of facts. It includes such concepts as the requisite, responsibility, values, attitudes, intentions, virtues, and conduct, at a minimum. As such, the moral realm is not limited to structures of codes, principles, or standards. In fact, the teaching of Hebrews 5 clearly indicates that rote adherence to such structures is not the stuff of Christian maturity; rather, maturity entails the habitual exercise of developed and honed ethical skills to pass moral judgment.

The exercise of such skills demonstrates that the individual thinks critically about moral matters, making her or his own decisions. Such thinking goes beyond external directives such as the Decalogue (witness Jesus' example of this type of thinking when he states multiple times in the Sermon on the Mount, "You have heard that it was said . . . But I tell you . . . ") to include traits such as honesty, love, consideration, and justice.

Finally, the moral sphere is not limited to the individual, but includes a societal element. Hebrews, most of the letters of Paul, and the teachings of Jesus were directed to groups, rather than individuals. For Christians, the most influential society in which they participate should be the local congregation. As a member of that society the individual participates as one

---

38. Frankena, *Ethics*, 3.

moral agent among many who seek to shape their common life by living faithfully to Christ, directed by the Jesus narrative they hold as their authority not only for faith, but also for conduct.

MORAL AUTHORITY

On occasion I still see a bumper sticker that reads, "Challenge Authority." The notion of authority generates a visceral, suspicious, and even negative response from many people, no doubt reflecting their personal experiences of imposition and coercion by authority figures or structures with whom they have come in contact. We encounter the concept of authority in the moral realm when considering a question such as, "What makes a decision right?" or "How do we know what is obligatory?" The subject of authority for ethics is a complex one and, as you probably suspect, is one on which there is considerable disagreement among ethicists. Yet, if we are to avoid the conclusion that commitments and decisions in the moral realm are simply arbitrary, it is essential to develop an understanding of, and convictions concerning, authority for ethics.

At the end of the Sermon on the Mount, Jesus' major moral teaching, we read these words: "When Jesus had finished saying these things, the crowds were amazed at his teaching, because he taught as one who had authority and not as their teachers of the law."[39] On another occasion, at the beginning of his ministry, Jesus was in Galilee teaching on a Sabbath. Luke indicated that the people "were amazed at his teaching, because his words had authority."[40] What was this authority Jesus wielded? How is it that this person, who held no lofty position in society, exercised much greater moral influence on the crowds than those who did?

Later in Matthew's Gospel, after the mother of James and John asked Jesus if they could sit at his right and left in the kingdom, he referenced the authority that the leaders of the gentiles exercise over them. Giving guidance to his followers he then said, "not so with you."[41] What is this authority utilized by gentile leaders that Jesus forbids? How does it compare with the kind of authority Jesus himself exercised over his listeners to the point that the crowds were amazed? What sort of authority is legitimate in the moral realm, and what sort is not?

---

39. Matt 7:28–29.
40. Luke 4:32.
41. Matt 20:26.

The Nature of Moral Authority

The struggle with authority—both its nature and our reaction to it—is nothing new. A general negative visceral response to the exercise of authority in society did not start with the counterculturalism of the 1960s. Frederick J. Adelmann, in the foreword to his edited work on authority, reminds us that "ethicians and political scientists over the centuries have been vague in their treatment of the notion of authority. The old scholastic textbooks referred to authority as the 'form' of society; the newer ones omitted the point altogether."[42] Not mincing words, he reflects the feelings of many who face any kind of authority when he writes, "Anyone committed to authority is considered a conservative in the pejorative sense, or perhaps a fascist, or at least unwilling to change in the inevitably changing world."[43] Over 100 years ago, in a book review on ethics within Christianity, the reviewer started by writing, "A recent important book by Dr. Hall has one central theme, however many its variations, viz., the rise of authority in Christian ethics and the successive efforts to work free from its control and reach a genuinely ethical, as distinct from legal, conception of conduct."[44]

It appears that whatever one's view of authority, in addition to a predominantly visceral aversion to the concept, lack of clarity on the subject is also common. Richard T. De George, an expert on ethical authority, commented that "those who challenge authority are no more clear in their protest than those who attempt to uphold authority are in its defense. Consequently there is need to get clear what authority means and what its possible justifications and limits are."[45] An environment devoid of authority is not necessarily a desirable or beneficial one, as much as we may object when confronted with authority or experience relief when we circumvent or avoid authoritarian encounters. John Wild cautions that "The most tragic state of a culture is to lack all authority. But next after this is the alienation of a culture from its authorities, which rapidly leads to the first."[46]

Why has authority been such a difficult subject for many people through the ages, including our own? Why has the notion of authority become so visceral for us, and negatively so at that? Why is authority something we often want to avoid? The answers, I suggest, have to do with our common experiences of authority, and subsequent convictions about

---

42. Adelmann, *Authority*, 1.
43. Adelmann, *Authority*, 2.
44. Tufts, "Authority in Ethics," 148. Courtesy of JSTOR.
45. De George, "Nature and Function," 76.
46. Wild, "Authority," 15.

the nature of authority and how it functions. One Harvard philosopher described our experience of authority like this: "the voice of authority is at least *prima facie* overriding for those subject to or obligated by the authority. Furthermore, the authority, or some other agency whose function it is, has the right and indeed responsibility to enforce compliance."[47] He goes on to explain that throughout society those constituted as authorities or having authority make decisions to which others are obligated to comply. Failure to comply results in the imposition of penalties, which are intended both to educate and to force compliance.[48]

If the exercise of authority of necessity entails the imposition of obligation, including coerced compliance and penalties for noncompliance when necessary, then it should not surprise us that the notion of authority often meets with negative responses on the part of many. Which individuals, believing themselves to be free and responsible moral agents, enthusiastically embrace a situation in which others make their moral decisions for them, and enforce compliance through threat of penalties? In short, who wants to live in a repressive environment?

The key to dealing in the moral realm with the common understanding of authority is to realize it is only one kind of authority. Moreover, as an authority for ethics it is often the wrong kind of authority. De George points out that an individual who is the type of authority we have been considering sees him- or herself as a moral legislator, one whose decisions or commands make actions either right or wrong. Obedience is obligatory simply because the legislator has commanded it.[49] Such authorities, for example, include parents of young children, the government, and religious leaders or structures.

When thinking about authority in the moral realm it is important to understand the relationships surrounding the authority. An authority is not one in isolation; rather, the authority engages in relationships by virtue of the fact that she or he is an authority for others, and is in relationship with them. Authority is not an absolute characteristic, such as an ability or a possession. Rather, it exists only in a particular context and between entities.[50]

A very helpful and clear description of moral authority, at its operational best, was provided by philosopher John Wild, whose distinguished twentieth-century career included faculty appointments at Harvard, Yale, and Northwestern universities. He observed that authority entails

---

47. Adams, "Philosophical Grounds," 6.
48. Adams, "Philosophical Grounds," 7.
49. De George, "Authority and Morality," 31, 37.
50. Jenkins, "Authority," 36–37.

transmission of value, without distortion, from the authority figure to free persons. As such, the authority functions as a mediator[51] who is responsible "to achieve a position of intimate closeness to the real value. His second duty is then to communicate it by thought and action to free minds without the loss of their freedom."[52] In a religious context, then, the authority figure mediates between God and others "without the use of force, and the loss of human freedom which brute force would imply."[53] Fundamentally, then, what is an authority according to Wild? An authority is "a person having some special access to a real value which he is able to transmit to other free minds, prepared to receive it with discipline and respectful attention, while it is still not yet fully actualized."[54] Such a notion of authority is a far cry, indeed, from the common understanding of authority within the broader society, one that is overriding and enforces compliance through the threat of punishment and penalties. The kind of moral authority described by Wild is the kind that enables individual moral agents who are seeking to live maturely and responsibly. This concept of authority, then, holds great promise for those believers who, according to Hebrews 5, are developing their skills habitually in order to be able to distinguish good from evil, and thus live in faithfulness to Christ.

Moral Authority Alternatives

Recall that Wild's description of an authority's function was to communicate by thought and action. Just how does this work? How is authority related to thought and action? By now it should be clear there are several possible kinds of authority in the moral realm, and they do not all function in the same way. Fundamental to all types of moral authority is what De George terms the authority of moral obligation. If one has a duty to act in a certain way, then that individual inherently has the authority to so act. One cannot be required to act in a certain way when the necessary authority to so act has been withheld. It is the moral sphere itself that requires the independent moral agent to act in a manner consistent with that obligation, and so imbues the agent with the authority to act.[55] This type of authority serves as a foundation for the others.

51. Wild, "Authority," 14–15.
52. Wild, "Authority," 15.
53. Wild, "Authority," 17.
54. Wild, "Authority," 12.
55. De George, "Authority and Morality," 38, 46.

Earlier we considered the type of authority that De George refers to as "executive authority."[56] Such an authority gives commands, and expects compliance simply by virtue of the fact that the commands have been given. What makes a given action right or wrong is nothing other than the will of the authority, and thus there is a fickle element to ethics as a result. What is right today can become wrong tomorrow, if the authority reverses the command. This is the kind of authority that enforces compliance, and removes from its subjects all freedom to choose compliance or not. It thus is a coerced authority—an authority from above—rather than one freely embraced by the independent moral agent.

Another type of moral authority—one that aligns with Wild's notion of communication by thought—is what De George terms "epistemic moral authority."[57] Such an authority has knowledge in the moral realm—a kind or level of knowledge by virtue of which he or she can become an authority for another if the other gives assent to and believes in the authority figure.[58] The authority becomes such for another by virtue of conveying knowledge, which knowledge is believed and held to be true by the other. The strength of the authority is determined by both the number who believe and the level to which his or her authority is endorsed.[59] "Epistemic authority is thus in principle substitutional in nature. Its purpose is to substitute the knowledge of one person in a certain field for the lack of knowledge of another."[60] Note that there is no element of coercion associated with this type of authority. Unlike executive moral authority, epistemic moral authority has no power of enforcement: rather, the subject of the authority, an independent moral agent, freely accepts the authority.

Over time the subject learns more and more, requiring the authority less and less. De George reminds us that, "it should be the aim of a moral teacher to enable the subjects of his authority eventually to make their own moral decisions, for it is only when they reach this level that they become fully moral and responsible."[61] This should sound familiar, for it is precisely what was referenced as Christian maturity by the writer of Hebrews 5: "But

---

56. De George, "Authority and Morality," 37.

57. De George, "Authority and Morality," 38.

58. De George, "Authority and Morality," 38, and De George, "Nature and Function," 78, 87.

59. De George, "Authority and Morality," 38–39.

60. De George, "Nature and Function," 82.

61. De George, "Authority and Morality," 39.

solid food is for the mature, who by constant use have trained themselves to distinguish good from evil."[62]

Wild's idea of communication by action finds a parallel in yet another type of moral authority—exemplary moral authority. This kind of authority has in view the authority's virtue, rather than knowledge as was the case with epistemic moral authority. Although the two kinds of authority often occur together, an epistemic moral authority need not be virtuous, or act consistently with the knowledge being conveyed to others.[63] An exemplary moral authority, however, "is one whose actions inspire others or one whose actions become a model for the behavior of others."[64] As was the case with epistemic moral authority, an exemplary moral authority is one by virtue of belief on the part of the subject that the authority is, in fact, morally authoritative for her or him. Also, an exemplary moral authority carries no authority of enforcement, but rather is dependent upon the affirmation of the subject.

The best moral authority is one that combines both epistemic and exemplary moral authority and so functions as a teacher who also demonstrates moral virtue. Recall from Wild that authority is relational. An authority transmits value to free persons, and thus serves as a mediator between the value source and those receiving the value. What does this mean for the Christian who is seeking to grow in maturity after the model of Hebrews 5? What is it that should function as an epistemic and exemplary moral authority for such a Christian? Wild sums it up, writing,

> Since God is transcendent, and since divine values are inaccessible to the unaided human faculties, the mediation must be initiated and sustained by God Himself incarnate. Thus the supreme, religious authority is the person of Christ, both man and God, the mediator *par excellence*, who spoke as one *with authority*. In exercising this mediating function he showed us the way in which all genuine, earthly authority of lesser kind and degree should be exercised.[65]

Notice that Wild includes both epistemic and exemplary moral authority when he describes Christ as one who both "spoke with authority" and "showed us the way."

---

62. Heb 5:14.
63. De George, "Authority and Morality," 41.
64. De George, "Authority and Morality," 41.
65. Wild, "Authority," 17; italics original.

Determining Moral Right from Wrong

We have now made the transition from thinking of a moral authority as one who enforces compliance with a set of rules through coercive and threatening enforcement to one whose teaching and conduct conveys moral guidance to those who voluntarily and freely accept it. Furthermore, I have suggested Jesus Christ should serve as the epistemic and exemplary moral authority for those who, following the admonition of Hebrews 5, seek to mature in their Christian faith. The next question is just how can we determine what we, or others, should do in particular situations? What is it that makes something morally right? How do we take what Jesus taught and did (or perhaps does) and interpret or apply it to our culture and situation in the time between the incarnation and the eschaton—a time when Jesus is no longer on earth, but rather is resurrected, ascended, and glorified?

In general ethicists have offered two broad approaches for determining what it is that makes something morally right or wrong. Each can function as an overarching hermeneutic to be applied to a moral authority, in our case the moral authority of Jesus. One approach is that of ethical teleology. As the term implies, teleological theories hold that obligation, or that which is morally good, is determined by the amount of benefit produced, compared with the amount of evil. Furthermore, the determination of that which is morally good or obligatory is assessed by measuring the amount of nonmoral good achieved.[66] "Teleological theories, then, make the right, the obligatory, and the morally good dependent on the nonmorally good."[67] Obligation and correct action are established when the intended or predicted amount of nonmoral good that will result is greater than the nonmoral bad.[68]

The other approach for determining if something is morally right or wrong—deontology—is the opposite of teleology. For the deontologist the morally good is not determined by intended or predicted consequences, but rather by other factors such as the inherent goodness of promise-keeping, acting justly, or emulating a moral architype, irrespective of the resultant outcome. "[A] deontologist contends that it is possible for an action or rule of action to be the morally right or obligatory one even if it does not promote

---

66. Frankena explains that moral good refers to such things as "persons, groups of persons, traits of character, dispositions, emotions, and intentions," whereas nonmoral good refers to items such as "physical objects like cars and paintings; experiences like pleasure, pain, knowledge, and freedom; and forms of government like democracy." Furthermore, he asserts that "it does not make sense to call most of these things morally good or bad, unless we mean that it is morally right or wrong to pursue them" (*Ethics*, 62).

67. Frankena, *Ethics*, 14.

68. Frankena, *Ethics*, 14.

the greatest possible balance of good over evil for self, society, or universe. It may be right or obligatory simply because of some other fact about it or because of its own nature."[69] One of those possible facts is simply that it is what God wants. In this case the moral good is determined by God's will alone and nothing more. The one huge question for those who support this approach is: How is God's will to be determined?

Jesus functions as our epistemic and exemplary moral authority by virtue of our acceptance of, and submission to, what he taught and what he did. How are we to move from this fact to determining God's will in the moral realm, and thus be able to distinguish moral good from moral evil? The key is to realize the close relationship between the One who conveys God's will and the One who serves as our moral authority. Richard J. Mouw, former president of Fuller Theological Seminary, captured this relationship well in his book, *The God Who Commands*. At the risk of appearing to endorse executive moral authority (which I do not), I suggest the thoughts of Mouw will help us bridge the gap. Mouw reminds us that "The God who commands is the same one who has, in the person of Jesus, entered into a human frame of reference. The Creator became Redeemer, stooping to become like one of us. When God commands, he does so with an intimate knowledge of our condition, having suffered in the same ways that we suffer."[70] The will of God the Creator is mediated through God the Son, by virtue of the life he lived and the things he taught. When he emptied himself of divine glory in order to become like one of us, Jesus conveyed through word and deed what God wants from us. Those words and deeds have been captured in the Bible. It behooves us both to learn from Jesus and to perceive him accurately in what we find in the New Testament. "The God who commands in the Scriptures is the one who offers the broken chariots of the Egyptians and the nail-scarred hands of the divine Son as a vindication of the right to tell us what to do."[71] Just how we are to approach the Scripture in order to understand Jesus, our moral authority, is our next challenge.

---

69. Frankena, *Ethics*, 15.
70. Mouw, *God Who Commands*, 19.
71. Mouw, *God Who Commands*, 20.

3

Determining a Biblical Hermeneutic for Ethics

WHAT IS THE ROLE of Scripture in ethical thinking and how is it to be employed by people of faith to inform our work in the moral realm? The difficulty we face in answering the question is determining the details of using the Bible for that purpose. In this chapter we take up an investigation of hermeneutics for ethics both as another tool we need to demonstrate our affirmation "Jesus is Lord," and also as a means of building a solid foundation for developing an ethic at the end of the book based upon the living Jesus.

AUTHORITY AND COMPLEXITY

Almost without exception all Christian traditions affirm that the Bible, both Old and New Testaments, is Holy Scripture. As such, it is authoritative for ethics in some way. The means by which Scripture is to be used in ethics, however, is a subject of much debate—one which began centuries ago, continues to the present, and will go on for the foreseeable future. A certain tradition may affirm a particular biblical hermeneutic for ethics, while other traditions are convinced alternative interpretive approaches are proper. Views change over time as cultural influences and theological trends shape the thinking of those seeking to remain true to the authoritative word while applying it to changing moral contexts. Some have found in the Bible theological concepts that should influence moral convictions, while others see the commandments of Scripture as paramount. Certain biblical values or the examples of those who led exemplary moral lives may serve to drive the fundamental ethical convictions of some Christians or Christian communities, whereas biblically informed character is primary for others.[1] The upshot is that not all individuals, traditions, and communities experience the Bible as authoritative in the same way, even though all affirm that Scripture is authoritative in the moral realm.

There is a sense in which attempting to use the Bible to inform moral thought entails a complexity, or perhaps difficulty, that theological efforts do not experience—or at least do not experience in the same way or to the same degree. Theological thinking can enjoy a level of abstraction from human experience that thinking in the moral realm cannot. If we make a biblical argument that God is eternal, for example, the truth of the statement is not contingent upon any human conduct, value, attitude, or anything else. Whereas there may be an absolute element about moral assertions, on the other hand, of necessity they must relate somehow to human contexts. One cannot make a biblical argument for an obligatory action, attitude, or value without including those accountable for such. Even when simply reading the Bible, one quickly realizes the authors and their various audiences worked in vastly different cultures, social contexts, and moral environments, even while the same Holy Spirit was actively inspiring all of them.

Fundamental to using the Bible for ethics, then, is the realization that even though it is God's written word, it is not monolithic, and contains a great deal of ethical diversity. Furthermore, the social and moral contexts of the first readers of the biblical writings were vastly different from our own. Bruce Birch captured this challenge succinctly when he wrote, "Differences between the biblical world and our own must be faced honestly and the use of Scripture as an ethical resource cannot be a simple pattern of emulating ancient ways, nor will we find a single, unified moral code to merely adopt."[2] Add to this the fact that at least some of the New Testament writers perhaps expected the *parousia* to occur imminently, and the complexity of engaging in New Testament-based moral thought in a postmodern context two millennia later is greatly heightened. Ethical prescription for those expecting the end to come within a very short period of time may not directly translate to societies and Christian communities that, while ever watchful for the Lord's imminent appearance, continue on for generations.

1. Cosgrove, "Scripture in Ethics," 13.
2. Birch, "Scripture in Ethics," 29.

Charles Cosgrove summarized his view of the challenge like this: "By the close of the twentieth century, the role of the Bible in Christian ethics had become a highly complex theological and ethical problem. Except in fundamentalist circles, one could no longer simply equate biblical ethics with Christian ethics. The diversity of moral perspectives in Scripture and the epochal difference between antiquity and modernity (or postmodernity) made it difficult to conceive the Bible as a direct source of Christian ethics."[3] Whereas we may not fully agree with Cosgrove, particularly when he suggests using the Bible directly for ethics is a difficult thing to conceive, he nevertheless captures the difficulty we face when using such ancient and diverse texts as an authoritative source for the moral realm in which we find ourselves.

How, then, have ethicists attempted to bridge the gap between the Bible and modern societies? In what ways have they tried to develop a biblical moral case when the Bible itself deals with a particular ethical situation in various ways? How can diverse treatments of the same subject in the Bible be used to develop moral prescription in the twenty-first century?

One approach is to attempt some sort of harmonization of biblical content.[4] Such an approach, however, runs the risk of misusing certain texts in order to get them to align with the harmonization attempt. Rather than allowing each text to speak for itself, harmonization imposes an artificial objective on all the texts.

Another approach is to seek for one text that somehow is overriding. That text—be it the Decalogue, the Sermon on the Mount, one of Paul's epistles, or something else—is viewed as primary, and others are read in light of that text. The difficulty of this approach is that not all texts seem to be equally authoritative, and certain ones are subordinated to others. The means by which the selection of the overriding text is accomplished is another area of controversy associated with using the Bible in this way.

A third way to apply the Bible to current contexts is to search for a fundamental theme that runs throughout Scripture. Examples include God's sovereignty, divine love, creation, and covenant. Whereas this may appear attractive at first and applicable to current social contexts, in the end all scriptural texts must be viewed in light of the theme, rather than be read for what they are in themselves. As was the case with harmonization, something—in this case the fundamental theme—is artificially imposed on all of Scripture.

---

3. Cosgrove, "Scripture in Ethics," 24.

4. All of the basic approaches are taken from the introduction by Green. See Green, "Introduction," 2.

Finally, some attempt to find in Scripture a unified metanarrative derived from God's character and conduct. Such a metanarrative finds expression in various ways throughout the many texts that make up the Bible. Similar to the difficulties with other approaches, viewing all of Scripture through a divine metanarrative reduces the texts of the Bible to irreconcilable examples of the larger concept, and robs them of their inherent authority as Holy Scripture themselves.

A wholly different approach to viewing the ethical meaning of Scripture is to focus on the experiences of the original believing communities, and to see the biblical texts as testimonies by the communities of their experiences with God. Thus much of the Old Testament is Israel's recorded recollection of their experience of God. King David captured his witness to God's working in the Psalms. The Gospel writers conveyed four different perspectives of their experiences with Jesus. The apostle Paul wrote to his nascent Christian communities about both their struggles and the way God desired them to express faithfulness to him. Rather than finding in the Bible God's will for the moral life of his faithful followers, we see how the faithful in various contexts lived in the moral realm. Birch writes, "a proper understanding of canon emphasizes that canon is not a definitive collection of timeless, divinely revealed truths. Canon is a collection of witnesses to an ongoing encounter with the presence of God in the lives of persons and communities."[5] The community, then, is paramount, and is the context in which an individual is to find moral guidance and accountability.

In spite of great attempts to develop means to use the Bible for ethics, there still is no agreement on how that is to be done. Furthermore, the means that have been developed all are less than ideal. All suffer from a range of difficulties, chief of which is that they appear to diminish the authority of the Scripture itself. As those who affirm it is the Scripture itself that is authoritative for our ethical lives we need a better biblical hermeneutic for the moral realm—one that neither imposes a predetermined schema on the text nor diminishes its authority. First, however, we need to understand how the primacy of Scripture works.

SOLA SCRIPTURA

For sixteenth-century reformer Martin Luther the work of God in the world "is known to us solely through the Scriptures open to interpretation by any Christian under the guidance of the Holy Spirit. Acquaintance with the original languages of the Scriptures is needful, and theological education

---

5. Birch, "Scripture in Ethics," 28.

should be concerned exclusively with these tools and with the understanding of the Scriptures."[6] Other reformers agreed with this same broad conclusion, although differences existed. For example, Luther allowed anything the Bible did not specifically prohibit, whereas Ulrich Zwingli permitted only what the Bible specifically articulated.[7] Their general perspective, however, has been classically known as the doctrine of *sola scriptura*.

Sola scriptura is Latin for "Scripture alone." It is one of several "*solas*" of the Protestant Reformation, and has come to hold the preeminent place among them. Since it rejects any infallible authority other than the Bible, the doctrine stands at odds with the Roman Catholic Church's view that tradition along with Scripture is authoritative, or perhaps that church tradition is authoritative over Scripture. Thus, *sola scriptura* comprises the central tenant of the Reformation.

Sola scriptura, however, did not have its start with the reformers. Rather, it has its roots in the consistent position of the church during the first centuries of its existence, which was that "the Scripture was the sole source of normative revelation in the post-apostolic era."[8] The reformers simply reiterated this ancient affirmation of the early Christians. However, they realized that fifteen centuries of biblical interpretation had occurred since the New Testament documents were written, and a body of doctrine based upon that collective interpretation defined orthodox belief. Whereas that collective did not enjoy the position of infallible authority as did Scripture, it did serve to inform future interpreters of what the church through the ages had held regarding biblical teaching. As such, that collective body of doctrine held a certain level of authority—known as the authority of tradition—albeit fallible and subordinate to the authority of Scripture. In an attempt to capture this concept, theologian Marty Foord writes,

> *sola scriptura* meant Scripture was the supreme authority over the church. It did not mean Scripture was the only authority. Luther, Calvin, and the other reformers used other authorities like reason and tradition. . . . Yet the Bible was the supreme authority that ruled reason and tradition because Scripture alone was infallible precisely because it is God's word. All other authorities (including church leadership) were fallible and must submit to Scripture.[9]

---

6. Bainton, *Christendom*, 12.
7. Bainton, *Christendom*, 31.
8. Mathison, *Shape of Sola Scriptura*, 256.
9. Foord, "Real Meaning of Sola Scriptura," para. 2.

One role of those "other authorities" was to judge any new interpretation of Scripture to determine if, in fact, it comported with the classic doctrinal position of the church through the ages.

This leads us to consider an aberration of *sola scriptura* affirmed by many modern Christians, unwittingly swayed by influences such as Western individualism and rationalism, who believe they are being true to the church's classic doctrine. In his outstanding book on *sola scriptura* Keith Mathison[10] credits Douglas Jones with coining the term "solo *scriptura*" in 1997 to describe this view. Fundamentally it asserts that the Bible is the only authority for the Christian, and it is infallible. The church's collective understanding of the Bible's meaning and teaching are of no consequence, and most certainly carry no authority. Solo *scriptura* affirms "a 'me and my bible' hermeneutic which allows 'each individual Christian' to maintain their own theological view point on a given doctrine."[11]

There are at least two threats to which the individual who supports solo *scriptura* is reacting. First is the notion that he or she should submit to, or be influenced by, past collective understanding of the message of Scripture. Asserting that the Holy Spirit is leading as he or she, even in isolation, studies the Bible, the individual believes that whatever conclusions emerge must be correct. Second, the term "tradition" often generates a negative visceral response, for it is associated with Roman Catholic belief and a subordination of the Scripture to the teaching of the ecclesiastical hierarchy. Yet *sola scriptura* is associated with a vastly different understanding of tradition—the collective body of orthodox doctrine developed over the centuries by thousands of biblical interpreters as they were led by the Holy Spirit. Both of the threats from *sola scriptura*, however, actually are nonthreats, for (1) the Holy Spirit was leading all of those faithful students of the Scripture in past ages, just as current students are being led, and (2) the collective results of past study should be welcomed by Christians today as a corrective to areas where their cultural limitations and less-than-perfect interpretive skills have led them to erroneous conclusions. The real question modern-day Christians should ask themselves is not whether or not they are being led by the Holy Spirit when they study the Scripture, but rather, "How do I know my conclusions are correct?" It is the witness of fellow believers for the past two millennia that should help answer the question.

Mathison gives us a good summary of the error of solo *scriptura*, and the threat it poses to the individual who adopts it:

---

10. Mathison, *Shape of Sola Scriptura*, 238.
11. McMahon, "Doctrine of Sola Scriptura in a Nutshell," para. 2.

> Proponents of solo *scriptura* have deceived themselves into thinking that they honor the unique authority of Scripture. But unfortunately, by divorcing the Spirit-inspired word of God from the Spirit-inspired people of God, they have made it into a plaything and the source of endless speculation. If a proponent of solo *scriptura* is honest, he recognizes that it is not the infallible Scripture to which he ultimately appeals. His appeal is *always* to his own fallible interpretation of that Scripture. With solo *scriptura* it cannot be any other way, and this necessary relativistic autonomy is the fatal flaw of solo *scriptura* that proves it to be an un-Christian tradition of men.[12]

Perhaps an example will help establish the wisdom of conducting ourselves according to *sola scriptura* rather than solo *scriptura*. Not long ago, a pastor friend loaned me a book written by a recent theology PhD. The author made a careful and solid case for a particular position. It was difficult to find a flaw in the author's reasoning. The exegesis was well done, and it was a piece of solid scholarship. In general the argument initially appeared convincing. However, it was not compelling for one reason: it was in conflict with the entire corpus of interpretation and understanding of the biblical content in question throughout the millennia of church history. In essence this author was asserting that the book's argument, divergent as it was from the church's historic and orthodox understanding, was correct whereas the collective understanding of thousands of scholastic predecessors was wrong (and had been for 2,000 years). Although it is theoretically possible for this to be the case, I suggest it is highly unlikely. In order to affirm the author's conclusion, one also would have to affirm that the Holy Spirit had misled thousands of other interpreters, or at least affirm all of them collectively had misunderstood the Holy Spirit's illuminating work as they pursued their scholarly tasks. Here we have a case, I suggest, of solo *scriptura* at work, rather than an approach that would affirm the historic Christian position of *sola scriptura*.

The point is *not* that individuals should avoid working with the Scripture. In fact, much the opposite is the case. However, they also should realize they stand in a line of succession of individuals through the ages of the church, including the present one, who also worked with the biblical texts. The consensus of their individual efforts, each of which was both led by the Holy Spirit and validated by millennia of Christian thought, is far more likely to be an accurate representation of God's word than that of an individual who believes his or her view of the Scripture in isolation from

---

12 Mathison, *Shape of Sola Scriptura*, 253; italics original.

the broader Christian community is accurate. Indeed, when using the Bible in the moral realm the church's classic doctrine of *sola scriptura* is to be our guide, rather than the modern aberration of solo *scriptura*.

A BIBLICAL HERMENEUTIC FOR ETHICS

When we look into Scripture with the objective of determining how Jesus—our ethical teacher and example—is depicted, we soon realize the task is anything but straightforward. First, there are several authors who attempted to convey their impressions of Jesus' teaching and conduct. In general the gospels written by Matthew, Mark, and Luke are rationalized fairly easily given the dependencies between them, even though each is written from a certain perspective and with specific goals. John's Gospel, however, is not as easily rationalized with the other three. The apostle Paul, who was not one of Jesus' disciples during Jesus' earthly ministry, conveyed an understanding of Jesus that began with his own Damascus road encounter of the resurrected, ascended, and glorified Jesus, not the Jesus who walked the earth. James, the half-brother of Jesus, was not a disciple until perhaps after the resurrection, but had family experiences with Jesus that the disciples did not. His epistle barely mentions Jesus, yet heavily reflects Jesus' teaching in the Sermon on the Mount. The author of the Epistle to the Hebrews leveraged her or his philosophical background in Alexandria while developing a picture of the living, glorified Jesus who is very active, yet not removed from us.

The interpretive question we have to face is how to utilize the various and varied pictures of Jesus we find in the New Testament in an authoritative way as we seek to follow Jesus faithfully while we live daily in the moral realm. There have been many attempts to answer that question.

The Hermeneutical Issue

We affirm the books of the Bible were all inspired by the Holy Spirit. Nevertheless, they were written in several languages by many authors in various historical and cultural contexts over hundreds of years. Many of them were written to discrete audiences with specific intentions and objectives. Even the books of the New Testament, written during a period of less than 100 years, reflect considerable appeal to the Old Testament, not to mention the varied backgrounds and perspectives of their respective authors. Thus, focusing only on the New Testament does not diminish the diversity and complexity with which we are dealing. The challenge before us, as the people of God seeking to be faithful followers, is the matter of appropriation: How is the biblical material to be appropriated in our historical and social context in a way that ensures we are not abusing it, but rather using it correctly as the authoritative source for ethics that we affirm it is?

In the 1970s, Raymond Surburg wrote an article dealing with historical hermeneutics in which he points out that since the inception of the church there have been not only many approaches to interpreting the Scripture, but also a wide range of conclusions about what the Bible teaches. "In the course of that long history a number of different kinds of schools of interpretation have arisen upon the scene utilizing methods which were significantly different from each other. The consequence of this situation resulted in different understandings and promulgations of what the Holy Scriptures truly taught and intended to teach."[13] We will be looking at some of those methods later in an attempt to paint a picture of our forebears' various assertions concerning appropriation of the biblical content for their own times and contexts. Now, however, we need to continue our effort to understand the hermeneutical issue.

At the foundation of the hermeneutical task is the question of the level to which the Bible is to be used not only for theology but also for ethics. Perhaps it should go without saying that, of course, the Bible is fundamental. Scholars across the theological spectrum appear to hold that their most important source is the Bible. In *Bible and Ethics in the Christian Life*, authors Bruce Birch and Larry Rasmussen observe that, historically,

> [t]he Bible has always been regarded as central for Christian morality and ethics. It has, in fact, been regarded as the charter document for the Christian moral life. Biblical materials have been enlisted again and again for the fashioning of character and conduct. They have been consulted repeatedly for guidance and authority. Every generation has drawn lines between its own moral wrestlings and those of the biblical communities. The scriptures have been a seminal source and resource for the moral life.[14]

They go on to assert that this is not just a historical position, but there is consensus among both theologians and ethicists that "for Christian ethics the Bible is somehow normative. *In what way normative* is a question with many proposed answers; but there is agreement that the Bible *is* the charter document that holds a place more authoritative than any other source."[15] Writers as wide-ranging as Bernard Ramm and H. Richard Niebuhr appear

---

13. Surburg, "Presuppositions of the Historical-Grammatical Method," 278.
14. Birch and Rasmussen, *Bible and Ethics*, 11.
15. Birch and Rasmussen, *Bible and Ethics*, 46; italics original.

to agree with Birch and Rasmussen. Ramm, focusing on appropriate use of the Bible, writes that it is fundamental to the hermeneutical task, *"to ascertain what God has said in Sacred Scripture; to determine the meaning of the word of God.* There is no profit to us if God has spoken and we do not know what He has said."[16] He goes on to argue that improper use of the Bible has resulted in affirmations that God supports polygamy, the divine right of kings, killing of witches, avoiding basic methods of sanitation, allowing women to suffer in childbirth, etc. Proper use of the Bible, however, would avoid the misapplication of Scripture in determining moral principles.[17] For Ramm, then, the Bible is the paramount source for ethicists.

Niebuhr, along with his co-author Waldo Beach, also affirms the primacy of God's word: "The Bible has always been and will doubtless remain the chief source book for the study of Christian ethics."[18] As basic and intertwined as the Bible, God, and Christian ethics appear to be, and given the degree of unconditional affirmation of such to be found across the spectrum of ethicists and theologians, there is, surprisingly, no universal agreement as to how to use the Bible in ethics.

Jack Sanders, in seeking to provide a partial answer for what he sees as a crisis in ethics, asserts that within our modern pluralistic society "there is hardly any hope of finding specific instructions that will still be valid after nearly two thousand years, but whether the New Testament provides a general ethical validity—middle axioms, norms, or even a mere direction of response—that will be the question."[19] In his initial focus on Jesus he references Albert Schweitzer's point that Jesus intended only an interim ethics,[20] and then concludes that "Jesus does not provide a valid ethics for today. His ethical teaching is interwoven with his imminent eschatology to such a degree that every attempt to separate the two and to draw out only the ethical thread invariably and inevitably draws out also strands of the eschatology, so that both yarns only lie in a heap. Better to leave the tapestry intact, to let Jesus, as Albert Schweitzer appealed to us to do, return to his own time."[21]

Can it be true that we should let Jesus return to his own time, since he does not provide any sort of ethic that is usable today? The vast majority of Christian ethicists would disagree, and see the attempt to relegate Jesus to the irrelevant as extreme and summarily dismissive of a vast amount of

16. Ramm, *Protestant Biblical Interpretation*, 2; italics original.
17. Ramm, *Protestant Biblical Interpretation*, 2–3.
18. Beach and Niebuhr, *Christian Ethics*, 10.
19. Sanders, *Ethics in the New Testament*, xii.
20. Sanders, *Ethics in the New Testament*, 3.
21. Sanders, *Ethics in the New Testament*, 29.

morally laden Jesus content that is somehow still normative for those seeking to be faithful and mature believers, even in a twenty-first century setting. Dismissing Jesus outright as inappropriate for the modern ethical context is simply too reductionistic, and perhaps reflects more the presuppositions of and influences upon those who hold such a position than it does a careful attempt to appropriate the Jesus material in a responsible manner. Or, in the words of ethicist J. Philip Wogaman, "Christian ethics certainly may not abandon the Bible, for the Bible remains the foundation sine qua non of basic theological insight."[22] Sadly, Sanders' perspective views an ethic based upon Jesus and the New Testament as a type of bondage, rather than the freeing and empowering moral foundation it truly is.[23]

How, then, should we view our task of developing a responsible, workable hermeneutic for ethics given the complexity of the Scriptures themselves, as well as the historical variation among ethicists regarding how the Bible should function in the moral realm? I suggest that as a starting point we should acknowledge that none of us is able to approach the Bible in a completely objective manner. No matter how committed we are to rise above cultural and contextual influences, we should adopt a humble attitude before God and our associates toward our own interpretive efforts and conclusions. We should agree with J. Severino Croatto that "it is a matter of common knowledge that all interpreters condition their reading of a text by a kind of *preunderstanding* arising from their own life context,"[24] and remain open to critique of our approaches and conclusions irrespective of our certitude that they are correct.

Assuming we come to the Bible with the appropriate humility, a simple reading of the text, or even more specifically the stories of Jesus' life, reveals that Scripture does not present a single moral approach. Rather, there is diversity within the Bible's moral content. Jesus does not always engage moral challenges in the same way. Sometimes he tells a parable. At other times he interprets and augments the Old Testament law. On occasion he doesn't offer any teaching at all, but instead engages in conduct that demonstrates the moral lesson he is trying to convey. In certain situations he

---

22. Wogaman, *Christian Ethics*, 278.

23. Sanders broadens his conclusion about Jesus to include the rest of the New Testament when he writes, "The ethical positions of the New Testament are the children of their own times and places, alien and foreign to this day and age. Amidst the ethical dilemmas which confront us, we are now at least relieved of the need or temptation to begin with Jesus, or the early church, or the New Testament, if we wish to develop coherent ethical positions. We are freed from bondage to that tradition" (*Ethics in the New Testament*, 130).

24. Croatto, *Biblical Hermeneutics*, 1; italics original.

requires his followers to conduct themselves in a specific way, and in others he seeks to instill a virtue or element of character that is to typify his disciples. Yet there is something common to it all, something that ties it all together. In the words of Wogaman, "For the Bible to be appropriated into the work of Christian ethics, it must be seen to have some core of unity. Otherwise, there would be no basis in the Bible itself for dealing with apparently conflicting elements in the biblical canon."[25] He then indicates that many ethicists establish the unifying core by prioritizing certain texts over others, and thus establish a canon within the canon.[26] Determining whether or not that is the best approach will be one of our challenges as we continue to pursue our hermeneutical task. Whatever may be the conclusion to that effort, discovering the unifying core is crucial to establishing a hermeneutic for ethics that accommodates the entire word of God.

Wogaman gives us a bit of guidance as we launch our effort to discover a hermeneutic by outlining six points of tension with which ethicists have struggled through the centuries.[27] We too should struggle with these tensions, for dealing with them honestly will help us develop a more accurate and useful approach to biblical interpretation for ethics.

First, both revelation and reason are important for ethics, although there is no agreement on how each should be employed. Second, the goodness of the creation is affirmed, but so are values that transcend the material world. Third, the New Testament refers to "the elect," but also expects the evangelistic task will spread the gospel to everyone. The scope of Christian ethics, then, is broader than those who are Christians. Fourth, Christian ethics needs to deal with both the biblical emphasis on unmerited love and its demand for justice against wrongdoers. Fifth, within the history of God's faithful there is reliance upon and use of the power of the state and employment of violence. Christian ethics needs to square this imagery with the picture of God's anointed as the suffering servant, as well as Jesus' call for, and example of, nonviolent response and love of enemies. Sixth, for certain individuals such as Abraham, Joseph, and Joseph of Arimathea, wealth is depicted as a sign of God's favor, or at least it is seen in a favorable light. Elsewhere, in books such as Amos, Micah, and James, there is a strong bias toward the poor and condemnation of the wealthy. In other places, such as Mary's Magnificat, the early church's redistribution of wealth, and the eighth

---

25. Wogaman, *Christian Ethics*, 3.

26. Wogaman, *Christian Ethics*, 3.

27. For an expanded treatment of each of these six items, see Wogaman, *Christian Ethics*, 3–15.

chapter of Paul's Second Letter to the Corinthians, there appears to be an endorsement of economic leveling among God's faithful.

Perhaps it is now clear that any approach to biblical interpretation for ethics has to accommodate not only moral tensions and diversity within the Scripture, but also a host of other hermeneutical challenges. Throughout history our forebears in the faith have developed many ways to use the Scripture, all with the same goal we have—to be mature and faithful followers of our Lord. Let's begin with an overview of the major approaches that have been developed since Jesus walked the earth.

Hermeneutics from the Birth of the Church

In the second chapter of Acts we read of Peter's speech to the stunned crowd on the day the church was born. Throughout that speech Peter interprets portions of Scripture both to explain the phenomenon the crowd was observing, and to convey the message of Jesus the Messiah. In the two millennia since that amazing day faithful followers of Jesus have continued to interpret the Bible as part of their commitment to God, affirming not just that the Bible records various witnesses of faithful communities, but also that it is divine revelation in written form.[28] The hermeneutical task, however, is anything but trivial, particularly if one extends the effort all the way to using it responsibly in a modern social context. The notion of hermeneutical stages proves helpful to understanding the overall hermeneutical task. Donald Bloesch explains the process, stating,

> First, one must come to the Bible with an open heart and a searching mind. This presupposes that the seeker is a believer, one who has already been grasped by the spiritual reality to which the Bible attests. We agree with Barth that one must approach sacred Scripture without any overt presuppositions or at least with a critical attitude towards one's presuppositions.[29]

This last caution reflects the sensitivity expressed by Croatto, namely that nobody comes to the hermeneutical task without at least some biases from the past.

With this necessary element of humility in mind, Bloesch goes on to indicate the next step is to approach the text with a critical outlook, leveraging the benefits of literary and historical criticism to determine the writer's intent, understood through the culture in which a specific passage was

---

28. *Encyclopedia Britannica* Editors, "Hermeneutics," 1.
29. Bloesch, "Primacy of Scripture," 143.

formed.³⁰ This has not always been the hermeneutical approach affirmed by God's people. Throughout the history of the church there have been not only this one, but several others. We will explore all of them later in this section, but now we will move on to the next hermeneutical stage.

Once the original writer's intent is determined, it remains to move to what Bloesch terms "theological exegesis," an interpretive step in which the specific text being investigated is seen in light of the Bible's overall message. The interpreter "must now subject his³¹ own preconceptions to the scrutiny of Scripture itself. He must listen to the voice of the living Christ within Scripture . . . The text no longer is the interpreted object, but now the dynamic interpreter."³² We have here a hint at what I will propose as the appropriate hermeneutical standard for ethics: not only the picture of the historical Jesus who walked the earth before the crucifixion, but also the Messiah anticipated in the Old Testament as well as the postcrucifixion, resurrected, ascended, and exalted Jesus. Much more will be said about this in the ensuing chapters. It is sufficient at this stage to introduce this broad image of Jesus as central for interpreting the Bible in the moral realm.

Lastly, Bloesch suggests the ethical element of hermeneutics when he writes,

> the interpreter must relate the text, now understood in the light of Scripture itself, to the cultural situation of his time. He must translate the theological meaning of the text into the language and thought forms of modern man so that his hearers are presented with a coherent and intelligible message . . . The illumination of the Spirit is necessary not only for the interpreter but is also for the hearer if a real translation of meaning is to take place.³³

Cognizant of this general approach to the hermeneutical task, how have our forebears in the faith come to understand the means by which the message of Scripture is to be understood and applied, particularly in temporal, cultural, and social contexts very different from those of the original authors of the Bible?

---

30. Bloesch, "Primacy of Scripture," 143.

31. Unfortunately, as we have seen elsewhere, this author's style reflects an outmoded writing standard in which male pronouns are used presumably to refer to both genders. If this is not the case, then the author must intend that only men be interpreters of the Bible. I assume, however, that this is not the author's intention, and he intends to include both genders when choosing to use male pronouns.

32. Bloesch, "Primacy of Scripture," 143–44.

33. Bloesch, "Primacy of Scripture," 144.

Traditional Hermeneutical Schools of Thought

Four major schools of thought encompass the majority of hermeneutical approaches developed over the centuries. There are many variations of each, and ethicists have leveraged them in a host of different ways when interpreting the Bible for ethics. At points the names of the schools have varied somewhat, but in the broadest and most basic form they are the literal, allegorical, moral, and anagogical.

The literal approach appears at first to be quite simplistic. It holds that the appropriate hermeneutic is to affirm the literal meaning of Scripture. This view extends at least as far back as the fourth century, and still is in common use today, particularly for devotional purposes. In its most responsible form it is not so simplistic as to ignore the various types of literature and figurative language found in the Bible. If a particular sentence, phrase, or image cannot be reasonably understood via the literal meaning of its words, then forcing such an interpretation is inappropriate. For example, "'The eye of the Lord is upon thee,' would be a figurative-literal sentence . . . The literal meaning is about God's omniscience."[34]

For many centuries the dominant hermeneutical approach was that of allegory, from the dawn of the church to the Reformation. This school regards a Scripture passage as having a second level of meaning beyond the obvious elements of the text, and ignores the historical context in which it was written. As such it reflects a metaphorical approach. Of primary importance is what the interpreter wants to convey. The first-century Jewish philosopher Philo employed the allegorical method to reconcile the literal meaning of Scripture with his much-beloved Greek philosophy. Second-century church father Origen also used this interpretive approach, as did a host of church leaders after him. Whereas this hermeneutical method may seem to be an abuse of the text, A. Berkeley Mickelsen reminds us:

> Through allegorizing, traditional Christianity became tenable for Augustine. Augustine was an incisive theologian and a clear thinker. He knew that sound principles are important for interpretation. Yet he himself allegorized extensively. For example, the psalmist talks about lying down, sleeping, and rising up again or awaking (Ps. 3:5). But what he really refers to is the death and resurrection of Christ! In the narrative of the fall, the fig leaves mean hypocrisy, the coats of skins are mortality, and the four rivers become the four cardinal virtues.[35]

---

34. Ramm, *Protestant Biblical Interpretation*, 49.

35. Mickelsen, *Interpreting the Bible*, 34. In this quote, Mickelsen uses material from both Augustine's *Concerning Christian Doctrine* and F. W. Farrar's *History of Interpretation*.

Whatever difficulties we may have with the allegorical approach (or any other major hermeneutical school, for that matter), we should be cautious about dismissing outright any hermeneutic that was employed and affirmed by a host of God's faithful who went before us.

The moral, or tropological, school views the text as a source of moral lessons, and seeks to develop interpretive tools or approaches that result in guidance regarding human conduct. Allegory was often employed when reading the Scripture as a means to arrive at moral conclusions. As an example, late in the first century the Letter of Barnabas viewed the Levitical dietary laws for Israel "as forbidding not the flesh of certain animals but rather the vices imaginatively associated with those animals."[36] We will see that many approaches to using the Bible for ethics have been developed since this school emerged, but the fact it was used so early in the history of the church indicates Jesus' faithful realized from the outset that the Bible somehow was authoritative not only for their theological affirmations, but also for their values and conduct.

Finally, the anagogical approach primarily sees the Bible in light of the future and the eschaton. All events of the Bible are viewed from the perspective of eternity, and are understood as symbols of heavenly realities. For each text or story there is an underlying vision of the future that is mystical, ecstatic, and hidden, and at times that vision is not clear or is beyond human understanding. Anagogical hermeneutics takes the reader on a journey from the present to the end times and beyond, and reveals what the faithful community will look like in the future.[37]

A poem from the sixteenth century captures in a nutshell the various schools of interpretive thought:

> The *letter* shows us what God and our fathers did;
> The *allegory* shows us where our faith is hid;
> The *moral* meaning gives us rules of daily life;
> The *anagogy* shows us where we end our strife.[38]

Mickelsen goes on to explain, "Interpretation could be literal, allegorical, moral, or anagogical. 'Jerusalem' for the medieval interpreters could refer to the literal city in Palestine. Allegorically it could mean the church. Morally (tropologically) it would refer to the human soul. Anagogically 'Jerusalem' refers to the heavenly city."[39]

---

36. *Encyclopedia Britannica* Editors, "Hermeneutics," 1.
37. "Anagogical," *Oxford Reference*.
38. Quoted by Mickelsen, *Interpreting the Bible*, 35; italics original.
39. Mickelsen, *Interpreting the Bible*, 35.

It should be noted that since the Reformation, a variation, refinement, and enhancement of the literal school of thought has been developed. Today it is the foundational hermeneutic for many who hold to the authority of Scripture in all matters of faith and practice (i.e., belief and conduct, doctrine and ethics). It is known as the historical-grammatical method of interpretation. This approach primarily grew out of the Reformation as a reaction to the allegorical hermeneutic that had dominated biblical interpretation for hundreds of years. Many of the reformers, including Luther, Calvin, Zwingli, and Knox held to this approach.[40] Fundamental to this hermeneutic was commitment to a scholarly exegesis of the text, including a focus on the original Hebrew and Greek versions rather than the Latin Vulgate. Only in doing so could the normal meaning of the text, understood to be the literal one, be determined accurately.[41] The historical-grammatical method was further developed in the seventeenth and eighteenth centuries through scholarship focused on the ancient manuscripts, historical contexts in which the biblical materials were written, and literary analysis.[42] In the nineteenth century, many exegetical commentaries were published that addressed matters such as a biblical book's main emphases, intent for the original readers, grammar, historical background, and linguistic analysis.[43]

Surburg uses nineteenth-century Old Testament scholar Milton S. Terry's statement as a summary of this hermeneutical approach:

> In distinction from all the above-mentioned methods of interpretation, we may name the Grammatico-Historical as the method which most fully commends itself to the judgment and conscience of Christian Scholars. Its fundamental principle is to gather from the Scriptures themselves the precise meaning which the writers intended to convey. It applies to the sacred books the same principles, the same grammatical process and exercise of common sense and reason, which we apply to other books. The grammatico-historical exegete, furnished with suitable qualifications, intellectual, educational, and moral, will accept the claims of the Bible without prejudice or adverse pre-possession, and, with no ambition to prove them false, will investigate the language and import of each book with fearless independence. He[44] will master the language of the writer, the

---

40. Surburg, "Presuppositions of the Historical-Grammatical Method," 278.
41. Surburg, "Presuppositions of the Historical-Grammatical Method," 281–82.
42. Mickelsen, *Interpreting the Bible*, 43.
43. Mickelsen, *Interpreting the Bible*, 47.
44. As we have seen with several other authors, Terry employs male pronouns presumably reflecting the convention of his day. I will assume his statements apply equally

particular dialect which he used, and his peculiar style and manner of expression. He will inquire into the circumstances under which he wrote, the manners and customs of his age, and the purpose or object which he had in view. He has a right to assume that no sensible author will be knowingly inconsistent with himself, or seek to bewilder and mislead his readers.[45]

Having understood the main approaches to biblical interpretation since the inception of the church, we now turn to the hermeneutical approaches developed by ethicists as they seek to use the Scripture as the authority for the moral realm. Whereas they do not exactly parallel the approaches just reviewed, they do leverage, extend, and apply them for doing ethics. At the end of the next section a hermeneutic for ethics will be proposed—one appropriate for our task of determining how to live as mature believers and be more faithful to God.

Hermeneutics and Ethics

Earlier in the chapter we saw that nearly all Christian ethicists hold that Scripture is authoritative for ethics, although there is broad diversity of opinion on what that means. Various ethicists emphasize the authority of theological concepts, commands, values, exemplary lives, community witness, God's character or conduct, and so on. Adding complexity to the hermeneutical picture are the social contexts of the biblical writings, sometimes vastly different from our own. There have been attempts to harmonize the biblical material in various ways, all of which appear to be less than ideal, while some ethicists simply encourage us to live with the moral tensions and incongruities found as one compares a certain passage with another that deals with the same subject. Whatever one's approach, realizing the hermeneutical task is anything but easy should serve as a reminder to adopt a humble and cautious position, always receptive to correction and improvement, when seeking to establish a biblical hermeneutic for ethics.

Our challenge, you may recall, is how to utilize the various and varied pictures of Jesus we find in the New Testament in an authoritative way as we seek to follow Jesus faithfully while we live daily in the moral realm. Soon we will review a number of ways ethicists have approached this in the past, but as we launch into the task we should keep in mind several notions

---

to women and men, rather than only to men as his language in today's context would indicate.

45. Terry, quoted in Surburg, "Presuppositions of the Historical-Grammatical Method," 280.

Richard B. Hays brings to our attention.[46] First, as interpreters we do not act in isolation. It is true we are accountable for whatever interpretation we assert, but we act as members of both the current and historic community of God. For 2,000 years, God's faithful people have been using the Bible for ethical guidance (and before the development of the New Testament, far longer). We interpret within the historical context of the church.[47] This is reflective of the notion of *sola scriptura*, in contradistinction to solo *scriptura*, as we saw earlier in the chapter.

Second, we need to be aware there are other sources of moral authority in addition to Scripture. Hays reflects traditional Wesleyan thinking when he mentions tradition, reason, and experience.[48] Ethicists have long struggled over the relationship between these three and Scripture, as Hays points out: "the interpreter must also reckon with the problem of how to coordinate the witness of the New Testament with the moral wisdom that comes from other sources: *tradition, reason,* and *experience*."[49] Again, reflecting a proper understanding of *sola scriptura*, we assert the three are both fallible and subordinate to Scripture, while remaining valuable resources for informing moral thought.

Third, not all passages in the Bible are written in the same mode. There is diversity of expression and approach within Scripture. The interpreter must be sensitive to this variation. More will be said about this later, but for now the interpreter must keep in mind that, "the hermeneutical task is—in part—the task of rightly correlating our ethical norms with the modes of Scripture's speech."[50] Of course this adds complexity to the interpretive effort, but ignoring the variations of moral expression found within Scripture leads only to erroneous ethical prescription.

What, then, are the typical ways ethicists have utilized the Bible through the ages? Let us start by looking into the ways the Bible has been viewed as ethically normative.

---

46. Hays has treated these and many other hermeneutical themes extensively in *The Moral Vision of the New Testament*. Only a fraction of these themes are addressed here. The reader is encouraged to read Hays' book to get a much more in-depth understanding.

47. Hays, *Moral Vision*, 305–6.

48. Hays, *Moral Vision*, 210.

49. Hays, *Moral Vision*, 295; italics original.

50. Hays, *Moral Vision*, 209.

Hermeneutical Approaches for Ethics

Many have written on the subject of how to use the Bible for ethics,[51] and there are various ways the options are defined and categorized. Whereas a defense could be made for any number of approaches, one used by many authors is to articulate common views of how the Bible serves as morality that God has revealed. We will start with this approach, then augment it by considering an overview of other ways to use the Bible for ethics. For a more comprehensive presentation other sources should be consulted.[52]

The Bible as Revealed Morality

The 1970s work of James M. Gustafson remains foundational for understanding the main ways Scripture can be employed as revealed morality. Gustafson first identified a view that sees the Bible as moral law. Those who violate Scripture's moral law should be judged morally wrong.[53] Birch and Rasmussen associate this view with fundamentalism, which interprets the Bible in a literal manner such that there is only one moral standard for all time. Scripture's norms, standards, and commands are to be directly applied to all current contexts.[54] One ethicist termed this the "prescriptive" approach, and linked it to historical figures such as John Calvin, John Wycliff, and the Anabaptists.[55] Another called this the "rules" mode of ethical hermeneutics.[56]

An example of a serious scholar who employed this approach is mid-twentieth-century ethicist and theologian Edward John Carnell. Carnell used the Scripture in many ways when addressing ethical subjects, but leveraging the Bible as moral law was one he used most often. In his book on Christian apologetics Carnell wrote, "Christ commands that those who love Him follow His words implicitly. 'If you love me, you will keep my commandments' (John 14:15)."[57] In a specific example, that of drunkenness,

---

51. Rather than attempting to be original regarding how the Bible has been used for ethics, the work of others will be leveraged to create an overview of typical approaches, with examples of each.

52. See, for example, Birch and Rasmussen, *Bible and Ethics*; Gustafson, "Place of Scripture"; Hays, *Moral Vision*; Siker, *Scripture and Ethics*; and Tambasco, *Bible for Ethics*.

53. Gustafson, *Theology and Christian Ethics*, 130.

54. Birch and Rasmussen, *Bible and Ethics*, 21–22.

55. Friesen, "Issues in Christian Ethics," 32, citing Edward Leroy Long.

56. Hays, *Moral Vision*, 208–9.

57. Carnell, *Introduction to Christian Apologetics*, 300.

Carnell quoted 1 Corinthians 6:9–10, then asserted, "The Scriptures promise to the unrepentant drunkard, eternal damnation, for the latter has spurned God's law by willfully destroying his body, the temple of the Holy Spirit."[58]

After articulating the first way to view Scripture as revealed morality, Gustafson quickly pointed out there are at least two significant issues with this ethical hermeneutic.[59] First is the question of which moral law is to be endorsed as authoritative and primary. There are many in the Bible, and whereas they are not in complete conflict, neither are they in complete harmony. Second, the way in which the moral law is to be applied is not at all clear. Which texts are to be applied to moral situations, and which are not? Alternatively, *how* are texts to be applied, and by what means do we know the application is the correct one?

Gustafson identified a second view of the Bible as revealed morality. In this view it is the Bible's moral ideals that are seen as authoritative. These ideals often are presented as principles to be applied to current contexts. Those who do not live up to the ideals or principles should be "judged morally wrong, or at least morally deficient."[60] If Scripture as moral law is associated with fundamentalists, then Scripture as moral ideals is linked to those of a more liberal persuasion.[61] Twentieth-century ethicist Reinhold Niebuhr can be understood as a proponent of this hermeneutic. According to Hays, Niebuhr

> shows no interest in applying Scripture's specific *rules* to the moral issues of his day; rather, he sees Scripture as providing, above all else, *principles* that guide moral reflection—or, at an even higher level of abstraction, ideals (for example, love), from which principles (such as equal justice) may be derived. Moral decisions must be made by deciding in specific situations which actions best correspond to these principles.[62]

The hermeneutical approach of moral ideals faces its own set of difficulties. First, Gustafson asks if Scripture warrants the use of the language of moral ideals, pointing out that such language is not as intrinsic to Scripture as the language of law.[63] The second issue is how to determine the content of the ideals themselves, and the third is establishing the basis for applying an ideal to a specific life situation.[64]

58. Carnell, "Is Drunkenness a Sin?," 6.
59. Gustafson, *Theology and Christian Ethics*, 130.
60. Gustafson, *Theology and Christian Ethics*, 131.
61. Birch and Rasmussen, *Bible and Ethics*, 22.
62. Hays, *Moral Vision*, 222; italics original.
63. Gustafson, *Theology and Christian Ethics*, 131.
64. Gustafson, *Theology and Christian Ethics*, 132.

In addition to the difficulties pointed out by Gustafson, both of these views of the Bible as a moral authority suffer from a common shortcoming: they do not show sufficient appreciation for the difficulty of taking documents that were written centuries ago in a range of cultural and social contexts and applying them to our current Western context. The gap is wide between biblical times and our own, and simply advocating a direct application of either moral law or moral ideals to the complexities of a twenty-first-century world betrays an insufficient awareness of the vast contextual difference between ancient societies and our own. A more responsible application of the Bible of necessity will address this challenge.

A third hermeneutical approach to the Bible as revealed morality is what Gustafson terms "analogy,"[65] which appears to be similar to what Hays terms "paradigms."[66] In this approach it is morally wrong to act in a way that was judged morally wrong in scriptural situations of similar circumstances.[67] One practical way to employ this approach is to see in Scripture an overriding thrust that can be applied to current contexts. Paul Ramsey, for example, holds that the Bible's central message "is that God means to mold human life into the action of God, human righteousness into God's righteousness, man's frequent faithlessness or maybe his fragile faithfulness into the faithfulness of God Himself."[68] Regarding the central motif of Scripture, Ramsey argues for the notion of covenant. "Covenant is *the* biblical theme around which he chooses to organize his appropriation of biblical ethics since covenant 'is not only frequently mentioned in the Bible but is its main theme.'"[69] Applying the covenant notion to practical situations, "Ramsey sees Paul as continuing and developing what Jesus had initiated, an ethic based on God's covenant righteousness and God's concern for humans that responds to neighbor-need with appropriate neighbor-love."[70]

One rather obvious problem of this approach is the difficulty of determining what constitutes similar circumstances between the biblical event and the one in question. A second is how to select the appropriate biblical situation that will serve as the basis for the analogy.[71] In situations where an overriding biblical thrust or primary theme is employed, the issue is how to develop a sufficient defense of the selected theme as primary.

65. Gustafson, *Theology and Christian Ethics*, 133.
66. Hays, *Moral Vision*, 209.
67. Gustafson, *Theology and Christian Ethics*, 133.
68. Siker, quoting Paul Ramsey in *Scripture and Ethics*, 83.
69. Siker, *Scripture and Ethics*, 85; italics original.
70. Siker, *Scripture and Ethics*, 87.
71. Gustafson, *Theology and Christian Ethics*, 133.

Some ethicists, while affirming the Bible as revealed morality, choose a blended sort of hermeneutic that includes various biblical norms, commands, laws, ideals, principles, analogies, themes, and the like. They appropriately perceive that hermeneutics for ethics cannot be reduced to one of the three views presented above, and assert that a broader and more open approach should be taken. This, of course, adds complexity to the hermeneutical task, and also exacerbates the difficulty with the other views of how to select and apply the appropriate hermeneutical element in any specific context. This, in my opinion, is such a glaring deficiency with the blended approach as to render it indefensible, with the one possible exception that the ethicist's subjective moral authority holds the slight potential for an accurate application. One should not count on correct application in a high percentage of cases, however, as the judgment of other ethicists most often would render different conclusions. It remains for us to seek a more reliable biblical hermeneutic for ethics.

The Bible as Revealed Reality

Birch and Rasmussen, in presenting various approaches to scriptural hermeneutics for ethics, point out that Gustafson contrasted the notion of the Bible as revealed morality with that of the Bible as revealed reality.[72] According to this concept the Bible does not so much present standards for morality as it calls for response to the God revealed in the Bible and who was active in historical events. "The God disclosed in the scriptures was a living, free God active in every historical present. The Christian life was centered in response to that God and that action."[73] The Christian or Christian community that seeks to use the Bible for ethics should first understand the God who speaks and acts in specific historical situations, then respond in faithfulness to God. According to Gustafson, the focus in any particular event is "not 'How ought we to judge this event?' nor even 'What ought we to do in this event?' but 'What is God doing in this event? What is he saying to us in this event?'"[74] Biblical theology provides a framework for answering the question.

A towering figure in Christian ethics in the twentieth century was that of H. Richard Niebuhr. Niebuhr serves as a prime example of an ethicist who held to the Bible as revealed reality, and the need for the faithful to learn of God and respond appropriately. Key to his understanding of Scripture

---

72. Birch and Rasmussen, *Bible and Ethics*, 23.
73. Birch and Rasmussen, *Bible and Ethics*, 24.
74. Gustafson, *Theology and Christian Ethics*, 135.

was his emphasis on the historical conditioning of its various writings, and thus he did not think it possible to apply biblical ethics directly to current contexts.[75] For Niebuhr, "to read the Bible is to hear various historically conditioned encounters between God and the people of God across time. And across time, certain patterns emerge that testify to the constancy of God in relation to humanity. Such cohesiveness provides the necessary unity to the biblical witness to God and to the community of faith even across time."[76] The documents of the New Testament do not comprise an apologetics book, nor are they a compendium of divine dictates. Rather, they are the records of early Christians' experiences of God through their encounters with the historical Jesus and the effect he had on his disciples. For Niebuhr, then, the only responsible biblical hermeneutic is one that affirms the historical conditioning of the biblical texts and sees in them the confessions of God's faithful communities.[77] When it comes to the specifics of an appropriate response, "Niebuhr identified Jesus' faithfulness to God especially in terms of his identity with the poor and the oppressed of the world, his inclusion of the enemy as neighbor, and his emphasis on the transformation of internal attitudes toward one's neighbor. For Niebuhr, these are characteristic of faithful responses of Christian communities in the world."[78]

Certain ethicists who work within the hermeneutic of revealed reality approach the Bible via a particular theme. An overarching concept used by many is to see in the Bible a predisposition or bias in favor of the poor, with a resultant dedication to pursue justice on their behalf. According to Stephen Charles Mott, "the biblical message of justice creates a basic loyalty to the poor and weak and a commitment to their defense. Scripture is then interpreted in the light of this biblically formed understanding.... The Bible is read with the expectation of answers to questions of social justice and human oppression."[79] The Bible, however, is not read in isolation. Rather, the disciplines of other fields of study are leveraged to bridge the gap between biblical social contexts and modern ones: "In aid of greater methodological self-consciousness in interpretation, modern sociological and ethical categories are applied to the materials of the Bible to suggest new possibilities of meaning and to provide a means of assessing the applicability of the results of exegesis to contemporary discussion."[80]

75. Siker, *Scripture and Ethics*, 52.
76. Siker, *Scripture and Ethics*, 47.
77. Siker, *Scripture and Ethics*, 48–49.
78. Siker, *Scripture and Ethics*, 54.
79. Mott, *Biblical Ethics and Social Change*, viii.
80. Mott, *Biblical Ethics and Social Change*, viii.

One outworking of this hermeneutical approach is that of those who, in one respect or another, emphasize the Bible's focus on liberation. For them the way God has engaged with history is through the liberation of his faithful people from the powerful who would abuse and oppress them. Often appeal is made to the story of the Exodus—Israel's liberation from slavery in Egypt—as the primary archetype which serves to inspire and direct the response of God's faithful who currently find themselves subjugated by oppressive regimes. Several examples will serve to clarify how this hermeneutic is applied in specific circumstances.

For Juan Luis Segundo, working in a Latin American context, a deep understanding of the real-world situation is primary. Only when such an understanding exists can the Bible be reinterpreted in such a way that it speaks to conditions of the current historical situation. A precondition to using the Scripture is a commitment to the poor. Although objective truth may be found in the Bible, the interpreter must use caution when selecting specific passages and applying them directly to any specific historic situation. Oversimplification in applying texts is a temptation, and thus the Exodus should not be seen as the complete biblical message. It must be realized that historical development of the Bible, including the teaching of Jesus, was a process, as is application of the Bible to current oppressive contexts in which the poor find themselves. Thus, concrete answers for today's problems cannot be found directly in the Bible. Learning to learn involves creativity, and so must development of answers.[81]

Another ethicist—one who focused on black liberation—is James Cone. For Cone, the liberation of blacks and God's revelation in Jesus as the liberator of the oppressed serve as the hermeneutical standard. The Jesus of the Gospels is seen as the Oppressed One who aligns with the poor and oppressed, both through what he taught and what he did. Just as the historical Jesus joined himself to the poor of first-century Palestine, the living Jesus of today is joined to oppressed African Americans, and thus must be viewed as a black Christ (just as in the first century he was viewed as Son of David, Son of God, and Son of Man). Regarding use of the Bible, Cone shockingly refers to the Christian Bible as a "poison book," meaning white Christians have obscured the Bible's true message of actual social liberation of the oppressed by spiritualizing such notions as the Sermon on the Mount's poor in spirit—all at the expense of African Americans. Proper response to Jesus entails his disciples identifying with his blackness, just as the historical Jesus identified with the poor and disenfranchised of Palestine. Faithfulness to

---

81. Tambasco, *Bible for Ethics*, 52–54, 135, 137, 142, 145.

God means the entire person—heart, soul, mind, and body—must be where the disposed are, and thereby be reconciled to God.[82]

Another take on the liberation theme is the feminist theology of Rosemary Radford Ruether. For Ruether, the Bible is a record of humans seeking to capture their visions of faithfulness to God. However, the Bible is so androcentric and patriarchal that it needs to be recontextualized in a way that it is freed from patriarchy. The tradition of the prophets is central to interpretation and response, and thus a feminist hermeneutic is simply an extension of the prophetic tradition whereby sacred texts are reinterpreted in the context of faithful communities. If a reinterpretation is liberating and promotes the full humanity of women, it is genuine; otherwise it simply perpetuates oppressive hierarchical domination. The example of Jesus is seen as normative. Just as he rejected the domination of social and religious elites, renounced the use of power to dominate, and identified with the poor, so God's faithful should do the same (particularly with regard to women). As Mary Magdalene freed herself from patriarchal repression, so women today should break the status quo of repression and servitude to men.[83]

Thinking of Scripture as revealed reality certainly has its benefits for those who would seek to be mature followers of Jesus and be more faithful disciples. Understanding how God has been active in history certainly gives us an insight into the heart and mind of God. Listening for and to God creates in us a humility and patience that otherwise would be missing, to our detriment. Seeking to respond to God keeps our attention appropriately focused, at least prior to engaging in any sort of activism. Yet this hermeneutic suffers from a number of difficulties and deficiencies that render it questionable as a sufficient and overall approach to using the Bible for ethics.

First and most basic is the understanding of the Bible as a record of the experiences of God's faithful. Of course there are elements of faithfulness expressed in the biblical documents. However, such an understanding certainly is quite selective. The Bible is far more than a recording of experiences; it is God's word to us. Its veracity and authority, as Calvin asserted, is equal to God speaking directly to us. Seeing Scripture only as a recording of experiences amounts to a belittling of the Bible. Second, this approach tends to select certain texts as primary while ignoring others. Thus, it takes a "text within the text" approach to hermeneutics that does not adequately accommodate the whole of the Scripture, but rather serves the agenda and preestablished conclusions of the interpreter. For example, liberation of the poor and oppressed may accurately be seen in stories such as the Exodus,

---

82. Siker, *Scripture and Ethics*, 159–64.
83. Siker, *Scripture and Ethics*, 171, 196–98.

but why are stories of domination (such as the conquest of Canaan) overlooked? Another example involves the images of Jesus affirmed by these interpreters. They often appear to reflect only certain aspects of the gospel stories, or perhaps only some of the gospel stories, but not the comprehensive Jesus picture. Furthermore, the biblical image of who the resurrected and exalted Jesus is now, what he is doing, and how he informs our ethics, is summarily ignored. Third, those who hold to a specific theme as an overriding hermeneutical approach fail adequately to defend the selected theme while ignoring others. For example, why is liberation the correct and sufficient hermeneutical driver, rather than another theme such as creation, covenant, or cross?[84]

The Bible and Character Formation

Certain ethicists assert the proper function of the Bible for ethics is to stimulate and guide character formation. The justification for this approach is that our conduct in the moral realm is an outgrowth of our character, and thus the best use of the Bible is not to extract moral standards, but rather to foster the development of moral character.

Just what does a hermeneutic for character formation look like? One ethicist asserts character ethics, at minimum, defines desirable characteristics, and even a critical biblical hermeneutic will generate the virtues Christian character should exhibit.[85] The Theology of Work Project holds that the starting point of this character approach is the question, "What type of person should I become?" because a person of good character is likely to do the right things throughout life. The proper character attributes should become "ingrained in us as default settings." Character ethics is "about how the character of God is shaping our own characters—about whether we are becoming more holy, just and loving people, to name three prominent character traits in the Bible."[86]

One challenge for those who affirm this hermeneutical approach is how to determine which passages are authoritative, and which virtues are normative for character formation. In addressing the issue, the Theology of Work Project appeals to the work of Glen Stassen and David Gushee, who argue Jesus is to be our model. We are to imitate him and develop in

---

84. For a more detailed critique, see Siker, *Scripture and Ethics*, 55–57, 146, 166–68, 199–201.

85. O'Neil, "On Hermeneutics and Ethics," referencing the work of Lisa Sowle Cahill.

86. Theology of Work Project, "Character Approach," paras. 1, 2.

ourselves the character of Jesus. More specifically, the virtues of the Sermon on the Mount, particularly those found in the Beatitudes, are the ones that are to be nurtured as Jesus' followers seek to grow in faithfulness.[87]

Birch and Rasmussen offer a good defense for this hermeneutic, as well as an explanation of how the Bible is to be used to form character. Their initial contention is a practical one and includes both individual and communal aspects: "the most effective and crucial impact of the Bible in Christian ethics is that of shaping the moral identity of the Christian and of the church."[88] They go on to argue that "rules, principles, and maxims are surely far less influential than dominating images and symbols, paradigmatic figures, rituals and stories."[89]

At this point we might ask exactly which biblical images, symbols, stories, and so on, Birch and Rasmussen think are to be used in the formation of Christian character. To this question they provide no specific answer, unlike Stassen and Gushee. Rather, they emphasize "the point is not *which* biblical materials generate *which* perspectives, attitudes, intentions and convictions, but *that* biblical materials *can and ought* to create a cast which has profound ramifications for character and conduct,"[90] and then go on to claim, "A singular presentation of the Bible's meaning for Christian character is not possible, nor is a singular presentation of normative Christian character. We wish only to suggest that the role of the scriptures in the nurturing of a basic orientation and in the generating of particular attitudes and intentions is a central one."[91] As frustrating as it may be not to have any specific guidance regarding which portions of Scripture should be employed with this hermeneutic, Birch and Rasmussen leave this determination up to the specific individuals and faith communities. For them not only can the way in which the Bible forms character be difficult to assess, but the elements of the Bible that effect such formation are equally elusive, and "may enter the process of character formation in ways very difficult to trace."[92] Their message to those who would grow in faithfulness to God "is to underline the moral importance of a continual immersion in biblical materials in worship and education. In a word, the starting point for moral identity is with the Bible in the life of the church as a gathered community."[93]

87. Theology of Work Project, "Character Approach," paras. 9, 10.
88. Birch and Rasmussen, *Bible and Ethics*, 104.
89. Birch and Rasmussen, *Bible and Ethics*, 105.
90. Birch and Rasmussen, *Bible and Ethics*, 108; italics original.
91. Birch and Rasmussen, *Bible and Ethics*, 108.
92. Birch and Rasmussen, *Bible and Ethics*, 109.
93. Birch and Rasmussen, *Bible and Ethics*, 111.

Jesus as the Normative Ethical Hermeneutic

There certainly is value to be realized from most of the hermeneutical approaches we have reviewed. In the appropriate context we can leverage the insights and affirmations of all the traditional hermeneutical schools of thought, as well as the hermeneutical approaches for ethics we explored. It would be a mistake, and an expression of hermeneutical hubris, to reject outright the spiritual and scholarly contributions of those from the broader family of Christian faith who have struggled honestly and humbly to formulate approaches to using Scripture in ways that reflect faithfulness to God while engaging the moral challenges of the specific contexts in which we find ourselves. Yet even though they may be quite helpful to us as we seek to use the Bible appropriately, all of them are inadequate in one fundamental way: they do not view the Bible's complete image of the Second Person of the Trinity—particularly the present, living, exalted Jesus specifically pictured in the Epistle to the Hebrews—as primary and fundamental to a hermeneutic for ethics. The challenge remaining before us is to appropriate the biblical material in our historical and social context in a way that ensures we are not abusing it, but rather using it correctly as the authoritative source for ethics we affirm it is. In an attempt to meet that challenge let me propose a six-element hermeneutic that will serve us well as we attempt to use the Bible for ethics in the actual contexts in which we find ourselves, while enabling us to grow in maturity as God's faithful people.

Scripture Has Primacy

Asserting that the primacy of Scripture is an element of a hermeneutic for ethics may first appear to be a penultimate concept to establishing such a hermeneutic. Earlier we saw that nearly all Christian ethicists affirm the Bible is fundamental to Christian ethics. However, there also was a wide variation of opinion among them regarding just how the Bible is fundamental. Thus, establishing what Scripture actually is in the context of doing ethics is basic to an ethical hermeneutic.

Once more we affirm Scripture itself is authoritative for our ethical lives. It is not simply the witness of faithful communities. Neither is its context so removed from our own or colored by the assumption of an immediate eschaton as to render its content inapplicable to our current situation. Rather, although it was written by many authors over hundreds of years in a variety of contexts, all of it was God-breathed, and thus is the timeless written word of God. Having one infallible divine source, by implication the

Scripture is characterized by some sort of singularity, continuity, or unity which is fundamental to using it in the moral realm.

The view of Scripture's authority asserted in the early years of the church, and reiterated by the reformers, is the accurate and appropriate one for ethical hermeneutics. A proper understanding of *sola scriptura* rejects any infallible authority other than the Bible, while allowing for the influence of other fallible sources of moral insight. Yet there is an implicit assumption that the Bible is to be viewed not simply as the source of moral content but as the challenger of our natural moral commitments. As such it issues a call to overturn or correct the moral effects of the fall to which we are all subject, and expects the believer, seeking to mature in faithfulness, will yield morally to the correcting work of Scripture. In short, we need to interpret Scripture with the intent, or goal, of altering our moral convictions.

It is important to affirm there is ethical velocity in the Bible. Revelation is progressive, and there is moral movement within the Scripture. At the same time the Bible displays singularity, it also demonstrates moral development; it is not morally static. The most beneficial aid to help us embrace Scripture's moral flow is to copy the interpretive approach of Jesus, when he declared, "You have heard it said to people long ago . . . But I say to you . . .,"[94] or when he indicated the Sabbath was made for people rather than people being made for the Sabbath. In using the Bible this way he created moral movement within the Scripture, and set a hermeneutical standard for us. This leads us to the second element of our moral hermeneutic.

Jesus Is the Interpretive Authority

In the last chapter we explored the concept of moral authority, and posed the questions, "What makes a decision right?" and "How do we know what is obligatory?" It is Jesus as the authoritative interpreter of Scripture who is the moral mediator between God and God's faithful. Jesus authoritatively conveys value when interpreting the Scripture, and thus conveys ethical rightness and obligation. Recall that a moral authority does not act in isolation, but rather in relationship with those who willingly accept and submit to his or her authority. An essential hermeneutical element, one that also may impress us as penultimate to the actual interpreting of Scripture, is to endorse the interpretive authority of the Second Person of the Trinity, not only the incarnate Jesus but also the Creator and the exalted Lord of All.

It is as we submit to and emulate the authoritative interpretive approach of the Word of God who was in the beginning—the one who was

---

94. Matt 5:21–22.

with God and was God, according to the first words of John's Gospel—that we ourselves understand what God wants of us, and are enabled as moral agents and interpreters of the word of God written. There is one word of God, but we experience it both as Living Word and as written word. To apply accurately the latter in the moral realm we first must yield to the way the former applies the latter.

Jesus' great moral teaching and reinterpretation of the Old Testament law found in the Sermon on the Mount ends with an observation: the people were amazed because of Jesus' authority, compared with that of their other religious teachers. Our hermeneutic needs to go a step past amazement to that of endorsement if we are to use the Scripture accurately in the moral realm. It needs to begin with the interpretive approach of Jesus.

Jesus Is Overarching

Some hermeneutical approaches to ethics focus on a single theme, such as love, community, justice, the poor and oppressed, liberation, the kingdom of God, etc. When this approach is selected of necessity a "canon within the canon" is created, for certain of the Bible's subjects and passages are granted primacy over others, and all passages are interpreted in light of the single theme. In our hermeneutic we seek to avoid this approach, preferring to accommodate the entire canon without having to filter it through a preselected theme.

The historical-grammatical method of interpretation requires that the interpreter show sensitivity to the language of the writer, pay attention to the literary form employed in any particular passage, and in general demonstrate commitment to a scholarly exegesis of the text. To this end, it is clear the dominant form employed throughout the Scripture, even from the creation account, is that of narrative. The Bible is God's story from its beginning to its end, and Jesus—at times preincarnate, at other times incarnate and walking the earth, and at yet other times resurrected, ascended, and glorified—is the central figure of the narrative. We must be quick to assert this Jesus is not to be seen as a theme in *contrast* to other possible themes (love, community, the oppressed, the kingdom of God, etc.), or in *parallel* with them, but rather as the one *overarching* them all. All of them are encompassed within the Jesus of the narrative. Jesus engulfs them all, and is their Creator, their Interpreter, their Overseer, and their Coagulator. They only have moral meaning when viewed in light of the overarching Jesus of the narrative.

The hermeneutical norm for those who would accurately use the Scripture in the moral realm is the one in the story of the fall who will crush the serpent's head while having his heal struck; the one who, as both David's son and Lord, is invited to sit at the right hand of the Lord; the shoot of the stump of Jesse as well as the suffering servant spoken of by Isaiah; the one glorious human-like figure high above the throne in Ezekiel's vision; the Jesus of the Gospel stories and Acts, as well as Paul's encounter on the Damascus road; the "one to come" (Rom 5:14) who is contrasted with Adam in the Epistle to the Romans; the Melchizedekian high priest of the Epistle to the Hebrews; and the one who walks among the seven golden lampstands, the Living Lamb who looks as if it had been slain, and the Alpha and Omega of John's vision. This figure is the paradigmatic interpretive grid for accurately applying the entire biblical narrative to today's social contexts, and is a compelling hermeneutical element for those who would mature as followers of Jesus.

Perhaps it goes without saying, but I want to make it clear: the narrative is not a single static lump. Rather, as was the case with Scripture itself, the narrative entails progression. It flows, and it develops. It has a beginning and an end, and the flow of the narrative's overarching Jesus affects how we interpret the narrative itself.

Jesus Is the Hermeneutical Core

It follows that if Jesus is the overarching figure in God's eternal story, then he also is the hermeneutical core for dealing with that story. Ethical hermeneutics cannot properly be done without Jesus at the center of the interpretive effort. There are several parts of this hermeneutical element.

First is the notion that the teachings and actions of the incarnate Jesus provide us with a tangible model for our own moral involvement. When we read the Gospel accounts we are to interpret them in such a way as to recognize the Jesus we are to follow. His teachings are not unattainable moral ideals or a vision of the eschatological kingdom, but rather tangible and actual ethical standards for those who claim to be Jesus' followers. Recall the historical-grammatical hermeneutic assumes the interpreter will affirm the most natural, simple, and direct meaning of the text. That being the case, enemies actually are to be treated as Jesus taught in the Sermon on the Mount. We are not to resist an evil person who abuses us. Just as Jesus told his disciples he refused to resort to violence when being falsely accused and accosted by society's established authorities, even though he had huge celestial armies at his disposal, so the mature follower of Jesus is to see in

Jesus' teaching (and associated conduct) an example to emulate and thus refuse to resort to violence even if the means to do so are available.

Jesus' predispositions in his conduct also serve as a moral standard for his followers. In the Gospels we see how Jesus engaged with various members of the society in which he lived. It is clear his moral commitments were to favor those to whom society had shown disfavor—the poor, outcasts, foreigners, women, children, the powerless, the despised, the contagious, the sinful, the oppressed, the accused. That conduct serves as a hermeneutical standard for how we are to interpret the Scripture.

Much more will be said about the earthly Jesus in the next chapter, but for now it will suffice to assert the earthly Jesus needs to be taken seriously as we read God's story. In short, the teaching and conduct of the earthly Jesus serve as epistemic and exemplary moral authorities when seeking to interpret the Bible correctly and apply it in the contexts in which we find ourselves.

Second, we need to view the Old Testament writings as Jesus did, and use them in our moral deliberations following the pattern he set. Fundamentally this means to view them as redeeming, not condemning. Stassen and Gushee rightly point out that Jesus adopted a prophetic stance toward the Old Testament rather than the common rabbinical one of his day.[95] When we look into the essential ethos of the Old Testament prophets we quickly realize they were the ethicists of their time, focusing on right attitude and conduct in the moral realm. As such, their emphasis when declaring the message of God was not on laws and rituals, but rather on the moral good. Theirs was a call to moral uprightness by the powerful, including a predisposition toward those who were victims of injustice or abuse and care for the poor, the outcast, foreigners, women, children, the suffering, and the sick. The prophets were not concerned about religious form, and neither was Jesus. Rather both sought goodness of heart among God's faithful, with the commensurate outworking of justice and grace within society.[96]

This prophetic mindset was, for Jesus, not only the definition of piety, but also the essential approach for interpreting the Old Testament. In adopting it he established a hermeneutical standard for his followers, and for all those who would be faithful to God. In short, the Scripture is to be interpreted and applied in the prophetic tradition as opposed to the tradition of religious ritual. The maturity called for in Hebrews 5 includes adopting the prophets' stance vis-à-vis society and the faithful community, for that is

---

95. Stassen and Gushee, *Kingdom Ethics*, 91–94.
96. As an example, see Isa 58.

what Jesus did. This naturally results in a much greater focus on the moral realm rather than religious correctness when interpreting Scripture.

Third, as its hermeneutical core, the living, exalted Jesus serves as a guide for interpreting the Bible and applying it in the moral realm. Not only are the narratives about his earthly conduct and teachings parts of our hermeneutical standards, but his current living conduct is overwhelmingly authoritative, for this Jesus is the one to whom we yield in all aspects of our existence. We do not seek to be faithful to the earthly Jesus *story* from 2,000 years ago, but rather the *living* Jesus portrayed in the Epistle to the Hebrews and present among us in the person of the Holy Spirit. The postresurrection Jesus is the one we call Lord. Both he and we live in a postresurrection era. Correct interpretation of the Bible can only be done when the interpreter is engaged in active, ongoing encounter with the glorified Second Person of the Trinity—the one who illumines the text about himself.

This presupposes the interpreter has yielded to the lordship of the hermeneutical center—the overarching Jesus who now is living and exalted—and seeks to emulate what Jesus currently is. Much more will be said about this in the fifth chapter, but for our current purpose of understanding the elements of a hermeneutic for ethics it will suffice to affirm we accurately interpret Scripture for today only when we view it via the Jesus of today.

There is biblical basis for seeing the living Jesus as a hermeneutical standard. In the fourth chapter of John's first epistle, he wrote about the divine indwelling of the believer. In the seventeenth verse we read these words: "In this world we are like Jesus." The Revised Standard Version adds clarity when it translates this phrase, "as he is so are we in this world." It is the current Jesus who is to be our standard for living in the world—the moral realm. The apostle Paul echoed this idea in his Second Epistle to the Corinthians when describing his conduct among that community of believers. In the thirteenth chapter he wrote of the resurrected Christ living by the power of God, and reminded those believers the same living Jesus is in them. The implication of that indwelling is the subject of his subsequent prayer—that they would not do anything wrong but that they would do what is right. It is the living Jesus that gives guidance to their moral conduct. We, as interpreters of the Scripture for ethics, primarily learn of that living Jesus in the Epistle to the Hebrews. It is the picture of Jesus in Hebrews—a piece of the Jesus story that is nearly totally ignored by the church—that augments and clarifies what has gone before, and brings us to the current element of Scripture's moral movement and progression.

Practical Implications Are Essential

Jesus used the Bible often during his ministry. In doing so, not only was he faithful to the Scriptures, but he used them in such a way that those he encountered realized practical benefits in their lives. For example, in defining his mission he used the words of Isaiah 61 to characterize his own engagement with the poor, the prisoners, the blind, and the oppressed.[97] He referenced an incident from the life of David when challenged by the religious authorities to justify his disciples' picking of grain on the Sabbath in order to have something to eat.[98] When asked to indicate which of the law's commandments was the greatest, he not only referenced the command to love God, but added to it a second that was of like character: "Love your neighbor as yourself."[99] By including the requirement to love one's neighbor, Jesus rendered a practical result to the observance of commands, one that would benefit the needy neighbor.

Through these events from Jesus' life in which he used the writings of the Old Testament, plus many more such instances, Jesus left us a clear hermeneutical element for our own application of the Bible to ethics: it must be used in such a way as to render practical moral benefits for others. It is not enough to use the Bible simply to articulate a notion of the good, define ethically desirable values, or formulate a concept of upright character. To do so likely would not be an abuse of Scripture, but it certainly would be an insufficient use of it. If our hermeneutic only produces ethical theory, then we have wasted the word of God, and failed to use it as Jesus did to benefit the needy among us. The need for practical results drives how we are to interpret the Bible.

Other Authorities Function as a Caution

Earlier it was mentioned the Bible is the supreme infallible authority for ethics. Without compromising that affirmation in any respect, it is also affirmed that three others—reason, experience, and tradition—remain valuable sources for informing thought while interpreting the Scripture, even though they are subservient to Scripture and remain fallible. How is it that they function as an aid to the one who would be faithful to God by using the Scripture accurately in the moral realm?

---

97. Luke 4:18–19.
98. Luke 6:1–4.
99. Matt 22:35–39.

Fundamentally these three serve as a check and balance on any results of the hermeneutic effort. If, for example, an interpreter draws a conclusion that violates reason, it is questionable whether the result appropriately utilizes Scripture. The historical-grammatical approach presupposes reason is not violated as the scholarly process proceeds. Reason is a mental trait granted to humans from the time of creation. Granted, the raw trait needs to be developed and nurtured, but application of this element of general revelation to the conclusions drawn from interpreting the special revelation of Scripture helps guide the interpreter when engaged in the hermeneutical task.

Individual experience, as well as the experience of God's faithful through the ages, functions in a similar way. Our individual continual walk with the living God—our individual experience—combined with that of our forebears in the faith yields a sort of commonality about God's working with his people. Through our collective experience and witness we learn certain basics about God's truth and values that assist the interpreter in the hermeneutical task.

The third nonbiblical authority is tradition. Previously we reviewed an example of how tradition works in the theological realm when we considered a theological assertion made by a current scholar regarding a certain passage. The assertion made sense and was intriguing, except for the fact that it violated the conclusions of hundreds of scholars over two millennia, and thus was highly suspect. Tradition aids the interpreter of Scripture for ethics in much the same way. It is a resource for the interpreter, reflecting thousands of years of faithfulness in the moral realm. The moral thought of Christians through the ages does not establish authoritatively how Scripture is and is not to be used in the moral realm today, yet it does serve to judge any new interpretation and to determine if it comports with the church's classic moral position. This certainly can result in significant disagreements within the Christian community, as many denominations have experienced in recent decades over various elements of sexual and gender ethics.

It must be emphasized that whereas these nonbiblical sources carry a certain level of influence when an interpreter is using the Scripture in the moral realm, it is the Bible alone that is infallibly authoritative for ethics. Where there is conflict, the Scripture must always prevail.

4

The Historical Jesus of the Gospels and the Moral Realm

WHEN WE LOOK AT Jesus as pictured in the Gospels it is crucial to remember we do not simply view Jesus as an historical figure whose life on earth was recorded by four of his followers. He is that, to be sure, but he is far more than that. As those seeking to grow in faithfulness to our Lord and to live maturely as his people, we understand Jesus is living—as the resurrection and postresurrection accounts so strongly attest—and that the Gospel accounts of his earthly life events are records of the living Second Person of the Trinity subsequent to his incarnation. As such, we do not only seek to emulate the archetypal earthly epistemic and exemplary moral authority; rather, we live our lives with the living Son of God, whom we see with increasing clarity as we view him in the Gospels.

This truth was explained profoundly by Søren Kierkegaard in *Training in Christianity*. He begins by pointing out that for any individual her or his reality is only that which is contemporary. Historical events are not an individual's reality.[1] Only that which an individual experiences in daily life is that individual's reality. What, then, of the historical events of Jesus' life as found in the Gospels? Kierkegaard asserts "Christ's life on earth is not a past event . . . [W]hat true Christians there are in each generation are contemporary with Christ . . . His earthly life accompanies the race,

---

1. Kierkegaard, *Training in Christianity*, 58–59.

and accompanies every generation in particular, as the eternal history; His earthly life possesses the eternal contemporaneousness."[2]

If the Jesus of the Gospel events is contemporaneous with us—part of our reality as we live it—then what does it mean to be a Christian? It certainly does not mean we simply affirm the truth of the historical events of Jesus' life. Many who are not God's faithful followers affirm the truth of the Gospel accounts. Rather, we commit ourselves to living as Jesus lived, and to becoming his followers. Kierkegaard explains,

> becoming a Christian in truth comes to mean to become contemporary with Christ. And if becoming a Christian does not come to mean this, then all the talk about becoming a Christian is nonsense and self-deception and conceit, in part even blasphemy and sin against the Second Commandment of the Law and sin against the Holy Ghost.[3]

As if this isn't strong enough language, he continues, "If thou canst not prevail upon thyself to become a Christian in the situation of contemporaneousness with Him, or if He in the situation of contemporaneousness cannot move thee and draw thee to Himself—then thou wilt never become a Christian."[4]

When one comes to the point of being a Christian who lives contemporaneously with the Jesus of the Gospels, what is one to do? Kierkegaard writes, "Now it is well enough to know that Christ constantly uses the expression 'follower'; He never says anything about wanting admirers, admiring worshippers, adherents; and when he uses the expression 'disciples,' He always so explains it that we can perceive that followers are meant, that they are not adherents of a doctrine but followers of a life . . ."[5] That life, it turns out, is one we are to emulate, for Jesus' life is to be his followers' pattern. "Christ came to the world for the purpose of saving the world, and at the same time . . . to be 'the Pattern,' to leave behind Him footsteps for those who would attach themselves to Him, who thus might become followers, for 'follower' corresponds to 'footsteps.'"[6]

In this chapter we will seek to discover what it means to live contemporaneously with the Jesus of the Gospels, for it is in those records that we find the pattern we are to copy, the footsteps in which we are to walk.

2. Kierkegaard, *Training in Christianity*, 59.
3. Kierkegaard, *Training in Christianity*, 58.
4. Kierkegaard, *Training in Christianity*, 59.
5. Kierkegaard, *Training in Christianity*, 215.
6. Kierkegaard, *Training in Christianity*, 216.

MISUNDERSTANDING THE PATTERN OF JESUS

It should not surprise us to learn there are those who somehow attach themselves to the Jesus pictured in the Gospels yet significantly or dramatically misunderstand what it means to be Jesus' followers. Two examples, at opposite extremes, will demonstrate what is not to characterize God's faithful people. Many others could have been chosen and would have served as examples equally well, so these two are by no means unique. The first was a prominent leader recently within the Religious Right subculture in the U. S., former Liberty University President Jerry Falwell Jr. Several Christian leaders who take seriously the teachings of Jesus in the moral realm were surprised when in an interview with the *New York Times* Falwell stated, "I don't look to the teaching of Jesus for what my political beliefs should be."[7] It is incontrovertible that if Jesus is Lord, he is Lord of all of life including politics and other areas of our human experience that involve ethics and the moral realm. During his lifetime, the Jesus of the Gospels actively engaged with the society in which he found himself. In seeking to walk in his footsteps, we are to engage with our society in the same way Jesus engaged with his. Falwell betrays his gross misunderstanding of the example and teaching of Jesus, and their applicability to the life of the Christian seeking to be faithful. We are to look to the teachings and conduct of Jesus in everything, not selectively exclude areas in which Jesus is at odds with those parts of our experience in which we would rather he not be Lord.

The example just cited by no means reflects careful thought regarding the span of the lordship of Christ, but rather a type of populism—understood as an approach intended to appeal to a common majority—in which Jesus is used when deemed to be of benefit, and rejected when not. As such it may quickly be dismissed as a viable option for the serious believer while realizing it continues to hold mass appeal.

Another extreme perspective is represented by theologian and ethicist Reinhold Niebuhr, professor at Union Theological Seminary for some thirty years in the mid-twentieth century. He is widely regarded as a foundational thinker in Christian ethics, politics, and social policy, and, as such, enjoys a level of gravitas in the moral realm that the first example most certainly does not.

---

7. For example, see the comments of Jonathan Wilson-Hartgrove in which he wrote about Falwell and others who share his views, "They seem bothered by Jesus & the Bible" (Wilson-Hartgrove, "So, about these Religious Right spokesmen"); or the more striking and terse comment by Shane Claiborne in which he wrote that Falwell "has denounced Jesus" (Claiborne, "BREAKING NEWS").

Upon reading Niebuhr's theological work one is immediately impressed with the seriousness of his Christology. The fact that he often challenges the conclusions of theological liberalism initially impresses one as a fairly orthodox theological approach. Upon further study, however, it becomes clear Niebuhr's thought, while leveraging orthodox language, is anything but orthodox. Theological symbolism and mythical notions play heavily in Niebuhr's writing. Since he is such a foundational figure in Christian ethics we need to take him seriously. A number of statements both from primary and secondary sources will serve to establish his view of the applicability of the Gospel stories to our goal of leveraging the life and teachings of Jesus in the moral realm.

In 1954, no other than Martin Luther King Jr. presented an essay to the Dialectical Society entitled "The Theology of Reinhold Niebuhr." In that essay he observed that, for Niebuhr, "Christ is the eternal in time, a breaking through of the everlasting mind of God which gives both meaning and consummation to process," then suggested this Christ "is not the Jesus of history that walked in Jerusalem rather he is a pure abstraction. Christ is only a symbol."[8] King strengthened his critique when stating Niebuhr's Christology "is so novel that he can make essentially symbolic the reality of Christ, the sinlessness of Jesus, and the resurrection. Indeed, his use of myth and symbolization to explain Christian doctrine is so thoroughgoing that hardly any denotative meaning is possible."[9]

If there is any doubt regarding King's analysis, Niebuhr himself clearly stated the same perspective. In his 1935 work *An Interpretation of Christian Ethics*, Niebuhr wrote of the Revelation to John:

> The apocalypse is a mythical expression of the impossible possibility under which all human life stands . . . The historical illusions which resulted inevitably from this mythical statement of the situation in which the human spirit finds itself do not destroy the truth in the myth; no more than the discovery that the fall of man was not actual history destroys the truth in the story of the fall.[10]

Speaking specifically of Jesus, Niebuhr continued:

> since myth is forced to state a paradoxical aspect of reality in terms of concepts connoting historical sequence, it always leads to historical illusions. Jesus, no less than Paul, was not free of

8. King, "Theology of Reinhold Niebuhr," 277.
9. King, "Theology of Reinhold Niebuhr," 279.
10. Niebuhr, *Interpretation of Christian Ethics*, 22.

these historical illusions. He expected the coming of the Messianic kingdom in his lifetime; at least that seems to have been his expectation before the crisis in his ministry.[11]

In general, then, Niebuhr asserted, "The ethical demands made by Jesus are incapable of fulfillment in the present existence of man.[12] They proceed from a transcendent and divine unity of essential reality, and their final fulfillment is possible only when God transmutes the present chaos of this world into its final unity."[13]

Some specifics may help clarify the extent to which Niebuhr rejected the moral teaching and example of Jesus. Regarding the typical moral conflicts we encounter on a regular basis, Niebuhr held that

> The ethic of Jesus does not deal at all with the immediate moral problem of every human life . . . The absolutism and perfectionism of Jesus' love ethic sets itself uncompromisingly not only against the natural self-regarding impulses, but against the necessary prudent defenses of the self, required because of the egoism of others. . . . It has only a vertical dimension between the loving will of God and the will of man.[14]

When analyzing Jesus' instructions about concern over daily needs in Matthew 6:25–32, Niebuhr concluded, "Every form of self-assertion is scrutinized and condemned in words which allow of no misinterpretation. . . . The prudent conscience will have an immediately unfavorable reaction to these words. No life can be lived in such unconcern for the physical basis of life."[15]

When focusing on a specific such as Jesus' instruction about enemies, Niebuhr showed his complete dismissal of the teaching of the historical Jesus. "Neither its inevitability nor its oral or social justification in immediate situations qualifies the rigor of Jesus' position . . . resistance and resentment are forbidden. . . . Nowhere is the ethic of Jesus in more obvious conflict with both the impulses and the necessities of ordinary men in typical social

---

11. Niebuhr, *Interpretation of Christian Ethics*, 22.

12. It has been pointed out in prior chapters that use of specifically male terms was intended or assumed by certain authors in past generations as representative of both men and women. Here and elsewhere Niebuhr adopts the same convention. He should be read in light of that convention even though today use of such language clearly refers only to males and specifically excludes females.

13. Niebuhr, *Interpretation of Christian Ethics*, 22.

14. Niebuhr, *Interpretation of Christian Ethics*, 15–16.

15. Niebuhr, *Interpretation of Christian Ethics*, 16.

situations."[16] His disdain for Jesus' ethic also extends to more personal aspects of human experience, such as family relations. After quoting Luke 14:26 and labeling it "ruthless" (as opposed to, say, "hyperbolic"), Niebuhr concluded "Surely this is not an ethic which can give us specific guidance in the detailed problems of social morality where the relative claims of family, community, class, and nation must be constantly weighed."[17]

We see, then, that when Niebuhr encountered the ethical demands of Jesus he responded in a reactionary manner by transforming the historic realities of Jesus into symbol, and claimed Jesus was plagued by illusions. He asserted Jesus' ethic cannot be applied to real-world moral issues, it conflicts with human moral necessities, and it cannot give guidance to the challenges society faces at any level. In short, Niebuhr rejects the notion that life can be lived according to the Jesus ethic. As was the case with the popularist approach viewed earlier, in which the ethical teachings of Jesus are rejected when they are deemed not to be of benefit, Niebuhr rejects Jesus as a moral norm or authority. Whereas he has produced highly laudable theological ethical argumentation that warrants the respect of any serious moral thinker, in the final analysis Niebuhr's view of the Jesus ethic betrays the fact that, for Niebuhr, Jesus is not Lord.

The question for us, as those seeking to grow in maturity and faithfulness to our Lord, is: Why did Niebuhr so thoroughly reject the clear moral teaching of Jesus as inapplicable to modern life? Niebuhr's conclusions are thoughtful and seem to reflect a significant level of practicality when applied to the entire society. This realization, however, accentuates a point that we must not, under any circumstances, miss. The ethic of Jesus was not directed to or intended for all individuals and the entire society. Rather, it was specifically directed to those who claim to be his disciples—those who seek to follow in his footsteps. Adherence to it is a demonstration of commitment to Jesus' lordship, as opposed to yielding to the draw and values of the general society. It is intended to be a witness by God's faithful to the broad society, rather than a reflection of a society that typically is not faithful to God. As such, questions like, "What if everybody took that approach?" are inapplicable since the teaching and example of Jesus in the moral realm are intended only for God's faithful. The way of Jesus is distinct from the way of the world, and this distinction is revealed most clearly as Jesus' followers yield to his authority without compromise. This reality helps shape our approach to adopting the way of Jesus as found in the Gospels.

16. Niebuhr, *Interpretation of Christian Ethics*, 18.
17. Niebuhr, *Interpretation of Christian Ethics*, 20.

REMEMBERING THE JESUS STORY

The earliest Christians formed themselves into local communities decades prior to the writing of the Gospels. As such, there was no written account of the Jesus story to which they could appeal. Rather, they had to rely on the verbal retelling of the story either by eyewitnesses to Jesus' life or by those who learned it from eyewitnesses. Faithfulness for those early Christians was contingent not upon reading accounts of Jesus' life, but rather upon remembering and retelling the story.

The storytelling approach to faithfulness by no means started with the early Christians, for Israel had practiced retelling the works of God throughout its history. In fact, telling the story of God's actions was an essential element of faithfulness for the Jews, and formed the basis of the social values by which God's people were to conduct themselves. The delivery from enslavement in Egypt was the basis for the prohibition against oppressing hired workers or depriving them of wages. God's miraculous gift of food during Israel's desert wandering yielded a moral standard of refraining from harvesting all of an entire crop, but leaving some of it for the poor.[18] Simply recounting the story, however, was not sufficient. Discernment of God's will and obedience to that will were also essential elements of faithfulness.[19]

The early church communities continued this tradition of both recalling God's story and determining what was obligatory for them if they were to live mature lives of faithfulness. Allen Verhey points out, "As a community of moral discernment each church tested all the reasons given in deliberation . . . against the story of Jesus of Nazareth. Its members transformed the question of what they should do into the question of how they might live the story they loved to tell."[20] Recall at the end of the last chapter the point was made that the Bible is God's story, and Jesus, from being preincarnate through his resurrection and glorification, is the story's central figure. There is movement and progression within the story, but Jesus remains the overarching One who gives the story its meaning and clarity. He is the story's hermeneutical core for the moral realm. Not only that, but as Verhey reminds us, by recalling the Jesus story those early Christian communities "situated the lives of their readers in relation to the living Christ, the *present* Christ."[21] Just as the early church communities looked to the Jesus story as a moral template by which they could live their lives, so the faithful and

---

18. For a more thorough explanation of this concept, see Verhey, *Remembering Jesus*, 24–25.

19. Verhey, *Remembering Jesus*, 24.

20. Verhey, *Remembering Jesus*, 21.

21. Verhey, *Remembering Jesus*, 22; italics original.

mature follower today sees in the Jesus story the pattern for life in the moral realm lived in relation to the living Jesus. Fortunately we now have the Gospels as written accounts of the earthly part of the Jesus story. Our goal is not only to embrace the Jesus story, but also to embrace the Jesus *of* the story.

THE JESUS OF THE GOSPELS

It should not be assumed this approach to faithfulness and maturity is something new or even something new for Western believers. Rather, embracing both the Jesus story and the Jesus of the story is the heritage we enjoy, and forms something of a foundation or lauchpad for faithful living in the moral realm today.

Nineteenth-Century Faithfulness

Two mid-twentieth-century Christian historians have undertaken studies that resulted in outstanding works which characterized the scope and tone of orthodox protestant faith in the nineteenth and early twentieth centuries: Timothy L. Smith and Norris Magnuson.[22] Smith points out faithfulness for believers in the U.S. during that period tended to minimize denominational differences while integrating practical piety and ethical vitality. "Though still centered in the historic Christian views of man and God and salvation through Christ, it was actively devoted to making the world a place where men might more readily choose the good path."[23] Notice for these believers there was no theological compromise in order to engage the society; rather, their conviction was that the orthodox faith included adherence to historical doctrinal positions as well as societal involvement for the purpose of helping people choose good. For them the Bible served as the final authority both for religion and politics, and in 1853 they built The Bible House in New York City for the express purpose of printing and distributing millions of Bibles.[24]

---

22. For an excellent overview of the history of orthodox protestant faith and social involvement during this time period, see Smith's *Revivalism and Social Reform*, which deals with the period up to the US Civil War, and Magnuson's *Salvation in the Slums*, which focuses on the 55 years after the Civil War. Together these two works paint a thorough picture of the heritage of twenty-first-century believers, and depict what faithfulness and maturity in the moral realm looked like during the revivalistic period of protestant history in the West.

23. Smith, *Revivalism and Social Reform*, 93–94.

24. Smith, *Revivalism and Social Reform*, 37. For more on The Bible House, see https://ephemeralnewyork.wordpress.com/tag/the-bible-house-nyc/.

Why, if social involvement by God's faithful was so pronounced during this time period, is that fact little known by modern-day believers or embraced as their own heritage? One reason, as Magnuson points out, is that copies of the relevant literature of the time were not preserved:

> Very few academic libraries bothered to save, if indeed they ever received, the literature of the Salvation Army, the Volunteers, and the Alliance, or of rescue missions and homes for derelict men and women. Even the *Christian Herald*, one of the most widely circulated religious magazines of that day, and a mine of information on evangelical humanitarian and religious activities, has rarely been preserved.[25]

The problem, however, goes beyond the issue of preservation of materials. Magnuson insightfully argues that,

> Even had these materials been widely available, the spirit of the age has not been conducive to an appreciation of the revivalistic sects. The triumph of liberal religion after decades of heated controversy, for one thing, did not make for a balanced evaluation of persons of a contrasting persuasion. The bitterness of that controversy, together with the conscious withdrawal of twentieth-century religious conservatives from an emphasis on social welfare, have greatly obscured the larger evangelical contribution to human welfare. The Fundamentalist withdrawal was itself, however, an accidental by-product of the fact that the era witnessed not only the severe social problems of an emerging urban-industrial society, but also widespread defections from historic Christian orthodoxy.[26]

Prior to the failure of the Fundamentalists of the early twentieth century to embrace the social activism of their revivalistic forebears, the gospel of Jesus was viewed by his earlier faithful followers as encompassing both evangelistic zeal and dedication to improving the social situation in which the beneficiaries of evangelism found themselves. Yet what specifically from the life and teachings of Jesus caught the attention of those revivalists and propelled them as they pursued their humanitarian objectives? These believers—our foremothers and forefathers in walking the life of faithfulness to God—came to be known as "gospel welfare workers." They focused more broadly on the wide range of social ills and suffering than more theologically liberal-minded people, who tended to concentrate on the problems

---

25. Magnuson, *Salvation in the Slums*, x.
26. Magnuson, *Salvation in the Slums*, x–xi.

resulting from industrialization. Thus, their efforts included all who were suffering due to ethnicity, gender, alcoholism, or other factors.[27] Their "combination of extensive personal knowledge of the slums with a teaching and experience that centered on the biblical meaning of love as practical helpfulness was primarily responsible for the philanthropy and the reform emphasis that marked the gospel welfare movement."[28]

The hermeneutical approach taken by these believers, unwitting as it may have been, was to adopt an overarching biblical theme or principle which they would leverage to direct their engagement with the needy of society: the notion of love. The primary exemplar of God's love, in their view, was the Jesus of the Gospels. They saw in his example divine love conveyed in tangible ways to all those Jesus encountered, and they sought to emulate Jesus as they encountered the needy in their own contexts. They primarily were revivalistic and pietistic people, rather than sophisticated scholars, and their conduct reflected that fact. They simply sought to follow the example of the Jesus they saw pictured in the Gospels. Reflecting this very realistic and historic picture of the exemplary earthly Jesus, Catherine Booth—who, along with her husband William, founded the Salvation Army—once confronted a church member who was telling of the great love the church had for an idealistic Jesus. She responded to him, "But suppose Jesus was to come to your chapel as He went about Palestine, with a carpenter's coat on, or as He sat upon the well, all over perspiration and dust with travel, where would your chapel steward put him to sit?"[29] For those reformers their authority, model, and teacher was the Jesus depicted in the Gospels' accounts of his life.

Charles Haddon Spurgeon and Thomas DeWitt Talmage

The Jesus of the Gospels was, for these faithful believers, both the one who walked the roads of Palestine in the first century and also the living resurrected Lord depicted at the end of the Gospels. As such, his teachings and conduct certainly served as a model for their own lives as mature followers of Jesus. But the fact he was alive called them to more than just emulation; it called them to commitment and obedience to their living Lord in all aspects of life, including life in the moral realm.

Two of the most well-known and influential Christian leaders of the time, both immovably "evangelical,"[30] were Charles Haddon Spurgeon in

27. Magnuson, *Salvation in the Slums*, 178.
28. Magnuson, *Salvation in the Slums*, 178.
29. As quoted by Magnuson in *Salvation in the Slums*, 170.
30. Magnuson, *Salvation in the Slums*, 25.

London and Thomas De Witt Talmage in New York. Their sermons give us great insight into the widespread understanding of Jesus, both historic and living, and the commensurate picture that motivated and directed Jesus' followers of the time.

Charles Haddon Spurgeon

One of Spurgeon's most illuminating sermons, published in 1857, was entitled "Christ's People—Imitators of Him."[31] In this sermon, Spurgeon described both the Jesus who believers are to imitate as well as the characteristics of believers who are faithfully imitating. At the outset of the sermon Spurgeon indicated he would "endeavor to stir up in your minds by way of remembrance, and urge you so to imitate Jesus Christ, our heavenly pattern, that men may perceive that you are disciples of the holy Son of God."[32] In this he leveraged the assessment by the Jewish leaders, upon seeing the boldness of Peter and John subsequent to their healing of a lame beggar, that they had been with Jesus.[33] He then went on simply to assert, "A Christian should be a striking likeness of Jesus Christ."[34] Expanding on the concept, Spurgeon wrote, "we should be pictures of Christ, yea such striking likenesses of him that the world . . . would, when they once beheld us, exclaim, 'He has been with Jesus; he has been taught of him; he is like him; he has caught the very idea of the holy Man of Nazareth, and he expands it out into his very life and every day actions.'"[35]

Spurgeon went on to identify four ways in which the faithful are to emulate Jesus, utilizing specific incidents from the Gospel accounts of Jesus' life to substantiate his points. First, referencing again the Acts 4 story of the healing of the lame beggar, he asserts "a Christian should be like Christ in his *boldness*,"[36] then argues that during his earthly life Jesus never catered to the rich, the great, or the noble, but remained bold in their presence.[37]

Next, Spurgeon claimed boldness should be amalgamated with the loveliness of Jesus, and cited specific events from Jesus' life in support:

---

31. For the entire text of the sermon, see Spurgeon, *Sermons*, 252–73.
32. Spurgeon, *Sermons*, 253.
33. See Acts 4:13.
34. Spurgeon, *Sermons*, 253.
35. Spurgeon, *Sermons*, 254.
36. Spurgeon, *Sermons*, 256; italics original.
37. Spurgeon, *Sermons*, 256.

> So, brethren, while we too are bold, let us ever imitate the loving Jesus. . . . A widow has just lost her only son; he weeps at the bier, and with a word restores life to the dead man. He sees a paralytic, a leper, or a man long confined to his bed; he speaks, they rise, and are healed. He lived for others, not for himself. His constant labors were without any motive, except the good of those who lived in the world.[38]

Notice Spurgeon concluded from the stories of Jesus' life a moral requirement for Jesus' followers: just as Jesus lived for others, so should they, motivated only by the good that can be achieved in the lives of others during their earthly lives.

Third, Spurgeon argued Jesus' followers should emulate his humility, and again referenced specific incidents from Jesus' earthly life: "if thou art a Christian, I bid thee look at thy Master, talking to the children, bending from the majesty of his divinity to speak to mankind on earth, tabernacling with the peasants of Galilee, and then—aye, depth of condescension unparalleled—washing his disciples' feet, and wiping them with the towel after supper."[39] Calling on Christians not only to focus on the Jesus of the Gospels, but also to adopt Jesus' humble attitude of service to the poor, Spurgeon urged them to

> Recollect, Christian, who your Master was—a man of the poor. He lived with them; he ate with them. . . . a friend of publicans and sinners, living and walking with them. So, Christian, be thou like thy Master—one who can stoop; yea, be thou one who thinks it no stooping, but rather esteems others better than himself, counts it his honor to sit with the poorest of Christ's people.[40]

Finally, Spurgeon encouraged Christians to copy Jesus' holiness by charging them, "Ever go about doing good."[41] Generally, being holy as Jesus was holy meant working for goodness in the moral realm. In the earthly life of Jesus the supreme example of this was Jesus' forgiveness of his enemies as they crucified him. Christians were to imitate their Lord even in this. "And best of all, as the highest portraiture of Jesus, try to forgive your enemies as he did; and let those sublime words of your Master, 'Father, forgive them, for they know not what they do,' always ring in your ears."[42] This absolute need

---

38. Spurgeon, *Sermons*, 258–59.
39. Spurgeon, *Sermons*, 260.
40. Spurgeon, *Sermons*, 261.
41. Spurgeon, *Sermons*, 261.
42. Spurgeon, *Sermons*, 262.

to forgive enemies led Spurgeon, in his own moral commitments and actions, to be "an aggressive Liberal politically, and, as one writer has judged, an 'extremely outspoken' critic of war and imperialism."[43] For Spurgeon, the "highest portraiture of Jesus" was not only to reject engagement in violence, but also to imitate Jesus by forgiving enemies.

Of particular interest to us as we seek to determine how nineteenth-century believers understood what it meant to be faithful in the moral realm is Spurgeon's entreaty of his listeners "to study Christ's character."[44] The notion we explored earlier of character formation is seen in Spurgeon as a hermeneutical standard for ethics. He goes on: "There is a wondrous power about the character of Christ, for the more you regard it the more you will be conformed to it. . . . study him in the evangelists,[45] studiously examine his character."[46] We see that not only are the works and teachings of the Jesus of the Gospels to be imitated, but his person is also to be studied and emulated. It is the full picture of Jesus in all its various moral facets that served as an example, including commands, attitudes, conduct, teaching, and character. As a final piece of guidance to his listeners Spurgeon commented, "Lastly, as the best advice I can give, seek more of the Spirit of God; for this is the way to become Christ-like."[47] Emulation of Jesus was thus seen as something that was spiritually alive, and driven by the living Spirit of God. This is not surprising, for the object of faithfulness ultimately is not to be the Gospel stories, but the living God behind the stories.

THOMAS DEWITT TALMAGE

The work of Thomas DeWitt Talmage had a thrust parallel to that of Spurgeon's, emphasizing both the absolute need for personal salvation and the requirement of the saved to be engaged in relieving the sufferings of the needy in society. His burden for social betterment was so pronounced he took on the job of editor of the *Christian Herald* in 1890.[48] Magnuson references a comment from Talmage's successors upon his death twelve years later: "his successors declared that the story of the cross and Christ's love had been 'the whole of his theology,' controlling his life and permeating

---

43. Magnuson, *Salvation in the Slums*, 26.
44. Spurgeon, *Sermons*, 271.
45. By the term "evangelists" Spurgeon means the four Gospels.
46. Spurgeon, *Sermons*, 271.
47. Spurgeon, *Sermons*, 272.
48. Magnuson, *Salvation in the Slums*, 25.

'every sermon he ever preached.'"[49] For Talmage, however, evangelism was not the whole of his understanding of what it meant to be faithful to the Jesus of the Gospels. Rather, "Talmage brought to his editorial task evangelical fervor, a keen interest in the contemporary scene, sympathy for the needy, and readiness to cooperate in matters of reform and charity. His fame aided the *Christian Herald* and his interests helped thrust it in the direction of welfare."[50] Yet in *Social Dynamite; or The Wickedness of Modern Society*, a collection of Talmage's sermons published in 1888, it is made clear in the preface that welfare was only one part of his social concern. For Talmage, municipal law was as good as dead, "and political reform impossible, so long as Christians are apathetic and politically negligent, and fail to aid those in authority by personally urging reform and standing by it in the name of Christ."[51]

Talmage saw in the Gospel recordings of the earthly life of Jesus the motivation for Christian involvement in society and the example for how it is to be approached. Showing a special interest in the cities where people suffer, he referenced specific events from Jesus' life, as well as his teachings, to link the needy of his day to the events of Jesus. In one sermon he used the image of Mary Magdalen prior to her encounter with Jesus,[52] as well as the teaching of the rich man and Lazarus,[53] to call Christians to emulate Jesus in thought and action in society, going to the worst places to help the suffering:

> There is a vast underground city life that is appalling and shameful. It wallows and steams with putrefaction. You go down the stairs, which are wet and decayed with filth, and at the bottom you find the poor victims on the floor, cold, sick, three-fourths dead, slinking into a still darker corner under the gleam of the lantern of the police. There has not been a breath of fresh air in that room for five years, literally. The broken sewer empties its contents upon them, and they lie at night in the swimming filth. There they are, men, women, children; blacks, whites; Mary Magdalen without her repentance, and Lazarus without his God! These are the "dives" into which the pickpockets and the thieves go, as well as a great many who would like a different life but cannot get it. These places are the sores of the city, which bleed

---

49. Magnuson, *Salvation in the Slums*, 25, 195n136.
50. Magnuson, *Salvation in the Slums*, 26–27.
51. Talmage, *Social Dynamite*, iv.
52. See Luke 8:2. Talmage may also have had in mind the association of Mary Magdalene with the sinful woman of Luke 7:36–50, an erroneous association first promulgated by Pope Gregory I in the sixth century AD.
53. See Luke 16:19–31.

perpetual corruption.... O, you never saw it, you say. You never will see it until on the day when these staggering wretches shall come up in the light of the judgment throne, and while all hearts are being revealed God will ask you what you did to help them.[54]

The last phrase of that excerpt is a veiled reference to Matthew 25, in which is pictured the judgment day where Jesus asks those who claim to be his followers what they did when they encountered the hungry and thirsty, strangers, those without clothes, the sick, and prisoners. Those who did not help the needy are judged guilty of not helping Jesus, and are cast into the eternal fire that has been prepared for the devil and his angels. This teaching of Jesus is one Talmage used elsewhere as a key incident from the life of Jesus that defines what Christian maturity and faithfulness look like. Describing a desperate situation in one group of cities, he referenced "two hundred and ninety thousand poor who are dependent upon individual, city and State charities. If all their voices could come up at once, it would be a groan that would shake the foundations of the city, and bring earth and heaven to the rescue."[55] He continued by rhetorically asking if he or any of his listeners have anything that belongs to the poor, such as an extra garment, some bread, a candle, something that could be used as a roof, a jewel, an extra pair of shoes, or a New Testament in which could be found the story of the one who came to seek and save the lost.[56] It is at this point that Talmage specifically referenced Matthew 25, in which Jesus says to those who claim to be his followers, "Inasmuch as ye did it *not* to these, ye did it *not* to Me."[57]

Thus, we see in the preaching of Talmage a joining of evangelistic fervor with intense concern for those who needed to encounter the Jesus of the Gospels, the man who addressed the physical needs of all who crossed his path, particularly the poor and suffering. This concern extended beyond individuals, to the reform of the political and social structures of society. The message delivered by Talmage, as well as contemporaries such as Spurgeon—that the Jesus of the Gospels was to be imitated and emulated, since his life was the standard by which they were to conduct themselves in society—had vast effects throughout both the United States and England, some of which we will review next.

---

54. Talmage, *Social Dynamite*, 195–6.
55. Talmage, *Social Dynamite*, 199.
56. Talmage, *Social Dynamite*, 199–200.
57. Talmage, *Social Dynamite*, 200; italics original. Talmage is quoting from the King James Version of Matt 25:45.

Practical Outworking in the Nineteenth Century

In the years leading up to the U. S. Civil War the dominant stance of revivalists regarding social issues was one of liberalism. The relationship between personal salvation and the improvement of society was carefully articulated, and individual spiritual regeneration was seen as the primary means of social reform. The gospel of Christ was viewed as the key to addressing society's ills, since legislation alone was deemed to be inadequate.[58] Yet simply preaching the evangelistic message of individual salvation was not only insufficient, it was a danger. According to Gilbert Haven, an abolitionist who became a Methodist bishop after the Civil War, ministers had to speak out on social and political issues, in addition to their evangelistic efforts. For Haven, the message of Jesus as found in the Gospels was all encompassing.[59] "The Gospel . . . is not confined to a repentance and faith that have no connection with social or civil duties. The Evangel of Christ is an all-embracing theme. It is the vital force in earth and in heaven. . . . The Cross is the centre of the spiritual, and therefore of the material universe."[60]

What was it about the life of Jesus that compelled these believers to see the entire society as the object of the gospel message? For some it was the spirit and principles that became evident as one learned about the life of Jesus.[61] They must be applied "not only to the ordinary labor and familiar relations of man's life in the world, but to all popular combinations of sin, organized iniquities, and public crimes, like intemperance, slavery, and war."[62] For others, devotion was the result of learning about the Jesus of the Gospels. Such devotion worked itself out socially in a life of "irreproachable morality and unceasing efforts to reform society." The issues particularly demanding attention included "slavery, intemperance, political corruption, and all other public vices."[63] Notice for these believers the focus of their attention was not limited to the specific human needs Jesus encountered. Rather, it was Jesus' engagement in the society in which he lived that propelled them to be active in the environments in which they found themselves, even though the specific human situations were not identical.

Revivalistic zeal for active involvement in the moral realm of society did not end with the Civil War. Instead it shifted focus somewhat, from

---

58. Smith, *Revivalism and Social Reform*, 151.
59. Smith, *Revivalism and Social Reform*, 35–36.
60. As quoted by Smith in *Revivalism and Social Reform*, 36.
61. Smith, *Revivalism and Social Reform*, 152.
62. Smith, *Revivalism and Social Reform*, 152.
63. Smith, *Revivalism and Social Reform*, 155.

commitment to abolition to the evils associated with growing urbanization and industrialization. For post-Civil War Christians, faithfulness to the gospel of Jesus meant focusing their efforts on the growing slums. "[C]ombining evangelism and welfare they formed one of the largest and most influential contingents of field workers in American cities during those decades."[64] What was it that propelled them into the most unpleasant places with their message of salvation, hope, and welfare reform? In studying the life of Jesus they would have read the passage in Luke 4 where Jesus defined his own mission as being driven by the Spirit of the Lord to proclaim good news to the poor, freedom for the prisoners, healing for the blind, release for the oppressed, and the year of the Lord's favor.[65] Devotion to Jesus led them to align their life missions with that of Jesus; thus, focusing on the suffering in the slums would have been a natural and obvious way for them to do so. For William Booth, who founded the Salvation Army in London in the mid-nineteenth century and later expanded it to the U.S., the focus was always "Souls! Souls! Souls!" as one issue of the Army's publications, *War Cry*, displayed in 1898.[66] Going after the souls, though, meant going to where they were, and that required Christians to "plunge down to the very depths of human contempt," since doing so was "the essence of the life of Jesus Christ."[67]

Relieving suffering was but the start of the revivalist's social goals in the post-Civil War era, even though they were an essential and necessary element of individual spiritual vitality. They also sought to reform society in general. The great Presbyterian minister and revivalist Charles Finney "insisted as late as 1868 that 'the loss of interest in benevolent enterprises' was usually evidence of a 'backslidden heart.' Among these, Finney specified good government, Christian education, temperance reform, the abolition of slavery, and relief for the poor."[68]

No one incident or teaching from Jesus' life was used by the nineteenth-century faithful to guide their moral work. Rather, the story of the Gospels in general motivated them in various ways. Only a few examples can be referenced here, but they should serve to show Jesus' specific teachings and actions, as well as his overall life as depicted in the Gospels, were influential in the attitude and conduct of the faithful, and functioned for them as both authoritative and exemplary in the moral realm.

64. Magnuson, *Salvation in the Slums*, 2.
65. See Luke 4 in which Jesus quotes from the prophet Isaiah in reference to himself.
66. As quoted and referenced by Magnuson in *Salvation in the Slums*, 6.
67. As quoted and referenced by Magnuson in *Salvation in the Slums*, 6.
68. As quoted by Smith in *Revivalism and Social Reform*, 60–61.

Specific stories formed a major element of Jesus' teaching and functioned as a strong motivator driving his disciples' conduct. Chief among those in the moral realm was the story of the good Samaritan.[69] Interestingly, in Luke's Gospel this specific story follows directly on Jesus' more general command to love neighbor as self, and was embraced by a wide range of revivalistic social workers. According to Smith,

> Individual churches soon joined the interdenominational societies in distributing food and clothing, finding employment, resettling children, and providing medical aid for the lowest classes. The revival of 1858 was in many respects the harvest reaped from this gospel seed. It convinced churchmen everywhere that the story of the Good Samaritan was a parable for their times.[70]

One of Jesus' most well-known teachings occurred as an answer to a request to be taught how to pray.[71] In Matthew's Gospel it is found in the middle of Jesus' most extensive ethical teaching, the Sermon on the Mount.[72] Although there are differences between the text of the Lord's Prayer as recorded by Luke compared with that of Matthew, both versions implore God to send his kingdom. Matthew added the request that God's will be done on earth as it is in heaven. This core teaching of Jesus found its way into the thinking and subsequent convictions and actions of the revivalists. Among their objectives was the establishment of holiness among the faithful. Instead of driving them to withdrawal and a life of contemplation, the holiness quest led believers to social service.[73] It was the Lord's Prayer that gave definition and focus to these efforts, and meant that "the triumph of the gospel calls for its victory over all evil, not a mere deliverance of individual Christians from harm."[74] Quoting from the March 26, 1857 issue of the Baptist newspaper *The Watchman and Reflector*, Smith demonstrates the influence of the Lord's Prayer on the revivalists' view of the gospel vison:

> It is something more than a gathering together of those who shall be saved in a future state, leaving the world to destruction; it contemplates the organization and supremacy of goodness in human society—the doing of God's will *on earth*—the coming

---

69. See Luke 10:25–37.
70. Smith, *Revivalism and Social Reform*, 177.
71. See Luke 11:1–4.
72. See Matt 6:9–13.
73. Smith, *Revivalism and Social Reform*, 175–76.
74. Smith, *Revivalism and Social Reform*, 152.

of His Kingdom hither, as well as our going hence to it.... [I]t is ours, not only to fit ourselves and others for a better world, but to labor to make this world better.[75]

The Lord's Prayer, then, was critical to the revivalists' conviction that their social efforts should focus on transforming their society into one whose moral characteristics paralleled God's kingdom in heaven.

In addition to the teaching of Jesus as found in the Gospels, his conduct also gave definition and content to the revivalists' work in the moral realm. That conduct provided them with an example to imitate as they attempted to help the poor and transform their society into the kingdom of God on earth. For example, after telling a paralyzed man his sins were forgiven, Jesus answered his critics by clouding the difference between forgiveness of sins and meeting physical needs when he asked them, "Which is easier to say to this paralyzed man, 'Your sins are forgiven,' or to say, 'Get up, take your mat and walk?'" (Mark 2:9). He then ordered the man to take up his mat and go home, and the paralyzed man was healed.[76] The influence of such events from Jesus' life became evident as spiritual and social service were married, and soul-winning was understood as a means to improve society.[77]

Finally, it appears an incident such as the triumphal entry[78]—in which the crowd, in all four Gospel accounts, ascribed to Jesus some sort of kingly function—served to form at least part of what the revivalists understood their mission to be. During that event the crowd did not just see Jesus as a religious teacher or compassionate healer, but ascribed to him political authority to exercise divine dominion over their social situation, free them from the oppressive Romans, and assume the role of king. The debate over slavery in the U.S. apparently had brought the revivalists to the point of seeing that the Bible did not condone oppression, and drove them beyond narrowly focusing only on immediate relief of human suffering to assert that "Christ must be king of the nation's affairs, economic and political, as well as religious."[79] In this they very much resembled the crowd that surrounded Jesus during the triumphal entry, and viewed his destiny in much the same way.

We can learn much from the nineteenth-century revivalists about Christian maturity and what faithfulness to God should look like in our daily lives. Their understanding of Jesus not only as individual savior but

---

75. As quoted by Smith in *Revivalism and Social Reform*, 152–53.
76. See Mark 2:1–12.
77. Smith, *Revivalism and Social Reform*, 173.
78. See Matt 21:1–11; Mark 11:1–11; Luke 19:28–44; and John 12:12–19.
79. Smith, *Revivalism and Social Reform*, 223.

also as the one they were to imitate was taken directly from the accounts of Jesus' life in the Four Gospels. For them the Bible was the final authority, not only for belief but for all of life. They were theologically uncompromising, being ardent adherents to orthodox doctrine, but at the same time seeing in the life of Jesus their pattern not only for evangelistic zeal but also for relief of human suffering and establishment of the reign of God on earth. Jesus was their king, and his kingdom was to be established both in the hearts of people and throughout the environments in which they lived. To that end they embraced his teachings and emulated his actions, motivated by the knowledge that Jesus was their living Lord.

A Normative View of Jesus' Life

The heritage of the nineteenth century has had great influence on later believers of orthodox faith who have sought to use the life of Jesus in a way that is ethically normative. Many of them have had the advantage of advancing scholarship regarding both the events of Jesus' earthly life and the broader Scripture, and thus have been able to develop ethical proposals that utilize Jesus' life in the present context in a way that is more responsible than the simple direct appropriation and emulation found among many of their nineteenth-century forebears. That greater understanding of the specifics of Jesus' life, the text in which it is recorded, and appropriate ethical hermeneutics to interpret that text have resulted in great benefit to those who seek to be faithful followers of Jesus.

Jesus in Context

The challenge of gleaning from the Gospels an understanding of Jesus' earthly life that somehow can be morally normative for God's faithful people in the twenty-first century can be met, in part at least, by appreciating that Jesus lived in a cultural/political/social/religious/geographic/temporal context very unlike our own. That context entailed conventions, limits, and standards significantly different from ours. To take some rather simple and obvious examples, in Jesus' context people reclined when eating rather than sitting at a table. Travel commonly occurred by walking, or perhaps riding a donkey. Foot coverings were quite different from ours, as were clothing conventions, and public interactions between the genders—not to mention those between Jews and Gentiles—were quite different from those in which we engage today (although in some non-Western cultures the cultural conventions may be much closer to those of Jesus' day than our own). English was not the dominant spoken and written language of Jesus' culture, with its biases and limitations of meaning and expression. In fact, in Jesus' context there was no single language used throughout the culture, but rather several, depending upon which element of culture one was found engaging.

In seeking to develop a picture of a morally authoritative Jesus from the Gospel accounts of his life it is necessary to discern which elements of Jesus' cultural context, as well as his teaching and actions within that context, are transcontextual, and which are not. Complicating the challenge is the fact that certain parts of Jesus' context and life may not be one or the other, but somewhere in between. Those seeking to be faithful followers of Jesus understandably have not always been as discerning as they might have been in this regard. Thus, during the Jesus Movement of the 1970s, for example, certain of the Jesus People sought to express their faithfulness by copying what they understood to be Jesus' outward appearance and daily routine. They wore robes and sandals according to their understanding of Jesus. Some were itinerate. Others renounced individual ownership, mechanization, and industrialization. To this day some Christians believe they demonstrate greater faithfulness and Christian maturity by adopting first-century Jewish worship elements, since Jesus was a first-century Jew, and they long to see a return to the temple conventions of Jesus' day as evidence that his return is imminent. Some of the Jesus Movement's leaders, seeking to be obedient to Jesus' command to deny themselves and take up their daily crosses,[80] actually dragged full-size wooden crosses behind them on occasion. The fact that certain of them would attach wheels to the bases of the crosses to ease the burden of dragging makes one wonder if they had an accurate understanding of Jesus' command.

It is questionable whether attempting to copy the physical routine and conventions of Jesus' context in Palestine has anything to do at all with Christian faithfulness and moral maturity in the context in which we find ourselves. Jesus lived within the situation in which he found himself, which is quite different from our own, or those of, say, Latin America or Africa. That does not mean, however, that he is irrelevant as our example. In fact, quite the opposite is the case.

Of all the elements that comprised Jesus' context, the one most distinct and fundamental was the religious one. Jesus was a Jew living in a Jewish context that was under the domination of Rome. The notion that made Jews distinct was they were "construed as a people under the special orders and protection of the one God."[81] Various groups of Jews held different opinions

---

80. See Luke 9:23.
81. Meeks, *Moral World*, 65.

regarding how the orders, or laws, were to be interpreted and used, but the need for adherence to them was something all Jews affirmed. The fact the Roman leaders under which the Jews in Jesus' day lived allowed Jewish laws to govern, to a certain extent, Jewish conduct was an incentive to codify the Jewish Scriptures into laws ruling civic life.[82] Wayne Meeks points out "most Jews agreed that God had given very specific commandments to his people and that the premier way in which one proved faithful was by obeying them."[83] Obedience was the means by which the entire community became and remained the one God wanted. God's law not only gave structure and meaning to the entire universe, but also reassured the obedient they were included within God's covenantal community. The way in which Jews obeyed varied, and there was disagreement about what obedience meant, but obedience was the central requirement.[84]

It is within this context of expected obedience to the law that Jesus lived. Much of the content of Jesus' life as recorded in the Gospels deals with obedience to the law, even though Jesus' timeless message and exemplary conduct may be better suited to a contextual environment different from that of outward obedience. In fact, a lot of the conflict Jesus encountered had to do with the difference between the core of his message and the outward obedience and conformity required by the religious and social context in which he lived. As examples, recall the challenges he encountered over legal matters such as healing on the Sabbath, eating that which the law forbade, or associating with the religiously or morally unclean.

Jesus, then, delivered his message and conducted his life within the milieu and mindset of legal obedience, yet represented a moral and spiritual reality far more extensive than law. Consider the incident in Jesus' life when he was confronted by a rich ruler about what must be done to inherit eternal life.[85] He addressed Jesus in moral terms, referring to him as "good teacher" (Mark 10:17; Luke 18:18). Yet Jesus' answer was strictly in the form of obedience to commandments. He recited from the Decalogue in Exodus 20 when responding to the man, for this was the moral and spiritual mindset the man understood, reflecting the context in which he lived. Jesus went on, then, to add elements beyond the Decalogue by telling the man to sell everything and give to the poor, followed by a directive to follow him. Jesus started his answer by speaking in the mode of the man's context, but then expanded to include a new moral and spiritual reality that was foreign to the

82. Meeks, *Moral World*, 94.
83. Meeks, *Moral World*, 95.
84. Meeks, *Moral World*, 95–96.
85. See Matt 19:16–30; Mark 10:17–30; and Luke 18:18–30.

man—the man had to become a follower of Jesus. This is what Jesus was after; moving the man from obedience to law to the moral realm of living life as a Jesus-follower. At this point the man's "face fell" (Mark 10:22), according to Mark's Gospel. Obedience to law was not Jesus' fundamental message, even though he worked in an environment in which such obedience was the accepted mindset. Later in the incident Jesus' disciples expressed a pessimistic response similar to that of the rich man when they asked "who then can be saved?" (Mark 10:26). They were beginning to realize the message of Jesus was far more extensive than obedience to the law, and did not receive that message as good news. Jesus reassured them, however, that whereas on the human level there was no hope, "all things are possible with God" (Mark 10:27).

Understanding that Jesus worked within this social and religious assumption—obedience to the law—yet conveyed a message more expansive and far different from it, yields great insight into how the life of Jesus as found in the Gospels may be understood properly as morally normative for God's faithful today. To that end, it is crucial to review Jesus' response when asked "Of all the commandments, which is the most important?"[86]

In the first century, Jews lived within their context of hundreds of laws, both commands and prohibitions, involving religious practice, personal conduct, interaction within the society, and other elements of their routine experience. The teacher of the law who asked Jesus the question about the most important commandment was reflecting that legal context, for he could do nothing else. In responding to the teacher, Jesus started within that context but then offered an expansion upon it and a corrective to it. Notice his initial answer referenced just one law, quoting Deuteronomy 6:4–5: "Hear, O Israel: the Lord our God, the Lord is one. Love the Lord your God with all your heart and with all your soul and with all your mind and with all your strength."[87] This answer was perfectly sufficient to address the question he had been asked. Jesus, however, realized the legal context in which the question was framed was an insufficient milieu to convey his message, and thus immediately upon giving the answer did something to challenge both the legal context and the sufficiency of the teacher's question, but once again did it within the legal context his hearers understood. In a recent article, Andrew Wilson described Jesus' challenging response like this: "Rather than stopping after his apparently straight answer, Jesus continues: 'The second is this: 'Love your neighbor as yourself.' There is no commandment greater than these' (12:31). But notice: That wasn't what the

---

86. Mark 12:28.
87. Mark 12:29–30.

scribe had asked. He wanted the commandments boiled down to one; Jesus refused to give him fewer than two."[88]

In answering by quoting two laws Jesus was showing that living a life of faithfulness to God in the moral realm is not a matter of fulfilling commandments, including a type of legalism that seeks a simple copying of the physical style and actions of Jesus, migrated directly from his cultural/political/social/religious/geographic/temporal context into one's own. Recall that, for Jews in the first century, faithfulness was understood primarily as obedience to the law. Instead of rote obedience, Jesus called his contemporaries as well as his faithful through the ages to emulate his *character*—a character he conveyed and demonstrated through what he taught and did in the context in which he found himself—and thus demonstrate they are his faithful and mature followers in the contexts in which they find themselves. The challenge is to determine which of Jesus' specific teachings and actions are transcontextual, and thus reflect his character irrespective of context, and which are specific to Jesus' context. The key to making this determination is to understand what Jesus meant by announcing that the kingdom of God had arrived.

Jesus' Earthly Life

Capturing a complete picture of the Jesus of the Gospels in a few pages will not be wholly successful, or even moderately so, but highlighting some significant normative elements from his life may help demonstrate what Jesus meant by the arrived kingdom of God. Although many scholars have written on the life of Jesus, two authors—John Howard Yoder and Glen Stassen—have produced studies that will be particularly beneficial in our attempt to picture the Gospels' Jesus in a way that can inform our thinking about mature and faithful living in the moral realm. For our present purpose select referencing of their works will suffice to demonstrate some of the points being made.

In the Magnificat[89] Mary gave us a hint at a proper understanding of her yet-to-be-born son. For those of us who prefer life in a comfortable and predictable social setting Mary's message is quite disturbing, for it envisions social upheaval at the hands of God, who has blessed her with the task of carrying the Savior. A simple reading of the text indicates that among God's mighty deeds is the scattering of the proud, the downfall of political leaders, exaltation of the humble, filling those who are hungry, and rejection

---

88. Wilson, "All God's Laws Are Equal," para. 3.
89. See Luke 1:46–55.

of the rich who simultaneously are sent away empty. It reflects a radical destabilization of social conventions. Yoder expresses the message of the Magnificat this way: "In the present testimony of the gospel we are being told that the one whose birth is now being announced is to be an agent of radical social change."[90] In the first century this change was understood in light of the common understanding of what the Messiah would be, that is, the one who would usher in social and political liberation to Israel and bring an end to its suffering.[91] Thus, at the outset of the Gospels, even before Jesus' birth, he is couched in the context of significant change throughout the society—something quite different from the spiritualized understanding of Jesus that dominates the thinking of many of those of orthodox faith in Western cultures today.

Defining Jesus

When reading the Gospels with a view toward understanding how Jesus' conduct and teachings may be normative for us in the moral realm, there emerge four general impressions. These four characterize the overall approach Jesus took to his earthly sojourn, capture in outward teaching and conduct the inward character of Jesus, and demonstrate the kingdom of God whose arrival Jesus announced.

First, Jesus was the deliverer of all who trusted in him. This was not an identity he pulled out of the air; rather, it came from the Old Testament background in which he was steeped, particularly the prophet Isaiah, and in which he participated as the one spoken of throughout Isaiah's prophecy.[92] Consider Isaiah 35, which references a parched land that is made glad, a wilderness that rejoices, feeble hands that are made strong, fear that is banished, blind who are made to see, deaf who hear, lame who leap, mute who shout, redeemed who walk in the way of holiness without fear of attack, the Lord who rescues his people, and much more. It is this background that gave definition to the kind of deliverance Jesus would bring. It should come as no surprise the specific actions and teachings of Jesus align very well with Isaiah's picture of deliverance, for it served as a type of template for Jesus' involvement in his society.

This approach to engaging in his context did not leave Jesus unscathed. Instead, it came at a significant cost, since his means of deliverance was not one of power and force but rather of vulnerability and identity with

---

90. Yoder, *Politics of Jesus*, 26–27.
91. Yoder, *Politics of Jesus*, 28.
92. Stassen, *Thicker Jesus*, 46.

those he came to deliver. When he touched a leper and healed him, Jesus exposed himself. When he engaged with the Gadarene demoniacs, he put himself in grave physical danger.[93] When he touched a dead body or an unclean woman he himself became ritually unclean, and when he associated with tax collectors and others considered "sinners" he willfully took on the criticism and ostracism of the community's spiritual elite.[94] Yet in doing so he also was showing those he encountered that God's deliverance was not the political one they were expecting, but rather the deep personal one experienced when the Spirit of God touches individuals where they are most sensitive and vulnerable.

The notion of Jesus as deliverer followed him from before the time he was born,[95] extended throughout his lifetime, and continued even after his death,[96] although Jesus' attempt to change the common understanding of a political deliverer to a spiritual and individual one was not always successful. Yet he was unwavering in his approach of active engagement in the society, rejection of the conservative social norms, and embracing identity and vulnerability rather than power and force.[97] Matthew captured this Isaiah-inspired approach when he wrote of Jesus, "This was to fulfill what was spoken through the prophet Isaiah: 'He took up our infirmities and bore our diseases.'"[98]

Second, throughout his earthly ministry Jesus confronted the unjust and powerful, and sought to establish justice. Even at his baptism we see this element of justice being a characteristic of Jesus' earthly ministry. Recall at his baptism the Holy Spirit descended on Jesus like a dove, and then the voice from heaven said, "'This is my Son, whom I love; with him I am well pleased.'"[99] At first this statement appears to have nothing to do with justice, but as Stassen and Gushee point out, the heavenly voice is quoting from Isaiah 42,[100] and by quoting just the first verse is indicating the broader

---

93. Notice that the demoniacs are described in Matthew 8:28 as "so violent that no one could pass that way."

94. Stassen, *Thicker Jesus*, 157, 159.

95. See Luke 1:68, in which Zechariah, the father of John the Baptist, expressed this same thought when he prophesied, "Praise be to the Lord, the God of Israel, because he has come to his people and redeemed them."

96. Consider, for example, the conversation of the two disciples on the road to Emmaus described in Luke 24, in which they said to the resurrected but veiled Jesus, "we had hoped that he was the one who was going to redeem Israel."

97. Yoder, *Politics of Jesus*, 98.

98. Matt 8:17, quoting Isa 53:4.

99. Matt 3:17.

100. Stassen and Gushee, *Kingdom Ethics*, 352.

message of the chapter is being applied to Jesus. Later in Isaiah 42 we see the one on whom the Spirit of God rests will bring justice to the nations, but through means so gentle as not to break a bruised reed or put out a smoldering wick. For Jesus, then, through his confrontation of the powerful and unjust, not only would he seek to bring peaceful justice, but would do so through peaceful means.

The first such confrontation occurred immediately after Jesus' baptism, when he encountered Satan during his forty days of temptation. Notice Jesus did not strike Satan, but rather confronted him through what he said. This means of confronting those who are powerful, while maintaining his own lowliness, would be Jesus' pattern throughout his time on earth.

Throughout the gospel records we see many occasions where Jesus sought to establish justice for the ones he encountered who had been denied justice, be they social outcasts, foreigners, the poor, or others abused by society. As an example, consider the incident recorded in Luke 7 in which a woman characterized as one "who lived a sinful life" (v. 37) wept at Jesus' feet, then dried them with her hair as Jesus was dining at the home of a Pharisee named Simon. Upon seeing the woman, the Pharisee began abusing her in his mind by labeling her a sinner. Jesus, aware of the Pharisee's judgmental attitude, came to the woman's aid by seeking that she be treated justly. He did this not by trying to exercise some sort of physical power, but rather by pointing out to the Pharisee his own failure to meet the social norms of his culture when welcoming Jesus to his home. Having pointed out the Pharisee's failure, he turned to the woman, forgave her sins, commended her for her love, proclaimed her faith had saved her, and sent her away in peace. Had the Pharisee had his way, she would have been thrown out of the house.

Jesus' actions, then, on behalf of those the powerful were seeking to abuse, were intended to bring them justice and were characterized by peaceful means. Even the incident of the cleansing of the temple[101] saw Jesus speak to the powerful who were taking advantage of others (notice he did not strike them, but only spoke to them). His use of a makeshift whip did not entail striking animals, but only moving them out of the temple area. According to Mark's account, in the middle of the incident Jesus began teaching, and in Matthew's account the blind and lame came to him for healing. So even in this incident from Jesus' life, sometimes used by certain

---

101. In order to gain a complete picture of this incident it is necessary to read all the accounts in Matthew 21, Mark 11, Luke 19, and John 2. The question over whether there were multiple temple cleansings or only one is irrelevant for our purpose, which is to understand how Jesus engaged with the powerful and unjust, and sought to establish justice for their victims.

Christians seeking to justify the use of violent means (particularly regarding capital punishment, police action, the military, and the like), Jesus' means actually were peaceful, and in the midst of it he took time to teach and heal.

Third, Jesus sought to build a community of those seeking to be faithful to God. Included in the community were those whom society sought to ostracize for not living lives that comported with the accepted societal and religious norms. Many of those who considered themselves pillars of the community would come to find themselves outside of the one Jesus developed. Such a reversal of position is to be expected, since earlier we saw a lot of the conflict Jesus encountered was a result of the difference between the core of his message and the religious and social expectations of his context. This reversal is reminiscent of Catherine Booth's challenge to the church member in which she asked where in that member's church would someone who looked like a dirty and dusty traveler, or who wore the clothes of a laboring carpenter, be directed to sit.[102] In other words, where would the socially unacceptable person's place be within that church's community?

Who were the kinds of people Jesus welcomed into his community? There are many examples in the Gospels, but let's look at one in Luke 14. Jesus was eating at the home of a Pharisee—one of the religious leaders of his day and a member society considered to be a prominent person in the community of God's faithful. Jesus said to his host that when he gave a banquet he should not invite the ones society expected to be invited: friends, brothers and sisters, other relatives, or rich neighbors. Rather Jesus told the Pharisee to invite the outcasts from the community: the poor, the crippled, the lame, and the blind. He went on to tell the parable of the great banquet, in which those expected to accept the invitation to the banquet made excuses why they could not come, whereas those who normally would not be included—the poor, the crippled, the blind and the lame—were compelled to come, attended, and became part of the banquet community. As a final indication Jesus' community was not the one of his host's expectations, Jesus declared, "I tell you, not one of those who were invited will get a taste of my banquet" (Luke 14:24).

Toward the end of his earthly ministry, Jesus gave another indication of the ones to be part of his community of faithful followers. In Matthew 25 we find Jesus' explanation of who will be included in his community at his second coming, and who will not. Simply put, those who fed the hungry, gave drink to the thirsty, invited strangers into their group, clothed those who needed clothing, cared for the sick, and visited those in prison are

---

102. See footnote 29 earlier in this chapter.

included in the community of God's kingdom and blessing; those who did not are excluded from the community and punished eternally.

We see in these two examples that which is characteristic of Jesus' community: certain virtues, priorities, values, attitudes, foci, character, and conduct, particularly applied to the suffering and outcasts of society. Stassen expresses the same truth a bit differently when he leverages the thought of William Telford's *The Theology of the Gospel of Mark*:

> Throughout the Gospel of Mark Jesus brings outsiders into community.... The father of the demon-possessed boy demonstrates faith, not the disciples. The woman outside of their circle, not those at the table, anoints Jesus for burial... 'It is a Gentile, a Roman centurion, not one of the twelve, who is the first human being to recognize and confess him to be the Son of God, and hence more than the Jewish Messiah.... Finally, it is the women, not the disciples, who come to anoint him after his burial and who receive the message that he has risen.'[103]

Perhaps his most striking notion regarding those invited into community is Jesus' teaching about love of enemies. "Jesus' central teaching of 'love your enemy' is not merely a feeling but an entering into the perspective of the other and bringing the other into community. Jesus' cross is the consequence of the anger of the authorities over his compassionate entry into the needs of outcasts and bringing them into community, and of the authorities' anger at his entering into their precincts and calling them to repentance."[104] We see Jesus included even enemies among those who could participate in his community. During his crucifixion he prayed God would forgive them, for they were ignorant of their actions, and immediately after his death the centurion overseeing his murder showed a hint of turning toward God when he "praised God and said, 'Surely this was a righteous man.'"[105]

Fourth, Jesus brought life in its various forms. This was most obviously and dramatically displayed when he raised people from the dead.[106] It was at the resurrection of Lazarus that he self-identified as the one who brings life to those who believe in him, even if they die: "I am the resurrection and the life. The one who believes in me will live, even though they die;

---

103. Stassen, *Thicker Jesus*, 161.

104. Stassen, *Thicker Jesus*, 166-67.

105. Luke 23:47.

106. During his earthly ministry Jesus raised three people from the dead: Jairus's daughter (Mark 5:22-43), the son of the widow of Nain (Luke 7:11-17), and Lazarus (John 11:1-44).

and whoever lives by believing in me will never die."[107] Yet bringing life to those he encountered also occurred when he interacted with the kind of people the social and religious norms dictated he should avoid. Think about the occasion when Jesus spoke with a Samaritan woman as he rested by Jacob's well in the Samaritan town of Sychar.[108] He asked her for a drink, and she responded by reminding him Jews are not supposed to associate with Samaritans. Jesus replied that if she knew God's gift and who he was, she would have responded differently: she would have asked him for living water. By the end of the incident many from the town believed in Jesus, acknowledging he is the Savior of the world.

We see in this very earthly incident of interacting with someone he was supposed to shun[109] that Jesus conveyed the life of God not only to the woman in the context in which she found herself—the moral realm—but also to all who acknowledged who Jesus was. Whereas he did not physically raise them from the dead as he had done with Lazarus, he did bring full life to those who were already alive, and he did it by means of a single social interaction with someone who was religiously, socially, and morally outside of what Jesus' contemporaries in their context erroneously asserted were the norms established by God.

When criticized by religious leaders after healing a man who was blind from birth,[110] Jesus indicated the purpose for his coming into the world was to bring life in its fullness.[111] This was an essential element of Jesus' self-understanding. Stassen confirms this truth by endorsing Bonhoeffer's thinking: "Life is what we see in Christ, which includes the No of judgment and death on our life that has fallen away from its origin and the Yes of creation, reconciliation, and redemption."[112]

These four impressions, then, characterized the overall earthly ministry of Jesus as recorded in the Gospels, and demonstrated the arrival of the kingdom of God he announced. He spent those three years as the deliverer of the oppressed, the one who confronted the powerful and sought to establish justice for the suffering, the builder of a community of the faithful, and the conveyor of life in all its forms. In doing this, he had a specific focus, which we will now explore.

107. John 11:25–26.

108. See John 4:4–42.

109. Notice in verse 27 that Jesus' disciples "were surprised to find him talking with a woman," an indication Jesus was acting outside of socially-accepted religious norms in order to convey to her and her fellow townspeople the life of God.

110. See John 9:1—10:21.

111. See John 10:10.

112. Stassen, *Thicker Jesus*, 45.

Jesus' Focus

We have seen what characterized Jesus' time on earth, but what was his specific focus? If the four impressions capture his overall conduct and teaching, what held them all together? In short, it was Jesus' announcement that his appearance ushered in the kingdom of God on earth. At the beginning of his ministry, right after John the Baptist was imprisoned, Jesus proclaimed the good news of God throughout Galilee saying, "The time has come . . . The kingdom of God has come near. Repent and believe the good news!"[113] The fact that the term "kingdom of God," or the synonymous "kingdom of Heaven"[114] used in the Gospel of Matthew on all but four occasions, occurs dozens of times throughout all four gospels establishes the centrality of the kingdom in Jesus' ministry. According to Stassen and Gushee, "this idea stood at the heart of his proclamation and self-understanding."[115] As was the case with the four impressions reviewed in the previous section, the idea of the kingdom of God was rooted in the prophet Isaiah. In his language of kingdom proclamation Jesus appears to have borrowed language from Isaiah's prophecy.[116] This suggests when Jesus announced the arrival of the kingdom of God, he had in mind Isaiah's thought about the kingdom. What, then, was Isaiah's understanding of the kingdom of God?

At its most fundamental, Isaiah's concept of the kingdom entailed the disclosure of God in the presence of humans. "The kingdom of God was understood as referring to the self-revelation of God and God's dynamic reign. . . . It was not a place but an action."[117] The specific kind of action we have already investigated; it was God's intervention on behalf of his faithful people. That intervention is not just providing personal salvation from sin and its affects, as many twenty-first century Christians assume. Neither is it limited to alleviating the immediate human needs of the oppressed, deprived, and suffering.[118] Rather, it is both, and entails deliverance, establishment of justice, the building of community, and conveyance of life in all

---

113. See Mark 1:14–15.

114. Matthew substituted "kingdom of Heaven" for "kingdom of God" to reflect the Jewish custom of refraining from saying or writing God's name, and employing a different word to reflect the same reality.

115. Stassen and Gushee, *Kingdom Ethics*, 13.

116. See the reference in Stassen and Gushee, in which they cite Bruce Chilton's *God in Strength*, wherein the following passages appear to be the basis of Jesus' kingdom proclamations: Isa 24:23; 25:6; 31:6; 40:10; 41:8–9; 42:1; 43:5, 10; 45:6; 49:12; 51:7–8; 53:1; 59:19; 60:20–22; 61:1 (*Kingdom Ethics*, 23–24).

117. Stassen and Gushee, *Kingdom Ethics*, 25.

118. Stassen and Gushee, *Kingdom Ethics*, 28.

of its forms. The kingdom of God means God's salvation has come. He "has acted to deliver humanity and now reigns over all of life, and is present to and with us, and will be in the future."[119]

Yoder expresses the reality of the kingdom of God on earth in somewhat different terms. Many find this view of the kingdom shocking, since it includes concepts they were taught from their earliest years were to be opposed in their conservative society. Yet it captures accurately the striking notion Jesus was conveying when he announced he was inaugurating God's kingdom on earth. Yoder writes, "We must conclude that in the ordinary sense of his words Jesus, like Mary and like John, was announcing the imminent *entrée en vigueur* of a new regime whose marks would be that rich would give to the poor, the captives would be freed, and men[120] would have a new mentality (*metanoia*), if they believed this news."[121] Although it was not clear at the time of Jesus' announcement (or those of Mary's Magnificat in Luke 1:46–55 and John the Baptist in Matt 3:1–3) what were the specific changes the kingdom would bring, "what the event was supposed to be is clear: it is a visible socio-political, economic restructuring of relations among the people of God, achieved by his intervention in the person of Jesus as the Anointed and endued with the Spirit."[122] This is a far cry from the context in which Jesus lived, in which obedience to law was the primary expectation. Having announced the kingdom of God, Jesus spent much of his ministry explaining the differences between the expectations of his context and God's expectations of those who would live faithfully in the kingdom.

Through his conduct Jesus demonstrated the kingdom at work in the lives of individuals and as present in the greater society in which he and his followers lived. It was through his teaching, however, that Jesus conveyed the expectations of the kingdom—the virtues, values, priorities, intentions, attitudes, foci, commitments, and conduct the participants in the kingdom were to embrace as they sought to be faithful and mature believers. Whereas these can be seen consistently throughout Jesus' teachings, they are no more pronounced or clarified than in the Sermon on the Mount. This is where we see the character of Jesus on display, and where Jesus conveys to his followers the moral example he expects them to embrace.

---

119. Stassen and Gushee, *Kingdom Ethics*, 29.

120. As we have seen elsewhere, the use of male language, although unfortunate, was the convention when Yoder wrote. He should be understood as referring to all people, not just men.

121. Yoder, *Politics of Jesus*, 39.

122. Yoder, *Politics of Jesus*, 39.

The Sermon on the Mount has served throughout the history of the church as Jesus' key teaching in the moral realm.[123] Although the Epistle of James, a thoroughgoing moral treatise, was written decades prior to the Gospels, it reflects much of the teaching of the Sermon on the Mount. As the sermon was spoken by Jesus prior to the writing of James' Epistle, and only captured in writing later by eyewitnesses of Jesus' teaching, it is the sermon that has been viewed as primary, having influenced even Jesus' half-brother James as he wrote his epistle.[124]

At the outset of our brief look at the Sermon on the Mount one thing must be made clear: the sermon is not a set of unattainable moral ideals. It is much more down to earth than that, and conveys Jesus' real expectations of his followers as they live in faithfulness to him. The sermon outlines "concrete ways to practice God's will and be delivered from the bondage of sin. In other words, he [Jesus] taught his followers how to participate in God's reign."[125] What many who hold that the Sermon on the Mount is idealistic, unattainable, and impractical fail to perceive is Jesus, throughout his ministry, sought to convey to his listeners that the kingdom of God and the society in which they lived are not on two different experiential levels. Rather, both of them exist in the same milieu, and are in conflict. Jesus rejected the moral conventions of the social norm in which he found himself, ushering in the alternative kingdom of God with its ethical standards.[126] In giving the Sermon on the Mount, as well as other teachings during his three years of earthly sojourn, he was calling his followers to embrace God's kingdom in their everyday lives in contradistinction to the moral norms of the dominant social context in which they found themselves.

Three examples will suffice to demonstrate how Jesus as pictured in the Gospels serves as an epistemic and exemplary moral authority for his followers. At the outset of the sermon, in Matthew 5:3–12, we find the fundamental values of the kingdom of God. This section, commonly known as the Beatitudes, reflects the character of Jesus. In beginning the sermon with moral self-disclosure Jesus sought to convey to his followers the standard for their character as well. Stassen and Gushee rightly assert "this picturing of Jesus is a crucial point: each virtue gets its meaning from Jesus' teaching

---

123. Stassen and Gushee, *Kingdom Ethics*, 31.

124. In 1 Corinthians 15:7, we learn that during the time between Jesus' resurrection and ascension he appeared to his half-brother James. A strong argument can be made that during this encounter Jesus conveyed to James the moral content we find in James' Epistle, thus connecting James to Jesus' teaching in the Sermon on the Mount.

125. Stassen and Gushee, *Kingdom Ethics*, 31.

126. Yoder, *Politics of Jesus*, 52–53, 99–100.

and embodying the reign of God."[127] They summarize the character virtues taught in the Beatitudes by indicating Jesus' followers:

- are humble before God, and identify with the humble, the poor, and the outcasts;
- mourn with sincere repentance toward God, and comfort others who mourn;
- are surrendered to God, committing ourselves to following God's way, and making peace;
- hunger and thirst for delivering, community-restoring justice;
- practice compassion in action, covenant faithfulness toward those in need;
- seek God's will with holistic integrity, in all we are and do;
- make peace with our enemies, as God shows love to God's enemies;
- are willing to suffer (just as Jesus suffered) because of our loyalty to Jesus and to justice.[128]

In conveying the sermon's virtues as its foundation, Jesus was clearly calling his followers to adopt a different character from that of the social status quo, with the attendant conduct such character implies. After articulating the Beatitudes, Jesus called his followers to live in a way that can be observed by others, like a brilliant city on a hill can be seen from a great distance, then launched into specific examples of the attitudes, commitments, and conduct he expected.

Throughout the Sermon on the Mount we observe a common theme: Jesus was attempting to move people from their legal context of rote obedience to the context of the kingdom of God. Through many examples he worked to change their understanding of faithfulness and moral uprightness from outward conduct that aligned with the dominant religious and social expectations to inward goodness that aligned with divine character. He did not, however, advocate antinomianism. Rather, he called people to something more than that to which they were accustomed.

After emphasizing antinomianism was not what he was advocating,[129] Jesus gave a number of examples of kingdom expectations in the moral realm, the first of which has to do with the very obvious moral matter of murder. He started by reviewing his listeners' common understanding of

127. Stassen and Gushee, *Kingdom Ethics*, 51.
128. Stassen and Gushee, *Kingdom Ethics*, 47.
129. See Matt 5:17–20.

the subject by stating, "You have heard that it was said to the people of long ago, 'You shall not murder, and anyone who murders will be subject to judgment.'"[130] The prohibition was limited to outward, observable conduct, strengthened by the threat of legal judgment and punishment for those who broke the law. This reflected the religious and social standards of the context in which Jesus and his listeners found themselves. He went on, then, to move their understanding of the consequences of murder from what normally occurred in their context to that which would occur vis-à-vis God's kingdom when he indicated the same penalty would ensue from anger with a brother or sister or showing contempt for another. Taking the situation a step further, Jesus taught that someone who called a sister or brother a fool risked eternal torture in hell.[131] Notice Jesus' focus was on the consequences, not the act, and taught that the same (or worse) severe consequences would be applied to actions not normally thought to be nearly as morally reprobate as murder. What Jesus was doing was attempting to open the eyes of his audience to the nature of the kingdom of God, to encourage them to internalize and embrace the character of the kingdom in their own attitudes and values, and to change their conduct accordingly.

Throughout the rest of the Sermon we see Jesus continued this effort to move his listeners from their current thinking to embracing the moral standards of the kingdom. This occurs not only in parts of the sermon that repeat the familiar "You have heard that it was said . . . But I tell you . . . " pattern, but also in parts that do not. Probably the most dramatic occurrence is when Jesus taught the kingdom's values regarding treatment of enemies.[132] The common understanding in Jesus' context was enemies were to be hated. Jesus, however, taught that the kingdom required enemies be loved, and abusers be the focus of prayer. Those who lived in the context of the kingdom of God were to love their enemies in the same way they loved their neighbors, and thus act like God. The last verse of the section expressed it this way: "Be perfect, therefore, as your heavenly Father is perfect" (Matt 5:48).

Jesus not only taught how the kingdom required enemies to be treated, he actually embraced the kingdom standard in his own encounter with enemies. When emissaries from the religious leaders armed themselves and sought out Jesus to arrest him, he healed one who had been injured by one of Jesus' well-intentioned disciples who had not yet embraced the character of the kingdom, and stopped the violent conduct that was driven by the

---

130. Matt 5:21.
131. See Matt 5:22.
132. See Matt 5:43–48.

commonly held view of how enemies were to be treated.[133] Even when he was being crucified Jesus displayed the values and attitude of the kingdom when he prayed for his enemies who were crucifying him.[134]

It is important to notice that between the lines in the sermon Jesus addressed the broader notion of retaliation, which would include not only treatment of enemies but all who do harm. When quoting from the Old Testament, he selectively omitted portions that endorse the use of violence as a way to respond. Stassen and Gushee point out that when Jesus referred to the Old Testament, "he always omitted any parts of the teaching that advocate violence or nationalistic triumph against enemies. He avoided the violent parts of the teaching so systematically that it must not be happenstance. Jesus' teachings are always consistent with the sacredness of human life."[135] We see this selective approach in places within the Sermon on the Mount, including when he quoted from Exodus 21, Leviticus 24, and Deuteronomy 19. "Jesus omitted 'life for life' and 'shall be put to death.' Again we see the pattern: he quoted Old Testament passages but specifically omitted the part that advocates the violent solution of taking the life of the murderer."[136] In his teaching, then, Jesus sought to move any who would be his followers from their understanding of ethics to the ethics of the kingdom. In his conduct he demonstrated the kingdom at work in the broader society, even when he was being crucified. Throughout it all, the use of violence was always prohibited for those who would follow the example of Jesus and live in the kingdom of God.

Toward the end of the Sermon on the Mount, Jesus, knowing that what he taught would not be readily accepted by those who heard him, emphasized in a number of ways that his teaching would not be endorsed by many. For those who wanted to be his followers, however, it was a requirement, for it demonstrated the character of God's kingdom. He indicated there was a narrow gate that leads to life, and few would find it.[137] Jesus reinforced that he actually expected his followers to do what he said when he concluded, "Therefore everyone who hears these words of mine and puts them into practice is like a wise man who built his house on the rock."[138] That was Jesus' standard in his day, and it remains the standard for Jesus' mature followers today.

133. See Luke 22:49–51.
134. See Luke 23:34.
135. Stassen and Gushee, *Kingdom Ethics*, 197–98.
136. Stassen and Gushee, *Kingdom Ethics*, 198.
137. See Matt 7:13–14.
138. Matt 7:24.

The Significance of the Cross

Any overview of the normative moral significance of the life of Jesus is incomplete without inclusion of his death on the cross. Yet how is the cross morally normative for the faithful? Earlier we saw Jesus' focus was the arrival of the kingdom of God in the context in which he walked the earth. In introducing the kingdom, Jesus was "the bearer of a new possibility of human, social, and therefore political relationships. His baptism is the inauguration and his cross is the culmination of that new regime in which his disciples are called to share."[139] Not only did Jesus introduce the kingdom, with all of its inherent relational differences when compared with the dominant society, but in the cross he showed the extent and the nature of what participation in the kingdom means. In short, Jesus was teaching that "to be a disciple is to share in the style of life of which the cross is the culmination."[140]

If Jesus' life was characterized by taking on the identity of the deliverer, the bringer of justice for those unjustly treated, the creator of a new community of the faithful, and the source of life in all its manifestations, how is his death to be interpreted in the moral realm? It is simply that Jesus' death must be seen in the context of the rest of his ministry. The cross was not a standalone event, but was integrated with Jesus' entire life. Stassen writes, "The cross needs to be seen in the light of Jesus' healings and his deeds of compassion, of his proclamation and embodiment of the reign of God, of his confrontations of the authorities and their injustice, of his actual ministry as a prophet, suffering servant, and Son of God."[141] The cross is not simply the chronological end of Jesus' earthly life, the finishing touch of his agitating involvement in his society. Nor does it mark the end of the kingdom of God that Jesus introduced on earth. Instead, the cross is the culmination of God's kingdom on earth, the fulfillment of what Jesus' ministry was all about. In Yoder's words, "The cross is not a detour or a hurdle on the way to the kingdom, nor is it even the way to the kingdom; it is the kingdom come."[142]

Think again about the Sermon on the Mount. In a nutshell, what Jesus was teaching is the way of the cross. In actually adopting, internalizing, and living the teachings of the sermon, God's faithful are taking up the cross and following the way of Jesus. They are not just living according to a certain teaching; rather, they are aligning themselves with Jesus in the social sphere.

---

139. Yoder, *Politics of Jesus*, 63.
140. Yoder, *Politics of Jesus*, 45.
141. Stassen, *Thicker Jesus*, 154.
142. Yoder, *Politics of Jesus*, 61.

For the one living faithfully in the moral realm the cross is not enduring the normal difficulties of life, but rather "the price of his social nonconformity. . . . it is the social reality of representing in an unwilling world the Order to come,"[143] the kingdom of God. It is a life in which "servanthood replaces dominion, forgiveness absorbs hostility."[144] In the Sermon on the Mount we see Jesus pointing his faithful toward the cross, and indicating how they can participate in it.[145] "When we go the second mile . . . when we give to the poor, we are participating in the way of Jesus who was crucified for us. We are participating in the grace of the cross."[146]

The cross, then, is crucial for a complete understanding of the moral example Jesus set during his days on earth. It is the visual culmination of Jesus' effort to bring the kingdom, and to live within his culture in a countercultural way. His intent was not to challenge the status quo simply for the sake of being an agitator, but to usher in the way of God in a society that either had missed God's way or had rejected it entirely. The cross is the Sermon on the Mount fulfilled, and an invitation to the faithful to adopt fully the way of Jesus as kingdom citizens.

Jesus, from the Resurrection to the Ascension

The gospel accounts of Jesus do not end with the cross. Rather, they record various incidents in which Jesus encountered a number of people during the forty days after his resurrection and before his ascension. This period has largely been ignored by the church through the ages. Of course the church strongly proclaims Jesus' resurrection subsequent to the grave, but what happened between that central event and the ascension, and what can we learn about faithfulness and maturity from the Jesus of that time period?

Scripture records ten postresurrection appearances of Jesus during the forty days between the resurrection and the ascension.[147] Five occurred on resurrection Sunday itself, one during the ensuing week, three during the subsequent few weeks, and one on the fortieth day. In Acts 1:3 we get a bit of insight about what Jesus was doing during that period of time: "He

---

143. Yoder, *Politics of Jesus*, 97.
144. Yoder, *Politics of Jesus*, 134.
145. Stassen and Gushee, *Kingdom Ethics*, 140.
146. Stassen and Gushee, *Kingdom Ethics*, 140.
147. Not all scholars agree on the number of post-resurrection appearances, or the order in which they occurred. An excellent presentation of both is found in Elizabeth Mitchell's article, "The Sequence of Christ's Post-Resurrection Appearances." I am assuming the accuracy of her study.

appeared to them over a period of forty days and spoke about the kingdom of God." Each of the recorded encounters between Jesus and various others was for the purpose of explaining or demonstrating the kingdom of God. This should not surprise us, for as we learned previously the kingdom of God was the singular focus of Jesus' time on earth. Yet as we shall see, Jesus' followers did not understand his focus during the three years of his ministry prior to his crucifixion.

It is significant that Jesus' postresurrection time on earth lasted forty days. Throughout Scripture the number forty is of grerat importance, particularly when referring to a period of time, and it has always been significant in the history of God's people.[148] The common characteristic of all of these periods is they were times of trial and testing. They were times of difficulty and challenge, fraught with risk, threats, and the unknown. In addition to proving Jesus actually was alive, the purpose of the forty days between Jesus' resurrection and ascension, which he spent focusing on the kingdom of God, was to show that the kingdom in which Jesus' followers would be participating after his ascension would be characterized by suffering, risk, and difficulty. Such had been the experience of all who had followed God faithfully throughout history. During the postresurrection period Jesus was attempting to convey to his followers that even though he had emerged as victor, his followers should anticipate that identification with Jesus would entail the same kind of suffering he had experienced.

It is clear from many of the encounters Jesus had during the forty days after the resurrection that his followers—both the eleven remaining disciples and others—had not understood Jesus' fundamental message about the nature of the kingdom of God, or their commission as participants in the kingdom. Four examples will serve to illustrate the range of the followers' misunderstanding as well as Jesus' correctives.

Jesus' first postresurrection encounter was with Mary Magdalene.[149] Upon recognizing Jesus she understandably addressed him as "teacher." At his crucifixion she had lost her teacher, and during the encounter she clearly wanted him again to be to her what he had been. Likely she hoped Jesus had returned to stay and set up his earthly kingdom. She wanted to cling to the Jesus she had known, rather than mature to being an emissary of the

---

148. As examples, recall the great flood took forty days to reach its height, the Israelites wandered in the desert for forty years prior to entering the promised land, Moses spent forty days on Mount Sinai receiving God's law and another forty to receive its replacement, the spies searched Canaan for forty days, Elijah was in the wilderness of Horeb for forty days, Nineveh was given forty days to repent in the time of Jonah, and Jesus' time of fasting and temptation lasted forty days.

149. See John 20:11–18.

kingdom Jesus had introduced during his earthly ministry. Jesus, then, had to offer her a corrective by indicating she could not cling to the precrucified Jesus and he had not returned to stay, but rather she should affirm the Jesus who was about to return to his father, the God of them both. Jesus was confirming to her the same message he gave to the Gerasene demoniac:[150] "Go home to your own people and tell them how much the Lord has done for you, and how he has had mercy on you."

On the evening of the same day Jesus encountered Mary Magdalene, he met up with two of his followers who were on their way to the village of Emmaus.[151] These two were not among the Eleven, but were some of the unknown others who followed Jesus. Aside from their encounter with Jesus and their subsequent reporting to the Eleven, they are not mentioned again in the New Testament. They reflected, however, a very typical Jewish understanding of the Messiah—one who would come as Israel's liberator. They wanted Jesus to be a Messiah who would act to their benefit. Notice their response when Jesus asked what they were discussing. They rightly understood Jesus was a powerful prophet, yet they were focused on what they could get from Jesus immediately. So they expressed their disappointment: "we had hoped that he was the one who was going to redeem Israel" (Luke 24:21). Jesus then offered them a corrective to their understanding of the Messiah by teaching them from their own Scripture what he, the Messiah, was to be: one who suffered, then entered his glory. The Messiah's purpose was not to be Israel's political hero. This same misunderstanding was expressed later by the Eleven when they were meeting with Jesus after the resurrection.[152]

In a third postresurrection encounter Jesus met seven of the Eleven as they were fishing.[153] Peter had decided to go back to his old profession, and the others went along. Upon recognizing Jesus on the shore Peter, thinking only of his own interests, jumped in the water to get to Jesus first, and left behind his companions. How did Jesus respond? He demonstrated to Peter, as well as the others, that as members of God's kingdom, no longer were they to pursue their own interests, such as fishing, nor were they to think only of themselves as Peter had just done. Rather, they were to adopt the position of servants, looking to the needs of others. In cooking for them and providing them with food Jesus was teaching them that the attitude

---

150. See Mark 5:1–20.
151. See Luke 24:13–35.
152. See Acts 1:4–8.
153. See John 21:1–14.

of kingdom participants was to be a lowly one, that of servanthood for the benefit of others.

Finally there is the encounter Jesus had only with Peter as John followed behind.[154] Peter, after being told individually three times to care for others and to follow Jesus, noticed John and objected to Jesus' individual instruction by asking, "Lord, what about him?" Jesus had to correct Peter's comparison of himself with others by telling Peter that following Jesus was the only thing that was to matter to him. Jesus may have a different plan for John. As an emissary of Jesus, Peter's priority and commitment had to be following Jesus.

What do all of these encounters have in common? In Matthew 16 we read of Peter's great confession at Caesarea Philippi, that Jesus was "the Messiah, the Son of the living God." Shortly thereafter, when Jesus indicated he was to suffer, be killed, and rise again, Peter rebuked him. Jesus responded to Peter by saying, "Get behind me Satan! You are a stumbling block to me; you do not have in mind the concerns of God, but merely human concerns." This was the "opportune time" after Jesus' forty days of temptation referenced in Luke's Gospel[155] in which Satan again confronted Jesus, this time in the form of Peter's rebuke, in an attempt to derail Jesus from his calling and mission. Notice the reason Peter produced this stumbling block: he had in mind human concerns rather than God's concerns. That was the issue Jesus addressed during the postresurrection encounters. As Peter still had in mind humans' rather than God's concerns, so Jesus' closest followers, having seen him alive subsequent to his crucifixion, still had in mind their own concerns rather than God's. During the encounters Jesus offered correctives to their errant thinking, and refocused them on God's concerns rather than their own.

Having offered correctives to his followers' misunderstandings concerning the kingdom of God and their roles in it, Jesus commissioned his followers. They needed to learn what it was they were to do when Jesus no longer was present with them. Jesus was soon to leave their society, and the context in which they had known him for three years. They, however, were to remain in that society, and were to work within that moral milieu. What were they to do?

The last appearance of Jesus on resurrection day occurred in the locked room where the disciples were huddled in fear of the Jewish authorities. Jesus suddenly stood among them, reassured them, and proved he was, indeed, alive. Then he gave them a commission: "As the Father has sent me,

---

154. See John 21:15–22.
155. See Luke 4:13.

I am sending you."¹⁵⁶ At the outset of his postresurrection ministry Jesus outlined in one simple phrase his followers' commission: they were being sent after the pattern in which Jesus was sent. Emulation of Jesus, and "follow me" was how they were to conduct themselves in the world. Their stance in their society and context was to reflect the stance Jesus assumed in his society and context.

Toward the end of the forty days, shortly before the ascension, Jesus gave his followers another commission. He openly told them he had been given all authority in heaven and earth,¹⁵⁷ and because of that fact he was empowering them to make disciples of all peoples. During his three years of earthly ministry Jesus' teaching and conduct amounted to a call to become Jesus' disciples. Now, in this commission Jesus charged his followers to make disciples of others. That making of disciples started with baptizing all subsequent followers of Jesus in the name of the triune God, and was the start of the "make disciples" task. Yet, it was only the start. The ongoing, continual, long-term part of disciple-making was to be the one that occurs in the moral realm: "teaching them to obey everything I have commanded you."¹⁵⁸ The obligation to obey is an ethical burden, not a theological one. The salvific message was to be first, without question, but the moral one of engendering obedience to Jesus and emulation of him was the rest of the disciple-making function; it is the one that consumes the lion's share of effort. This commission, located squarely in the moral realm, is in complete alignment with the teaching of Hebrews 5 and 6 concerning Christian maturity and faithfulness, which we reviewed in the first chapter.

There is one more significant ethical learning from Jesus' earthly ministry subsequent to his resurrection. Already, through review of the correctives Jesus provided during postresurrection encounters as well as the commissions to his disciples, we have seen that the vast majority of what it means both to be a disciple and a disciple-maker is focused in the moral realm. Being like Jesus in every way was the goal as well as the requirement, and it would take more than a mature, faithful follower's lifetime even to approach the goal.

The need for his followers to transition from what they were to what they should be was not the only transition Jesus explained during the forty days. He also conveyed he was about to transition. Just prior to his ascension Jesus "lifted up his hands and blessed them."¹⁵⁹ Nowhere else in the Gospels

---

156. John 20:21.
157. See Matt 28:18.
158. Matt 28:20.
159. Luke 24:50.

are we told Jesus lifted up his hands.[160] Why is this? What did his uplifted hands signify? What Jesus was doing was assuming the stance of the high priest, following the pattern of Aaron,[161] the first Levitical high priest.[162] This stance would have been recognized immediately by Jesus' followers.[163] The message he was conveying was that he was transitioning to a heavenly high priestly function at the same time as they were transitioning to be his emissaries. It was during the blessing he was taken up into heaven.

It is altogether fitting that at the end of his time on earth Jesus would give a hint of his future function, and it is that future function—what Jesus is doing subsequent to his earthly sojourn—to which we now turn.

160. Gansky, *40 Days*, 186.
161. Gansky, *40 Days*, 188.
162. See Lev 9:22.
163. Gansky, *40 Days*, 188.

5

The Living Jesus of Hebrews

THERE IS NO LIMIT to the moral guidance that can be gleaned from the life of Jesus, even regarding the complex moral situations of the information age in the twenty-first century. Even so, the picture of the Second Person of the Godhead found in the Gospels is incomplete. It depicts the Son of God only during about three decades, and that period limited to Palestine in the first century. We see in Jesus a very constrained member of the Trinity. The kenosis passage in the second chapter to the Epistle to the Philippians paints a picture of Jesus who, compared with what he was prior to the incarnation, conducted himself during his earthly sojourn as a nearly infinitesimally small and limited figure, even while his divinity was completely uncompromised. To be sure, during his earthly ministry Jesus' teaching and actions amazed his audiences and silenced his critics, being both profound and at times miraculous. He both defied and controlled the normal course of nature and social interaction,[1] and thus lived in a way that was beyond that of common human experience, while at the same time being limited in his ability to heal by virtue of the lack of faith of members of his home community.[2] According to the Philippians passage, he did not retain all of

---

1. Consider, for example, the incidents from the life of Jesus in which his actions multiplied the volume of available food, healed those who had been infirm for many years, raised to life those who were demonstrably dead, controlled and altered weather, and provided answers to questions that confounded those who were seeking to entrap him.

2. See Mark 6:1–6.

what he was prior to the incarnation, but divested himself to the point of becoming empty. He adopted the status of a slave to all, and took on himself human form. He obediently submitted to the will of the First Person of the Trinity, even to the point of being publicly humiliated and tortured to death.

Is this not a picture of a Jesus who, while on earth, was only a very small fraction of what he was prior? We tend to focus our worship, particularly when participating in the Lord's Supper or during Passion Week, on the suffering and death of Jesus as the substitutionary yet necessary sacrifice for our salvation, and rightly so. Simultaneously Christians tend to minimize the kenosis—the self-emptying—of Jesus. Consider for a moment how much the preincarnate Son of God gave up during the time he was on the earth. Can it reasonably be asserted that during that time he was completely the same as prior to the incarnation? Clearly the answer is "no." Instead, he was significantly limited, in spite of his magnificent life and uncompromised divinity.

If the self-emptied Jesus of the Gospels was subsequently exalted to the "highest place," given the highest name, worshipped by all in heaven and earth, and acknowledged as Lord by every tongue so that the First Person of the Trinity may be glorified,[3] should not this Jesus also somehow inform our values, virtues, attitudes, commitments, intentions, conduct, and other elements of our moral life? Should we not learn this picture of Jesus and combine it (at a minimum) with the picture of Jesus we find in the Gospels, thereby expanding and completing our understanding of the one who serves as our standard for faithfulness, maturity, and life in the moral realm? Jesus did not remain emptied; rather, he was restored to what he was prior to his incarnation, and perhaps to something more.[4]

In our daily spiritual sojourn we are not following one who is now walking the dusty roads of Palestine as the emptied Second Person of the Trinity. While God is not limited by the sequential events that characterize time, we as humans are; thus it is appropriate for us to differentiate in our worship and study the Son of God of eternity prior to the incarnation, the Son of God during his sojourn on earth in the first century AD, the exalted Son of God now, and the Son of God of the eschatological future. It is the exalted Son of God now with whom we commune and in whom "we live and move and have our being."[5] The present Jesus, the one exalted after the ascension, is pictured in the Epistle to the Hebrews. That picture is quite

---

3. See Phil 2:9–11.

4. The picture of Jesus found in the Revelation to John includes elements that are not found prior to his incarnation, and thus Jesus' exaltation and restoration may not be exactly identical with his pre-incarnate state. Whether or not Revelation's eschatological picture of Jesus should inform our moral thought prior to the *parousia* is another matter altogether.

5. From Paul's sermon in Athens, quoting the philosopher Epimenides. See Acts 17:28.

different from the picture of Jesus we find in the Gospels. The Jesus of Hebrews is not physically limited to Palestine in the first century. As a member of the Trinity he is not constrained, he is not divested, and he is not being publically humiliated and tortured to death.

The Jesus pictured in Hebrews completes the picture of Jesus found in the Gospels, and thus is a necessary and essential standard for understanding Jesus as our moral authority. Without it our source for ethics is incomplete, and to the degree it is incomplete it also is deficient. It is quite tempting to approach an investigation of Jesus as presented in Hebrews by focusing on the *titles* that the author of the epistle uses. Our desire, however, is to draw out the full *picture* of Jesus found in Hebrews, not just the activities Jesus performs. To that end, we will be best served if we divide the picture into three constituent elements: Jesus the human, Jesus the Son, and Jesus the High Priest.

JESUS THE HUMAN

In Hebrews we find the author went to great lengths to confirm to the readers that Jesus was intensely human. Donald Hagner observed, "It is worth noting that two of the New Testament writings that are the clearest on the deity of Christ—the Gospel of John and Hebrews—are also writings that emphasize most the full humanity of Jesus."[6] As was the case with the Gospel writers, the author of Hebrews presented Jesus' humanity in a positive light.[7] The presentation does not occur in only one place, however, but rather the "emphasis on Jesus' humanity runs like a scarlet thread throughout the epistle."[8] Since the complete picture of Jesus' humanity is nowhere found in a single passage of Hebrews, it is not easy to discern. Yet it is there, emphatically presented with strong emotions. Over 100 years ago, Scottish theologian H. R. Mackintosh wrote "Nowhere in the New Testament is the humanity of Christ set forth so movingly."[9] At the end of the nineteenth century, Scottish New Testament scholar Alexander B. Bruce described the picture of Jesus' humanity found in Hebrews:

> [N]owhere else in the New Testament are the earthly lot and human behavior of Jesus depicted in such vivid and lifelike

---

6. Hagner, *Encountering the Book of Hebrews*, 54.

7. See Parsons, "Son and High Priest," 204, in which he quotes David Mealand's 1979 article "The Christology of the Epistle to the Hebrews."

8. Parsons, "Son and High Priest," 204, again quoting Mealand.

9. Mackintosh, *Doctrine of the Person of Jesus Christ*, 79.

colours. Not even all the Gospels (not Luke, *e.g.*) show us Jesus in the weakness of His flesh side by side with the purity of His spirit, as He is exhibited here. We are so accustomed to one-sidedness in human thought, even in the case of philosophers, that we hardly expect one whose delight it was to contemplate the Divine dignity of the Son to display such masterliness in the treatment of His lowliness.[10]

We will see that participation in humanity in all of its aspects and fullness is the picture of Jesus the author sought to paint. His focus was not on *how* the incarnation took place, but rather the *fact* of the incarnation[11] and Jesus' total embrace of the human situation. Jerry Harvill captured the intent of the author of Hebrews when depicting the humanity of Jesus:

> We see a real person who at a real time and a real place had a real birth and real ancestors . . . who had real social relations with real people . . . who faced real opposition from foes who really did not like him . . . who experienced real pain, which made him cry in agony real tears . . . who knew real fear . . . and what it means to have real trust in God . . . There is here none of the 'other worldly,' innocuous unreality often surrounding our portrayal of him, but the hard, crisp lines of not-always-pleasant reality. Here are the sights, the smells, the sounds of real life.[12]

What, then, do we find when looking for the humanity of Jesus in Hebrews?

Jesus Was Completely Human, Yet Unlike Any Other Human

In Hebrews 2:9, we encounter the use of the term "Jesus" for the first time in the epistle. The term is used a total of ten times in Hebrews, and in this verse it is in an emphatic position, stressing Jesus' humanity.[13] What does it mean to be completely human? Most basically, it is essential that one who is human possess a body[14]—something affirmed twice in chapter 10, first when the author quoted from Psalm 40[15], and second in reference to the crucifixion.[16] Reference to possession of a body, particularly in light of any

10. Bruce, *Epistle to the Hebrews: First Apology*, 443.
11. Mackintosh, *Doctrine of the Person of Jesus Christ*, 83.
12. Harvill, "Focus on Jesus," para. 28.
13. Montefiore, *Commentary on the Epistle to the Hebrews*, 58.
14. Thiessen, *Introductory Lectures*, 301.
15. See Heb 10:5–7.
16. See Heb 10:10.

gnostic thinking that may have crept into the beliefs of the recipients of the epistle, was intended to affirm in clear and strong language that Jesus was undeniably and fully human. According to Donald Hagner, the Septuagint version of Psalm 40 as quoted by the author—"a body you prepared for me"—"jumped out at our author as a reference to the incarnation of Christ. The full, physical humanity of Jesus is a particularly important point for Hebrews."[17] Earlier, however, Jesus' participation in the physical elements of humanity was affirmed as part of the author's argument that he frees those who fear death.[18] This participation in "flesh and blood,"[19] as the author put it, was intended to show Jesus was fully human *in his essence*,[20] not simply donning certain human elements during his earthly sojourn.

Jesus' full humanity did not include participation in sin, according to the author. Depravity is not an element of human essence, but rather a result of the fall. For Jesus to be fully human did not require he become sinful as are other human beings, a point the author makes more than once in verses 4:15 and 9:14.[21] Göttlieb Lünemann expressed the author's concept of the human yet sinless nature of Jesus as follows:

> the author characterizes the human form of Christ's existence, in all its correspondence with the form of existence of other men,[22] as still different from the latter. And rightly so. For Christ was no ordinary man, but the incarnate Son of God. He was distinguished from His human brethren by His sinlessness.[23]

The sinlessness of Jesus may suggest to some that he was not, then, actually fully human. The author anticipated this objection in 2:17 when

---

17. Hagner, *Encountering the Book of Hebrews*, 130.

18. See Hebrews 2:14, which clearly argues that Jesus was human by virtue of the fact that he possessed the same kind of flesh and blood as other humans.

19. See Thiessen, *Introductory Lectures*, 301.

20. See Montefiore, in which he writes, "Flesh and blood form a constant and essential characteristic of human life . . . They bind men together in the solidarities of human existence. The Son of God, by an act of condescension, himself assumed complete humanity. His flesh and blood were similar to and as real as his brothers" (*Commentary on the Epistle to the Hebrews*, 65).

21. See Strong, in which he cites these two verses in support of his assertion that Jesus was "free, both from hereditary depravity, and from actual sin" (*Systematic Theology*, 676–77).

22. Here again we encounter the regrettable convention used in past centuries whereby male language was employed in reference to both genders. This will occur elsewhere throughout this chapter, as many of the references are taken from works written in the nineteenth and twentieth centuries.

23. Lünemann, "Commentary on the Epistle to the Hebrews," 441.

writing that Jesus "was made like them, fully human in every way." How is it that "every way" does not include sin, something in which all other humans participate? Lünemann goes on to explain that "every way" "is not: 'to be made the same or equal,' but expresses, as always, the notion of *resemblance*. Christ was in all things *similar* to men, His brethren, inasmuch as He had assumed a truly human nature; He was distinguished from them, however, by His absolute sinlessness."[24] Hagner asserts:

> Christ's full humanness and his sinlessness are not contradictory. Being sinful is not intrinsic or necessary to being fully human, nor, to state the opposite, is being sinless an obstacle to full humanness. . . . Since Christ has been tempted or tested, he can 'sympathize with our weaknesses.' . . . He knows well what it is to be in our position of human weakness.[25]

Hebrews, then, paints a picture of Jesus as fully and completely human in his essence, yet distinct and unique in his sinlessness.

The question that follows is, "Why did Jesus have to be human?" The response is found primarily in verse 2:17—in order that he could function as the high priest on behalf of all other humans, and in order that he could atone for humanity's sins. Regarding the first, Hagner focuses on priestly duty when he points out "humanity is stressed as a necessary qualification for Christ to become a 'high priest.' . . . a priest is a representative of the people, and as such, must be one of them. Therefore, to accomplish this priestly duty, Christ had to become like us 'in every respect'—except, of course, that he was without sin."[26] Much more will be explained later about the role of the high priest, but for our current purpose it is necessary to understand Jesus' humanity was a precursor to and prerequisite for the role of high priest. Without being human at the incarnation, Jesus could not later serve as high priest. Drawing on verse 2:10 while commenting on 2:17, F. F. Bruce emphasizes the solidarity with humanity that qualifies Jesus to be high priest:

> Any priest must be one with those whom he represents before God, and this is equally so with Christ as His people's high priest. In order to serve them in this capacity, He was obliged to become completely like His brethren—apart from sin, of course . . . He suffered with them and for them, and through His sufferings was made perfect—qualified in every way to be their high

---

24. Lünemann, "Commentary on the Epistle to the Hebrews," 444; italics original.
25. Hagner, *Encountering the Book of Hebrews*, 78.
26. Hagner, *Encountering the Book of Hebrews*, 60.

priest. He is merciful, because through His own sufferings and trials He can sympathize with theirs; He is faithful, because He endured to the end without faltering.[27]

The second purpose for which humanity was required of Jesus was so he could atone for the sins of all others. This flows from the fact that his complete humanity qualified Jesus to be high priest. Chief among the work of a high priest is the reconciliation of people to God, as William Lane points out.[28] In order to accomplish reconciliation, in some way atonement for sin had to be made, and in God's economy atonement involved the shedding of blood. Yet only by being linked with other humans could Jesus' self-sacrifice effectuate atonement for them. Lane observes this linking in 2:17 when he writes,

> The reason for the necessity contemplated in verse 17 is explained by two purpose-clauses, which follow in sequence. (1) *Only by standing with us in human solidarity could the exalted Son of God be qualified to participate in the life of the people as a merciful and faithful high priest.* . . . (2) *Only by standing with us in human solidarity could the exalted Son of God provide atonement for his people.* The second purpose clause is the natural extension of the first, and it describes the activity of the incarnate Son in distinctly priestly terms.[29]

Jesus Fulfilled a Specific Purpose

There was a specific purpose associated with Jesus' incarnation. Many effects of the incarnation become clear by reading the Gospels, but the specific purpose is articulated in Hebrews 2:9, 2:14, and 2:15. In short, Jesus became human in order to die. In the previous section it was pointed out that atonement for the sins of humanity was the result of the death of Jesus. Yet basic to the achievement of atonement was death itself. The picture of Jesus we find in Hebrews reveals a fully human person whose one purpose was to die. There are several particulars that are integral to this purpose. Verse 2:9 makes it clear Jesus' death was a tasting on behalf of others. The notion of tasting death "is a Semitic expression which captures vividly the reality of the violent death on the cross which Jesus endured for others."[30] He died a

27. Bruce, *Epistle to the Hebrews*, 52.
28. Lane, *Hebrews*, 53.
29. Lane, *Hebrews*, 53; italics original.
30. Lane, *Hebrews*, 45.

violent death involving intense suffering for a long period of time, and the entire social context surrounding Jesus' death included extreme humiliation, extensive injustice, gross misunderstanding, and many other elements of human experience that rendered his particular experience leading up to death a negative one in the extreme. All of these he underwent on behalf of others, experiencing what he did, tasting death for them, in a manner more extreme than they would ever experience.

Another particular specific to Jesus' death was the conquering "of him who holds the power of death—that is, the devil" (2:14). The death of Jesus was not like that of others in that his was a victorious death that vanquished an enemy of all humans, namely Satan.[31] Within a generation of Jesus' death "His followers were exultingly proclaiming the crucified Jesus to be the conqueror of death and asserting, like our author here, that by dying He had reduced the erstwhile lord of death to impotence. . . . for He, in the language of His own parable, had invaded the strong man's fortress, disarmed him, bound him fast and robbed him of his spoil."[32] Jesus died a death no one else could: a death that broke Satan's power over death.

Finally, a particular of Jesus' death was the freeing of those whose fear of death had enslaved them (2:15). The fear of death is a great motivator. It controls and guides humans to engage in all manner of conduct and compromise in order to avoid it, and thus enslaves them. Those who fear death are not free. However, the conquering death of Jesus "has transformed the meaning of death for them. To them His death means not judgment, but blessing; not bondage, but liberation. And their own death, when it comes, takes its character from His death."[33] The death of Jesus was unique in that it freed all other humans who embrace the one who tasted death for them.

The picture of Jesus' humanity in Hebrews, then, is a specifically purposeful one. Whatever may be gleaned from Jesus' sojourn on earth, his journey had a singular and pointed purpose: Jesus became human in order to die on behalf of others.

---

31. See Bruce, in which he points out that "The prince or angel of death is here identified with the devil—that is, Satan. It is not easy to parallel this outright identification, but it is not inconsonant with the general teaching of the New Testament" (*Epistle to the Hebrews*, 49).

32. Bruce, *Epistle to the Hebrews*, 49. See Luke 11:21–22.

33. Bruce, *Epistle to the Hebrews*, 51.

Jesus Experienced Intense Suffering

It follows from Jesus' complete humanity that he should undergo the normal experiences common to humans. He did not need to experience anything and everything that humans experience, but he had to experience that which all humans experience in order to be truly human. One thing all humans experience is suffering, and the life of Jesus was no exception. In Hebrews we find this first expressed in 2:9–10. The author introduced suffering in a dramatic fashion, citing Jesus' death as the first example of this component of Jesus' humanity. In 2:10, however, the author quickly shifted the reader's attention from Jesus' suffering at the end of his life to the suffering he experienced prior to his death. Curiously, such suffering, whatever it was, is presented as something that was for Jesus' own benefit, rendering him "perfect." That term itself was employed in the philosophical school in Alexandria, where the author studied, to convey such notions as perfected virtues, full actualization, maturity, completion lacking nothing, and the achievement of total humanity.[34] With that understanding as background, the author used the term not to convey that an imperfect Jesus had to be made perfect, but rather that the complete humanity that qualified Jesus to become humanity's high priest had to be fully experienced by Jesus, including the experience of suffering.[35] Having experienced suffering Jesus was perfected, or fully qualified, for what lay in the future. It was this fully qualified Jesus that ultimately brought "many sons and daughters to glory," as the author expressed at the beginning of 2:10. Bruce puts it this way: "the perfect Son of God has become His people's perfect Savior, opening up their way to God; and in order to become that, He must endure suffering and death."[36]

In chapter 5, the author gave us a clue regarding the form of Jesus' suffering. In 5:7, we read of Jesus' "prayers and petitions with fervent cries and tears." Many believe this is a direct reference to Jesus praying in the garden of Gethsemane just prior to his arrest,[37] although some see it as an expression of broader experience during Jesus' lifetime.[38] Whichever it may be, it

---

34. See *TDNT*, 8:67–70.
35. See *TDNT*, 8:83.
36. Bruce, *Epistle to the Hebrews*, 43.
37. See, for example, Lünemann: "the author has present to his mind, according to the prevailing and, beyond doubt, correct view, the prayer of Christ in Gethsemane, as this was made known to him by oral or written tradition" ("Commentary on the Epistle to the Hebrews," 508).
38. See, for example, Parsons: "There is no reason to limit the reference to the Gethsemane scenario; these verses may best be understood as a general reference to the

is clear Jesus experienced the normal and natural human fear of death. With this agonized prayerful response, particularly his "fervent cries and tears," his conduct "demonstrates his real humanity, for deity has no need to make supplication.... It was a natural human prayer for delivery from the cup of suffering and for escape from imminent death."[39]

Adding an insight from ancient Jewish understanding of prayerful expressions, James Moffatt notes,

> Later Rabbinic piety laid stress on tears . . . 'Rabbi Jehuda said, all things of this world depend on penitence and prayers, which men offer to God . . . especially if one sheds tears along with his prayers'; and . . . 'There are three kinds of prayers, entreaty, crying, and tears. Entreaty is offered in a quiet voice, crying with a raised voice, but tears are higher than all.'[40]

It is clear Jesus experienced and endured human suffering through intense anguish over what lay ahead of him, including death. Yet anguish was not the only aspect of his suffering.

In 5:8, the author referenced Jesus' sufferings as the means by which he learned obedience. This is a crucial element of Jesus' humanity, for in some way this suffering and obedience, when "perfected," rendered Jesus the source of salvation for other humans and qualified him to be high priest. The notion of being perfected and becoming qualified as high priest echoes what we have already seen in 2:10 and 2:17. It is true that learning often comes through the consequences of disobedience, and "'Son though He was'—that is to say, Son of God though He was—even He was granted no exemption from the common law that learning comes by suffering."[41] What else about obedience was it that Jesus, the sinless one who always obeyed the Father, had to learn through suffering? The key is to realize certain elements of learning come not through study, but through human experience. For Jesus, "He set out from the start on the path of obedience to God, and learned by the sufferings which came His way in consequence just what obedience to God involved in practice in the conditions of human life on

---

whole course of Jesus' passion and humiliation" ("Son and High Priest," 205).

39. Montefiore, *Commentary on the Epistle to the Hebrews*, 98.

40. Moffatt, *Critical and Exegetical Commentary*, 65.

41. Bruce, *Epistle to the Hebrews*, 103. See also footnote 67 on page 103 in which Bruce explains there were "many epigrams in Greek literature to the effect that learning comes by suffering." The author of Hebrews, who gives clear evidence of having been educated in Alexandria, likely had her or his Greek background in mind when expressing that Jesus learned obedience through suffering.

earth."[42] What Jesus had to learn experientially about obedience was what it is like to be a human who endured the painful consequences of obedience to God. Only then could it be said he experienced humanity while simultaneously remaining true to the path God had laid out for him.

Jesus Endured the Fullness of Temptation

There is one particular component of Jesus' suffering that warrants specific focus, for the author of Hebrews singled it out and distinguished it from Jesus' other suffering. In 2:18 we learn Jesus suffered while enduring temptation, and was thus qualified to help others when they suffer temptation.[43] In 4:15, we find the extent of Jesus' temptation at least matched that of other humans. In actuality, however, his suffering was greater since he endured temptation without succumbing to its lure: he never sinned.

Not only does the temptation he endured at the beginning of his ministry give us insight into the nature of Jesus' suffering,[44] but so do the temptations he endured from his closest followers.[45] Jesus endured a particular type of temptation throughout his life on earth, starting from his boyhood when his parents rebuked him.[46] We saw earlier that Jesus had a particular calling, and he suffered throughout his life because of it. The associated particular temptation was to avoid suffering by deviating from his calling. Bruce expresses the nature of Jesus' particular temptation and its accompanying suffering like this:

> He endured keen trials and temptations Himself, not only the trials incidental to our human lot, but those subtle temptations which attended His messianic calling. Time and again the temptation came to Him from many directions to choose some less costly way of fulfilling that calling than the way of suffering and death, but He resisted it to the end and set His face steadfastly to accomplish the purpose for which He had come into the world.[47]

42. Bruce, *Epistle to the Hebrews*, 103.

43. See Strong regarding Jesus' temptation: "He was subject to the ordinary laws of human development, both in body and soul" (*Systematic Theology*, 675).

44. See Luke 4:1–13.

45. See Bruce: "His friends' attempts to restrain Him (Mark 3:21 [and 31?]) and Peter's well-meant remonstrance (Mark 8:32), in which He recognized another form of the temptation which He faced earlier in the wilderness and later in Gethsemane; hence His rebuke to Peter (Mark 8:33) took the same form as His reply to the tempter in the wilderness (Matt. 4:10)" (*Epistle to the Hebrews*, 53n88).

46. See Luke 2:48–50.

47. Bruce, *Epistle to the Hebrews*, 53.

It was particularly important to the author to focus on Jesus' conduct when facing temptation, for the readers of Hebrews themselves were enduring the stress associated with the temptation to abandon their faith for a safer religious affirmation.[48] They were failing to resist temptation as Jesus had, and so the author set before them the example of endurance by the one they claimed to follow, as both a challenge they should meet and an example they should emulate.

In 4:15, the author extended the thought of 2:18 beyond simply suffering through temptation as a qualification for helping others to emphasize that Jesus' ability to align with those who are tempted—to know experientially what it means to endure the same kind of temptation they are enduring—is fundamental to his high priestly function on their behalf. He did not just imagine what they were going through and extend compassion to them on that basis. Rather, "he sympathises because he has, through common experience, a real kinship with those who suffer."[49]

All other people have succumbed to temptation and, by so doing, have truncated the level of suffering they endured. Jesus, however, did not sin and thus endured the full extent of suffering associated with temptation. Not only has Jesus suffered *as* all other humans, he has suffered *more* than they have by virtue of enduring temptation without succumbing.[50]

Jesus Bore the Effects of Guilt and Sin

Jesus indeed was fully human, suffered, bore temptation like no other, and fulfilled the purpose of the incarnation: to die. Yet why did he have to die, and what happened when he did? In 2:11, the author spoke of "the one who makes people holy and those who are made holy." How did this making of people holy occur, and what were they prior to being made holy? As sinful humans they were rendered guilty before God. That was their ongoing state. Annually

---

48. See Bruce, "Now His people were not only enduring those trials which are common to mankind, but were being tempted in their turn to be disloyal to God and give up their Christian profession. What a source of strength it was to them to be assured that in the presence of God they had as their champion and intercessor one who had known similar and even sorer temptations, and had withstood them victoriously!" (*Epistle to the Hebrews*, 53).

49. Montefiore, *Commentary on the Epistle to the Hebrews*, 91.

50. See Bruce, in which he cites B. F. Westcott: "He endured triumphantly every form of testing that man could endure, without any weakening of His faith in God or any relaxation of His obedience to Him. Such endurance involves more, not less, than ordinary human suffering: 'sympathy with the sinner in his trial does not depend on the experience of sin but on the experience of the strength of the temptation to sin which only the sinless can know in its full intensity. He who falls yields before the last strain'" (*Epistle to the Hebrews*, 85–86).

the animal sacrifices commanded by God served as a reminder of human guilt, but did nothing to assuage that guilt or render people holy, according to 10:1–4. The animals were a reminder, but only a human could pay the penalty for human guilt, and only a holy human could render others holy.[51] In becoming human—but remaining sinless and thus holy—Jesus was qualified to be an unblemished sacrifice on behalf of the guilty. In short, he was able to assume their guilt for he had none of his own for which to atone, and became the holy sacrifice God would accept on behalf of all other humans. There was a judicial exchange between Jesus and other humans: he would take on their guilt and pay the penalty for it, and they would take on his holiness.

Jesus Bonded with the People of God

There is another piece of the picture of Jesus' humanity that shows Jesus was not an isolated person, distinct from all others, as may be assumed because of his uniquenesses. Instead, we see much the opposite. Not only was he a suffering human who sacrificed himself for others so they might be holy and free of guilt, he actually was in solidarity with them. We see this clearly in 2:11, which indicates those who are made holy and the one who makes them such are of the same family. It is through the familial concept the author expressed the solidarity Jesus had with others. Not content to view them only as recipients of the holiness he provided, Jesus willingly endorsed them as his siblings. The author strengthened this notion by quoting three times from Psalm 22 and Isaiah 8 in 2:12–13, and crediting the language to Jesus himself. "These three different proofs are given to show that Jesus asserts his kinship with other members of God's family; firstly, he calls them brothers, secondly, he shares with them the human attitude of faith in God, and thirdly, he speaks of them as children of God."[52]

Before whom does Jesus assert the familial relationship he has with others? The answer lies in realizing those Jesus made holy were made such *in the sight of someone else, namely God*. The context for the declaration of a sibling relationship between Jesus and others is the presence of God. In 2:12–13, "Jesus is understood to stand before God together with those whom he has redeemed."[53] Not only are humans regarded as Jesus' siblings, but the family relationship is extended directly to include God. The last quote from Isaiah "is a text which is used to show Jesus' kinship with his

---

51. See Berkhof, "Since man had sinned, it was necessary that the penalty should be borne by man" (*Systematic Theology*, 319).

52. Montefiore, *Commentary on the Epistle to the Hebrews*, 64.

53. Hagner, *Encountering the Book of Hebrews*, 58.

followers. The Son of God is regarded as the speaker; and in his keeping are placed the children of God. The Son and the children are both members of the same family."[54] That family is none other than God's.

Jesus Lived as the Perfect Example, in Humiliation and Disgrace

In Hebrews 2:6–8, the author appealed to Psalm 8 to express the ideal and exalted nature of Jesus subsequent to his earthly human experience, even though the readers' understanding of Jesus was not nearly so lofty. In verse 9, we find a link between the Jesus the readers knew and the one they did not: Jesus is now exalted because of his human experience of suffering and death on behalf of other humans. By sacrificing himself so others might become holy, he demonstrated how others are to live, and thus became the example they are to emulate. Raymond Brown captures this concept of example by declaring,

> With the aid of Psalm 8, the writer wants to emphasize not only that Jesus has entered fully into our humanity, but more especially that he is the ideal man, man as God really intended him to be. The phrase *But we see Jesus* (2:9) brings the quotation from the Psalm to a dramatic climax. . . . Jesus has come into the world to show us what man is like in God's original purpose and what man can be through Christ's effective work.[55]

Hebrews 12 is a chapter of encouragement to those whose faith was faltering due to outside pressure and even persecution. In verses 2–4, the author revived the earlier idea of Jesus as an example the Hebrews were to emulate. The focus, however, is not on Jesus' exalted state—although that is mentioned in verse 2—but rather on his work as faithful pioneer on behalf of others through his endurance of opposition, shame, and the crucifixion. The degree to which Jesus endured such humiliation is explained by Bruce:

> To die by crucifixion was to plumb the lowest depths of disgrace; it was a punishment reserved for those who were deemed of all men most unfit to live, a punishment for sub-men. From so degrading a death Roman citizens were exempt by ancient statute; the dignity of the Roman name would be besmirched by being brought into association with anything so vile as the cross. . . . But this disgrace Jesus disregarded, as something not worthy to

---

54. Montefiore, *Commentary on the Epistle to the Hebrews*, 64.
55. Brown, *Message of Hebrews*, 57; italics original.

be taken into account when it was a question of His obedience to the will of God.[56]

The example the author presented, then, is more specific than simply the life Jesus lived on earth. Rather, it was the specific elements of Jesus' life and death in which he was opposed, humiliated, shamed, and tortured to death in a way that was most reviled in the culture. In Jesus the readers come face to face with the most extreme level of disgrace imaginable within their social context.

Why did the author hold out before the readers such a vile picture of the example Jesus left for his followers? Perhaps the answer is to be found in 12:3-4. Odd as it may seem at first, the author is attempting to encourage the Hebrews by putting before them the most repulsive picture of what Jesus endured in order to be faithful to God "so that you will not grow weary and lose heart." The encouragement continues with mention of the fact that irrespective of the level to which the readers had suffered, it did not compare with the suffering endured by Jesus. He had endured the worst of all possible humiliations and deaths; they had not even endured to the point of shedding their blood.

The final piece of this element of Jesus' humanity—his example in humiliation and disgrace—is found in Hebrews 13. This chapter includes the final exhortations to the readers, and verse 11 cites the practice whereby Israel's priests burned the bodies of the Day of Atonement sacrifices outside the camp.[57] The parallel with Jesus' death is not exact, of course, for Jesus' body was not burned, and Israel's sacrifices actually were offered within the camp prior to disposal of the carcasses.[58] Precise parallelism, however, was not the goal of the author. Rather, the author sought to impress upon the readers a further example Jesus left: execution of criminals outside of Jerusalem—a practice designed to maintain the ritual purity of the city[59]—was yet another social humiliation and ostracism that Jesus endured on their behalf, and his

---

56. Bruce adds validity to his assertion by quoting from Cicero: "Let the very mention of the cross be far removed not only from a Roman citizen's body, but from his mind, his eyes, his ears" (*Epistle to the Hebrews*, 352-53n42).

57. See Lev 16:27.

58. See Bruce, referring to Num 19:3, "The fact that the bodies of the animals sacrificed on the day of atonement were burned outside the camp suggests a parallel to the fact that Jesus was crucified outside one of the city gates of Jerusalem. The parallel may seem inexact, since the animals of the sin-offering were actually slaughtered within the camp; our author may, however, have also in mind the fact that the red heifer, which was a kind of sin-offering, was slaughtered outside the camp" (*Epistle to the Hebrews*, 402).

59. See Montefiore: "Criminals were customarily put to death outside of the city gate in order to avoid the ritual pollution of the city. Jesus' crucifixion was no exception (John xix. 20)" (*Commentary on the Epistle to the Hebrews*, 245).

followers were to be willing to endure it in emulation of their master. To follow Jesus, according to 13:13, meant to emulate him in his disgrace, distinct from the relative safety of the old Judaism they were tempted to reembrace.

The human Jesus portrayed in Hebrews is presented as the Jesus of the past, the Jesus who sojourned on earth for a while but who does so no more. Notice that the language employed to describe Jesus' full humanity, suffering, temptation, adoption of human guilt, sacrifice on behalf of others, humiliation, and crucifixion is past tense. In presenting the human Jesus this way the author was building a link to the Jesus the readers understood from the oral traditions and eyewitnesses they had heard. The Jesus they knew was not rejected by the author; rather, the author fully embraced this Jesus. In presenting the humanity of Jesus in the past tense, the author was attempting to show the readers what Jesus was and had done while on earth, but also to suggest the Jesus of the present is far different. That picture of Jesus is what we will take up next.

JESUS THE SON

At the beginning of the letter the author of Hebrews sought to present a powerful picture of who the Second Person of the Trinity is *at present*, distinct from who he was during his time on earth. To call attention to this distinction, the term "Son" is intentionally and consistently used throughout the first chapter, as opposed to other terms for the Second Person of the Trinity, such as "Jesus" or "Christ," which do not occur until chapter 2 or later. There was a purpose behind the author's selection of "Son" at the outset: to create a very different picture from the readers' understanding of the earthly Jesus—one that would convey to the readers who their Savior is and what he is doing in the present.

The concept of the Son in Hebrews cannot be underestimated. It is the second-most-frequently used term for the Second Person of the Godhead. One commentator asserts "this concept colors all the others, for again and again it is precisely because Jesus[60] is Son that the other titles and functions have special meaning."[61] The author chose to use "Son" not only with a specific intent, but in a specific way, since there is no definite article used

---

60. Many commentators, when writing on the use of "Son" in Hebrews, utilize terms that the author of Hebrews did not, particularly in chapter 1. In this instance, the term "Jesus" is used. Whereas this utilization is imprecise, it may have the benefit of being less cumbersome than the more precise terms "Second Person of the Trinity" or Second Person of the Godhead.

61. Harvill, "Focus on Jesus," para. 8.

before "Son." This is unique among biblical authors. The author of Hebrews evidently took this approach "to lay stress on the nature or character, rather than the personality of Jesus[62]. . . . we see One who is Son, that is, One who possesses all the characteristics and qualities to which that title points."[63] In short, use of "Son" rather than "the Son" points to what the Second Person of the Trinity is *inherently*. This picture of "Son" will prove valuable when discerning the moral guidance contained in Hebrews.

There is an overall characteristic that is fundamental to the relationship between the Father and the Son; one that underlies all elements of the picture of the Son as depicted in Hebrews. One commentator writes, "Everywhere the son is viewed as dependent on the Father—for appointment as heir of all things (1:2), for calling as High Priest (5:5), for resurrection (13:20), for exaltation (1:13)."[64] Whereas this is an accurate observation, it is only a partial one. In fact, the relationship between Father and Son is one of mutual dependency. In addition to the Son being dependent upon the Father, the Father is dependent upon the Son. As examples, see 1:2, in which the Father has spoken in the last days, but by means of the Son. In the same verse we learn when the Father created, the creative agent was the Son. In Hebrews, neither Father nor Son is independent, but each is dependent upon the other. The mutuality, which the author established at the very outset of the letter, is the background upon which the picture of the Son is painted, and will aid in understanding how the Son serves as a moral example for those seeking to be faithful.

If one studies Hebrews with the view to perceiving the Son as depicted by the author, soon four facets of the image emerge. Although somewhat intertwined and overlapping, investigation of the Son reveals one who is exalted, superior, eternal, and divine.

The Son as Exalted

In writing about the Son in the first chapter of Hebrews Mikeal Parsons observes, "The overall structure . . . seems to point to exaltation as the underlying motif,"[65] and later asserts the commentary on 1:1–4 found in subsequent verses "indicates that Christ is exalted because he is both divine ('the Son')

---

62. Here is a second instance of the imprecise use of "Jesus," rather than the more precise but cumbersome "Second Person of the Trinity." Many more instances will be seen of this utilization of substitute titles to refer to the Son, although they will not be footnoted.

63. Harvill, "Focus on Jesus," para. 10.

64. Mackintosh, *Doctrine of the Person of Jesus Christ*, 85.

65. Parsons, "Son and High Priest," 206.

and human."[66] The exaltation of the Son, of necessity, was from a certain state to another that is qualitatively different. It was from the humility of humanity that the Son was exalted to the state in which he now exists. After completion[67] of his earthly assignment—to make purification for human sin through his substitutionary death—the Son resumed his status as exalted. This resumption is simply that: it "did not involve a new status for him, but his re-entry into that which had always been his lawful place."[68]

In speaking of the relationship between the Son's purifying death and his exaltation "at the right hand of the Majesty in heaven," Alexander B. Bruce comments, "a celestial throne is the place that *fits* the Son; having made purification of sin, He *deserves* it. The purification is antecedent to the exaltation,"[69] and F. F. Bruce expands on the notion of the deserving Son when he writes, "He who was the Son of God from everlasting entered into the full exercise of all the prerogatives implied by His Sonship when, after His suffering had proved the completeness of His obedience, He was raised to the Father's right hand."[70] Although the Son's obedience during his earthly sojourn was total, his exaltation was not a gift bestowed upon him by virtue of his obedience. Rather, the Son's obedience during his earthly stint as a human demonstrated that exaltation—a return back to his state prior to his incarnation—was his rightful status, one on which he had rightful claim by virtue of who he is at the heart of his being. Thus, the Son had a dual claim on exaltation: one grounded in his completion of his earthly work as a human among humans, and the other based upon who he is at his core.

Note the author has thus established a link between Jesus on earth and the essential nature of the Son as the Second Person of the Godhead. The readers of the letter knew the first by verbal attestation and eyewitness accounts; the author was developing for them the picture of the second, and binding the two into one. This concept was repeated in 4:14 when the author, in speaking of the high priestly work of the Son, referred to "Jesus the Son of God."

---

66. Parsons, "Son and High Priest," 207.

67. In Montefiore, the author points out "the aorist tense of the participle emphasises that the act of purification has taken place in the past." (*Commentary on the Epistle to the Hebrews*, 38). Since the work is completed and in the past, the Son is now, in his exaltation, engaged in other activities.

68. Montefiore, *Commentary on the Epistle to the Hebrews*, 34. Compare Heb 1:3 with Phil 2:6–9.

69. Bruce, *Epistle to the Hebrews: First Apology*, 41; italics original.

70. Bruce, *Epistle to the Hebrews*, 13.

There is a final observation regarding the Son's role as the Exalted One. The tense of the command to sit in 1:13 shows the exalted state continues.[71] The exalted Son is not in the middle of a stint in that state; instead, exaltation is the normal, natural state associated with Sonship, and it continues indefinitely. The earthly sojourn was for a brief period in order to accomplish a specific objective. Having accomplished that goal, Jesus the Son returned to his natural, elevated status.

Inherent Characteristics

Hebrews 12:2 explains that, while being crucified, Jesus the Son not only endured but also scorned the shame of his execution. The reason given is he was looking forward to the joy he was to experience when seated at the right hand of God's throne, the place of his exaltation. Joy in exaltation characterizes the Son's ongoing position. Why joy? One theologian asserts, "His joy was largely the joy of anticipation (Heb. 12:2)—the joy of seeing millions of souls saved and with Him forever in Glory."[72]

There are four other characteristics of the exalted Son in which the author presented him as rather passive. First, he is heir of all things. Nothing is outside of his possession or accommodation. Not only was he the agent in creation, but all he created is now his. Just as a human heir simply inherits, so the exalted Son is depicted in his essence as Inheritor of All. Presented as the first characteristic of the exalted Son (1:2), the author is using the concept of heir to convey the expanse of the Son's exaltation: it includes everything.

God's glory is the next element the author introduced as characteristic of the Son's essence. This would have been an aspect of the earthly Jesus the readers would have understood well only if they had comprehended fully the resurrection. Realizing the readers had missed the resurrection's significance, the author specifically emphasized the Son's glorified state; being an ultimate one, it reflected the very glory of God. One commentator, in seeking to express the importance of the Son's glory as compared to his lack thereof during his earthly sojourn, writes,

> The inclusion of the Son's session here emphasizes his glory above all things. The very definite act of sitting down at the right hand of God is an unmistakably powerful biblical image. . . .this is not done at the expense of the power and glory of God, but

---

71. See Montefiore: "The present tense of the imperative κάθου implies that the Lord has not only taken his seat but continues his heavenly session" (*Commentary on the Epistle to the Hebrews*, 49).

72. Thiessen, *Introductory Lectures*, 310.

nonetheless underscores the unsurpassable exaltation of the Son after his having undergone the humiliation of death on a cross.[73]

The third characteristic is that the Son sits in the place of ultimate honor. The readers, being Jews, would have been familiar with the story from 1 Kings, in which a second throne was placed to the right hand of Solomon as the honored place for his mother to sit (see 1 Kgs 2:19).[74] Upon his exaltation the Son is specifically seated "at the right hand of the Majesty in heaven" (1:3), an image the author borrowed from the 1 Kings passage. The author later repeated the imagery, first in 1:13, when demonstrating the superiority of the Son, and next at the end of the letter, when encouraging the readers to emulate Jesus as they seek to live faithfully (12:2). The Son's exaltation to the place of honor is thus used in the moral sense as an example that should motivate and inspire his followers.

Finally, the exalted Son is pictured as vindicated vis-à-vis his adversaries. In 1:13, subsequent to the Son's seating at God's right hand, enemies are made the Son's footstool. This is not a goal the Son pursued; rather it is an action of the Father taken on behalf of the Son as a means of vindication. In his exalted state the Son is declared to be triumphant, and continuously remains the Vindicated One. Enemies have been eternally conquered.[75]

Active Characteristics

If we think for a moment about the offices, or titles, that characterize the exalted Son, it quickly becomes apparent from the early part of Hebrews that he holds the three understood and affirmed by Jews for centuries: prophet, priest, and king.[76] In 1:2, it is the Son who has spoken "in these last days," just as the Old Testament prophets had spoken in the past (see 1:1). It could be argued that a secondary purpose of the incarnation, in addition to the primary one of providing salvation for humankind, was to speak God's prophetic word to his fellow humans. The Exalted One acted as God's final prophet, and continues to serve as the means by which God's word is conveyed.

In 1:3 we find the first hint that the exalted Son plays a priestly role. The providing of purification for sins was distinctly and exclusively a function of the priest. "At this point, however, the writer does *not* say that Jesus

---

73. Mitchell, *Hebrews*, 44.
74. Montefiore, *Commentary on the Epistle to the Hebrews*, 38.
75. See Mitchell: "The image of enemies being transformed into a footstool indicates that the Son has been given power in exaltation. It speaks of vindication as well, for the Son is not actually subduing his enemies. Rather, God does this for him" (*Hebrews*, 50).
76. See Hagner, *Encountering the Book of Hebrews*, 45.

is a priest. He simply ascribes to the Son a distinctively priestly action."[77] Later we will investigate in detail the priestly function of the Son, but it is noteworthy at this point to understand the author linked the Son as high priest with the Son as exalted (see 8:1 and 10:12).

The role of king is specifically introduced in 1:8, where the Son is said to have a throne and scepter, and where justice is noted as the character of the Son's kingdom. In the next verse, the Son's anointing with oil is mentioned, referencing the practice of anointing Israel's kings; a practice that started with the anointing of Saul as Israel's first king.[78] Of these verses one commentator notes, "Now we are assured that Christ is sovereign. He is not only the prophet who speaks, and the priest who saves, but also the king who rules."[79]

We get a hint at when the kingship of the Son began in 1:5. The first quote is from Psalm 2:7 and likely originally referred to the coronation of a king in Israel, who was then designated as a son of God.[80] It was on coronation day that the new king took on this designation. Regarding the author's view of the kingly status of the exalted Son, F. F. Bruce writes, "In view of the emphasis laid throughout the epistle on the occasion of Christ's exaltation and enthronement, it is probable that he thought of this occasion as the day when He was vested with His royal dignity."[81]

From 1:8 it is clear the Son as king is administering justice "for ever and ever," and the statement in 1:3 that he is "sustaining all things by his powerful word" indicates he is administering the universe through exercise of the power associated with his exalted state. Thus, the enthroned king is active in the moral matters associated with the entire creation. Not wanting the readers to forget the royal status of the exalted Son, the author later returns to this theme when in 2:9 the readers are reminded the earthly Jesus has now been crowned with glory and honor.[82]

The Son as Superior

The author of Hebrews perceived the readers needed to be taught the way the Son's exalted status was superior. Largely this perception was driven by the readers' Jewish background, in which the prophets and Moses were

77. Lane, *Hebrews*, 34; italics original.
78. See 1 Sam 10:1 for the anointing of Saul as Israel's first king.
79. Brown, *Message of Hebrews*, 41.
80. Hagner, *Encountering the Book of Hebrews*, 46.
81. Bruce, *Epistle to the Hebrews*, 13.
82. See Mackintosh: "God set the seal upon His work by crowning Him with glory and honour (2:9)" (*Doctrine of the Person of Jesus Christ*, 82).

held in honored positions. Also, because of outside influences on the readers' thinking—perhaps those grounded in Gnosticism and/or the Qumran community—the vaulted position of angels required addressing. Thus, at the outset of the letter and occasionally throughout the rest of it, the author showed the various ways in which the exalted Son is also superior.

Superior to Prophets

The Epistle to the Hebrews begins by recalling that in the past God communicated with humans "at many times and in various ways" (Heb 1:1) through the prophets. It speaks of a time when God communicated occasionally, and then in an incomplete fashion. Each prophetic word was spoken for an immediate specific purpose, and in some cases also for a longer-term or eschatological one. None of them individually or taken as a whole was complete. With the speaking by the Son, however, there was something qualitatively new and different being conveyed. William Lane insightfully observes, "Only one expression descriptive of the old revelation is not taken up and developed in setting forth the distinctive character of the new revelation. It is the adverbial phrase 'at various times and in many ways.' The omission of this phrase implies that when God spoke his word through the Son he spoke *with finality*."[83] The word spoken by the Son was not simply the most recent in a chain of God's speaking throughout history; rather, it was the culmination of God's speaking.

That which the Son spoke was God's final revelation, but it also was superior to the words formerly given by the prophets. Another commentator reflects this idea when he writes,

> in Christ he spoke fully, decisively, finally and perfectly. The first-century Christians must listen to him, the greatest prophet of all times. Ezekiel portrayed the *glory* of God, but Christ reflected it (1:3). Isaiah expounded the *nature* of God as holy, righteous and merciful, but Christ manifested it (1:3). Jeremiah described the *power* of God, but Christ displayed it (1:3).[84]

The divine word spoken by the Son, being both final and superior, brought to an end God's speaking through the prophets "many times and in various ways" (Heb 1:1). That which God spoke through the Son was more than simply new content, or even final and superior content. God's final word ushered in a new age; a new covenant between God and his faithful people, as the author expressed it in 8:13—a covenant that obviated the old one

---

83. Lane, *Hebrews*, 31; italics original.
84. Brown, *Message of Hebrews*, 28; italics original.

under which God's people had lived during the times the prophets spoke. The readers of the letter needed to understand that in order to be God's faithful in the future they could not live as they had in their Jewish past, for God had given them a new and final word through the Son. Nineteenth-century theologian Alexander B. Bruce offers this explanation of why the Son's word is superior and final, as well as the launch of a new relationship between God and his faithful followers: "A Son dwelling in the bosom of God, His Father, and having access to His inmost thoughts, is . . . the perfect exegete of His mind . . . This implies that the Son must be the last speaker: no more remains to be said; it implies further that He is the only Speaker of the new era."[85]

What the readers had missed was that in the life of Jesus God was actually speaking his final word, and that through his Son. The author, then, had to paint for the readers a picture of the Son that was more extensive than the earthly life of Jesus with which they were familiar, and so explained how God had ushered in a new covenant by speaking his final word through the Son.

Superior to Angels

The situation of the readers was the likely motivation for the protracted focus in chapter 1 on the place of angels compared to that of the Son. Donald Hagner references Colossians 2:18 in pointing out that among the early Christians were those who worshipped angels, then writes, "People inclined toward Gnosticism—that is, people who regarded materiality as intrinsically evil—might well conclude that angels as spiritual beings, were superior to Jesus, who had been incarnated in human flesh."[86]

To counter the tendency for the readers of Hebrews to reason that angels were superior to the incarnated Jesus—now the exalted Son—the author directly juxtaposed the Son and the angels. The picture of the Son as superior to the angels is implicit in the introductory language of the letter. Among the various ways God's message to the prophets was delivered, one was through angels. Yet that word, being partial and incomplete, was inferior to the final word delivered directly by the Son. In 1:4 we learn even the name of the Son is superior to that of the angels. How is this so? Later in the chapter the author reasoned that the name "angel," which means "messenger," is the descriptive term for those beings who do God's bidding, and that they are so volatile that at times they appear as wind or flames.[87] Elsewhere

85. Bruce, *Epistle to the Hebrews: First Apology*, 32.
86. Hagner, *Encountering the Book of Hebrews*, 45.
87. See Hagner: "the changeability and transitoriness of wind and fire are contrasted with the permanent and unchanging character of the Son, which will be stressed

they are referred to as those who serve "those who will inherit salvation" (Heb 1:14). Angels, then, are servants who do as they are told, and as such bear a name that is far inferior to the Son of the Father. When comparing the Son to angels, one commentator writes, "Being called Son is what sets him apart from them, so it is all the more likely that the name he had been given was precisely for that function and was therefore 'Son.'"[88]

How is it the angels are inferior to the Son since both live in God's presence? The author's argument in chapter 1 lends itself to various images when viewing the Son next to the angels. One interpreter, commenting on the seven quotations in verses 5 through 13, explains:

> let us note the broad contrast which runs through the group of quotations. There is only one radical contrast, but it has three aspects: Son and servants, King and subjects, Creator and creatures. Christ is the Son of God, angels are the servants of God. . . . Christ is a Divine King, sitting on a throne of omnipotence exercised in behalf of righteousness. The angels are His subjects. . . . Christ is the Creator, and the angels are His creatures: He everlasting; they, like all created beings, perishable.[89]

Another commentator sees the contrast more in terms of traits rather than titles. He writes, "The comparison between Jesus and the angels considers four points: (1) his name is greater than theirs: he is acclaimed as 'my Son' (v. 5); (2) his dignity is greater than theirs: he is worthy of worship (v. 6); (3) his status is greater than theirs: he remains unchanged (vv. 7–12); (4) his function is greater than theirs: he reigns at God's right hand (vv. 13–14)."[90] There is no need to argue for one of these perspectives against the others; instead the careful student of the Son as pictured in Hebrews will realize the author has skillfully developed the picture so as to support many ways of observing the details of how the Son is superior to angels.

Superior to Moses

The author included a short section in chapter 3 showing how the Son is superior to Moses. Moses was not denigrated by the author, similar to the way the prophets were not attacked earlier, nor the angels charged with wrongdoing. Rather the place of each, including Moses, is affirmed. Why is

---

especially by the quotation in verse 12 (cf. 13:8)" (*Encountering the Book of Hebrews*, 48).

88. Mitchell, *Hebrews*, 39.

89. Bruce, *Epistle to the Hebrews: First Apology*, 57.

90. Lane, *Hebrews*, 35.

it, then, that the author chose to single out Moses, particularly right after affirming in 2:16 that Jesus helps not the angels, but Abraham's descendants?

For Jews at the time of the writing of Hebrews, Moses was not viewed as simply a prophet. Rather,

> Moses was the man with whom God had spoken more intimately and directly than with an ordinary prophet. The classic passage for demonstrating this fact is God's own witness in Numbers 12:6–8 . . . In some strands of the later Jewish tradition the testimony to Moses' faithfulness in Numbers 12:7 was used to prove that Moses had been granted a higher rank and privilege than the ministering angels.[91]

The reason the author felt compelled to establish the Son's superiority over Moses was that the prior arguments regarding the prophets and the angels, taken by themselves, still left open the possibility that the Son was not superior over all. Exalted though he was, he still could be inferior to the venerated Moses.

To establish the superiority of the Son over Moses, the author chose to begin with the very passage from Numbers that Judaism had used to assert Moses' superiority. That passage first distinguished Moses from other prophets, then pictured Moses as the faithful one in God's house. The author of Hebrews agreed with that passage, affirming the status of Moses as God's faithful servant. However, she or he also pointed out that Moses is limited in his stature, just as the household servant is limited when compared with both the house's builder and the builder's Son who oversees the house. Such a situation does not dishonor the servant, but rather shows there is a place of honor above that of the servant. Hugh Montefiore expresses the relationship like this: "The status of Moses as servant is contrasted with the status of **Christ** as Son . . . The nature of God's household has not been changed by the advent of Christ, nor has the status of its members been altered. He is simply pointing out the difference in a household of a son and a servant, however honoured the servant may be."[92]

The roles of Moses and the Son in the house are simply different, and that of the Son is superior. The house, according to the author, is God's faithful people—those for whom the Son had made atonement during his earthly sojourn. Moses had not made atonement for God's people, but rather was a witness to what God later would do through the Son.

---

91. Lane, *Hebrews*, 58.
92. Montefiore, *Commentary on the Epistle to the Hebrews*, 73; bold original.

Superior to Creation

At the very outset of the letter the author started to establish the Son's superiority over creation. In 1:2, the Son is referred to as God's agent in the creation of the entire universe, a theme repeated later in verse 10. In addition to being the agent in creation, the author seeks to establish the superiority of the Son over creation. Prior to quoting from the Septuagint version of Deuteronomy 32:43, the author in 1:6 mentions "when God brings his firstborn into the world." The Greek word translated "firstborn" (*prōtotokon*) is used to convey the notion of rank, rather than simple chronology. Given the context of the earlier verses, the exalted Son is in view here,[93] rather than one brought into being as the first of all that was created. David Hagner comments that the use of this word in its context "refers not to Jesus being created at the beginning of creation, but to his primacy of rank over all of creation, his superiority or preeminence over it."[94]

Expansion of the Son's creative function occurs in 1:10, a quote from Psalm 102 in which God is said to have created both the heavens and the earth. However, in Hebrews this divine creation is credited to the Son, thus elevating the Creator Son to a position superior to that of the creation. The author then added one final element to solidify the Son's superiority to the creation: in continuing the quote from Psalm 102, the creation is shown to be transient whereas the Son is eternal. Alan Mitchell comments, "As the Psalm text continues, so also the comparison of the Son, now to the creation. It is a perishable entity whereas he is eternal; thus he remains."[95]

With the addition of the Son's superiority over creation the author's picture of the Son's overall superiority is now complete. He not only enjoys preeminence over the created beings who were held in great honor by the author's readers—prophets, angels, and Moses—he is preeminent over all of creation; an ultimate position.

The Son as Eternal

Theologian Henry Thiessen cites Hebrews 1:2 and 11:3 to substantiate the following assertion he makes about God: "He is also the cause of time."[96] Hebrews 1:2, however, clearly teaches God's instrument in creating the universe was the Son; there was no creation without the Son. The question we

---

93. See *TDNT*, 6:871, 880.
94. Hagner, *Encountering the Book of Hebrews*, 48.
95. Mitchell, *Hebrews*, 50.
96. Thiessen, *Introductory Lectures*, 123.

need to ask is: Was time included in the scope of the Son's creation of the universe? We can glean a bit of an answer by considering the word the author chose to convey "universe." It is not the common word for the ordered physical, created world—*kosmos*—but rather a form of the word *aion*—the word normally translated "age" and indicating a very long period of time. The author chose to use *aion* because the intent was to capture a concept more extensive than the physical creation, extending to everything including time.[97] The word had long been used to describe the eternality of God, extending both before the beginning of time and after its end, but also in certain contexts would carry the sense of that which had been created.[98] However translated, the word retains its base temporal sense. The author, by choosing this word, was introducing the notion that the creative Son is outside of creation, including time, and thus is eternal. This notion is reinforced twice by use of "all things" as equivalent to *aion* in 1:2 and 1:3, where the Son both inherits and sustains everything.

As the author developed the notion of the eternality of the Son, several elements were added to fill out this aspect of the picture.[99] First, if the Son is outside of creation it follows that he is preexistent, not created. Since the Son sustains all, as indicated in 1:3, there is nothing in the created order he does not sustain, and thus is not among that which was created. As not only the sustainer, but the one by whom God has spoken his final word, the Son is outside of creation *as a person*, not a concept or force. At the beginning of the twentieth century, H. R. Mackintosh affirmed this element of the eternality of the Son when he wrote, "it is safe to say that Hebrews can be quoted for the pre-existence of Christ, and that this pre-existence is specifically conceived as personal. . . . His earthly life is an episode, though not an episode merely, in a history without beginning and without end."[100] The use of the word "firstborn" in verse 1:6 may at first appear to argue against the idea that the Son is both outside of and prior to creation, suggesting that at some point he was born. Yet the point of the verse is not a temporal one,

---

97. Regarding the use of *aion*, Lünemann writes that the word "is to be understood of the *worlds*, of the totality of all things existing in time (and space)." He asserts that whereas the word "has always . . . the strict notion of duration of time; . . . this notion might easily pass over into the wider notion of that which forms the visible contents of time, thus into that of the complex of all created things" ("Commentary on the Epistle to the Hebrews," 395; italics original).

98. See *TDNT*, 1:197–204.

99. There are places throughout Hebrews where the eternality of the Second Person of the Godhead is asserted or referenced, particularly in regard to the role of high priest. Those references are intentionally omitted in this section, since they will be addressed in the section on Jesus the High Priest.

100. Mackintosh, *Doctrine of the Person of Jesus Christ*, 83.

but one of rank. The Son, being superior to the angels, has always ranked above all else from eternity, before even the angels were created. He eternally proceeds from the Father, and is superior to all else. The use of the term "firstborn" simply indicates "the fact of the eternal generation of the Son. It simply means that He was before all creation."[101]

Second, the author linked the Son to the Jewish understanding that Wisdom was with God from eternity. The author drew upon his or her philosophical background to convey in yet another way that the Son is eternal, and joined that philosophical understanding with that of his or her Jewish readers regarding the role of Wisdom. One commentator points out, "The unique relation of Christ to God is one of the unborrowed truths of Christianity, but it is stated here in borrowed terms. The writer is using metaphors which had been already applied in Alexandrian theology to Wisdom and the Logos."[102] Thomas Long, in commenting on verse 1:2, states, "The irony is that the Son, who is heir of all things, also created all things. . . . The writer of Hebrews here connects Jesus to the figure of Wisdom, who was understood to be the inventive hand of God in fashioning the creation (see Prov. 8:22-31; Wisd. Sol. 7:22)."[103]

Just what was it that characterized this Wisdom that existed with God from eternity past, and which the author sought to include in the picture of the Son? In studying the first few verses of Hebrews William Lane observed that the author's melding of the wisdom notions from the Old Testament and Alexandria can be illustrated by the description of Jesus as the eternal, pre-existent Son through whom God created the world, who now sustains everything by his powerful word (1:2b-3). That manner of describing God's Son draws on a tradition in the Bible and in older Jewish literature which makes reference to God's Wisdom, to Divine Wisdom. In this tradition Wisdom is treated as a person who was with God from the beginning. In Proverbs 8:22-31, for example, Wisdom is associated with God in his creative activity as "the craftsman at his side" (Prov. 8:30).[104] Lane goes on to list the four activities of Wisdom that were articulated by later Jewish writers: "(1) the creation of the world; (2) the providential sustaining of the world; (3) the revelation of God's truth; and (4) the reconciliation of persons to God."[105] After arguing that the readers of Hebrews would have been familiar with this understanding of Wisdom from their Jewish background, Lane

101. Berkhof, *Systematic Theology*, 92.
102. Moffatt, *Critical and Exegetical Commentary*, 6.
103. Long, *Hebrews*, 15.
104. Lane, *Hebrews*, 32–33.
105. Lane, *Hebrews*, 33.

makes the obvious connection to the description of the Son in 1:2-3, showing that the author repeated the four activities of Wisdom in describing the eternal Son.[106] The author, then, did not paint for the readers a new picture of the Son, but rather copied one that they already affirmed. In assigning it to the Son the author was arguing for the Son's eternality in a way that was difficult to deny.

Third, the name "Son" is presented in such a way as to argue for eternality. In verses 1:4-5 the Son's name is presented as superior to that of the created angels, and the close linkage between the Son and the Father is made explicit. The notion of inheriting the name Son, taken in isolation, suggests that there was a point in time prior to the inheriting in which the Son's name was not "Son." Yet the order of verse 1:2, in which the Son's inheriting all things is placed prior to his creating the universe indicates that the Son's quality as the inheritor is an essential one, and therefore an eternal one. F. F. Bruce remarks, "If He is said to have 'inherited' the name of Son, this does not mean that the name was not His before His exaltation; . . . He inherits the title 'Son', as He inherits all things (verse 2), by the Father's eternal appointment."[107] Thus the Son inherits an essential element of his nature from eternity; one title of the Son could be "The Eternally Inheriting One."

Recall that the Son, as eternally distinct from creation, created all, including time. According to the author, however, he did this *as Son*, not as something or someone else. His eternally generated name from the eternally generating Father links him so closely to God that the two are inseparable at the time of creation, even the creation of the heavens according to verse 1:10. The eternality of the Father is also characteristic of the Son, just as the two were one during creation.

Finally, the author argued that the eternality of the Son is one that extends to the future. In verse 1:8 we learn that the Son, at that point referred to as "God" by God, has a throne that is eternal into the future. Characterized by justice and righteousness, it will never end, even after the end of all creation, according to verses 1:10-12. Alan Mitchell writes, "Here, just as one rolls up a cloak when done with it, so the heavens and the earth will perish at an appointed time, having accomplished the purpose for which they were created. . . . The Son, however, endures forever."[108] When one realizes that the author in this passage has chosen to quote from a Psalm[109] that

---

106. Lane, *Hebrews*, 33.
107. Bruce, *Epistle to the Hebrews*, 8.
108. Mitchell, *Hebrews*, 50.
109. Ps 102:25-27.

clearly referred to the eternality of God, the argument for the eternality of the Son into the future is greatly strengthened.

The picture of the Son painted by the author of Hebrews shows that the continuity of his eternality is incontrovertible, and along with the Son's exaltation and superiority should be a strong encouragement to the readers to live lives of faithfulness. The author has nearly completed the image of the Son. All that remains is to paint the Son as divine.

The Son as Divine

The constituent elements of the portrait presented to this point, taken collectively, are true only of God. Yet making the divinity of the Son explicit was deemed by the author to be an essential task so that no misinterpretation of the author's portrait was possible. Demonstrating the divinity of the Son was done in three ways.

The Son is Called God

Three verses in the first chapter explicitly indicate that the Son is God: verses 6, 8, and 10. Verse 6 is a quote from Deut 32:43 in the Septuagint, and calls all angels to worship God. The term for "God" is YHWH, God's formal name. Donald Hagner writes, "In the Deuteronomy text, the pronoun 'him' in the quotation refers to the Lord (YHWH—the Tetragrammaton, the personal name of God, 'Yahweh'), and by applying these words to the Son, the author in effect affirms the deity of the Son."[110] This is a case of "two things equal to the same thing are equal to each other."[111] In the Deuteronomy passage the pronoun refers to God; in verse 6 the author used it to refer to the Son, thus creating such a strong link between God and Son that the two are equivalent.

In verse 8 the pronouncement from God changes from addressing angels to addressing the Son. The verse is a quote from Ps 45:6, which was broadly understood as Messianic.[112] Hebrews exegete James Moffatt argues that the Psalm's correct understanding should be, "'Thy throne, O God (or, O divine One), is for ever and ever.' This . . . may well explain the attractiveness of the text for a writer who wished to bring out the divine significance of

---

110. Hagner, *Encountering the Book of Hebrews*, 48.
111. This is one of Euclid's axioms.
112. See Lünemann, "Commentary on the Epistle to the Hebrews," 406.

Christ."[113] The author of Hebrews thus employed the Psalm to create an image of God speaking directly to the Son *as God*. Having not only used God's formal name to refer to the Son, but also having created an image in which the Son is addressed as "God" by God, it remained for the author to show that the Son bears a name that historically was regarded as the highest of all.

In verse 10 the author quoted from Ps 102:25, a portion of a Psalm in which the speaker is addressing God. In the Septuagint the verse specifically contains the Greek word for "Lord" (*kyrios*), making explicit that the reference is to God as the one who created the heavens and the earth. When the author of Hebrews used the Psalm, however, it was in the same context as that of verse 1:8: God speaking to the Son, and in this case addressing him using the highest name there was—Lord. F. F. Bruce captured the strong connection between the Son being addressed as "God" in verse 8 and as "Lord" in verse 10: "If in the preceding quotation the Son is addressed by God as 'God', in this one he is addressed by God as 'Lord'. And we need not doubt that to our author the title 'Lord' conveys the highest sense of all, 'the name which is above every other name.'"[114]

In this three-pronged effort, then, the author made a strong case for the divinity of the Son, ascribing to him the very name of God without qualification.

The Son Performs God's Actions

There are places throughout the first chapter of Hebrews where the author presented the Son engaged in actions that only God does. It is another case of "two things equal to the same thing are equal to each other": if God does certain things that are characteristic only of the divine, and the Son is seen to be doing them, then the Son is divine. In verse 1:3 the Son is said to be the sustainer of all by his powerful word. That word, though, is the word of God, as clearly taught in verse 1:2. The Son is engaging in only what God can do through his word, sustaining all. H. R. Mackintosh sees this active, sustaining word to be a clear indication the Son is God: "The Divine place of the Son is signalised by the fact that in 1:3 He is said to uphold all things by the word of His power."[115] Furthermore, the sustaining of all is subsequent to, but also closely tied to, the creating of all, something ascribed to God at the beginning of Genesis. In Hebrews, however, the author presented the creating of everything as something that was done by the Son (see 1:2 and

113. Moffatt, *Critical and Exegetical Commentary*, 13.
114. Bruce, *Epistle to the Hebrews*, 23.
115. Mackintosh, *Doctrine of the Person of Jesus Christ*, 81.

1:10). If God was the creator, and the Son was the creator, then the Son is God. Another commentator expresses this concept a bit differently:

> Since the instrument of sustenance is the powerful word of God, the sense is that the universe continues to exist because of the powerful word, which caused it to exist in the first place. . . . The difference, of course, is that here it is the Son's word that does the sustaining, so he has been given the role of the creator God in keeping all things in existence.[116]

Receiving worship is the final example of the Son being engaged in the activities in which only God is engaged. Although a passive participant in that he is the recipient of worship, God is nonetheless fully engaged in the action. In 1:6 the author quotes from Deuteronomy 32:43 the invitation for the angels to worship God. The object of worship, though—the one engaged in the receiving of worship—is the Son. F. F. Bruce asks, "Since in its original setting it is Yahweh, the God of Israel, whom all angels are to worship, why is their worship here said to be paid to the Son?"[117] It is because God himself, the only one deserving of worship, views the Son as divine and equal to God himself.

Having shown the Son is both called God and participates in activities in which only God participates, there remains but one more way the author of Hebrews sought to paint the Son as divine; by showing the Son's essence is that of God himself.

The Son Is God's Essence

The author of Hebrews took a unique approach to make the point that the Son's essence is the essence of God. Two words, occurring in the New Testament only in Hebrews, were used to demonstrate the Son is God and reveal the author leveraged his or her philosophical background to convey a specific point. Both words occur in 1:3. First, the word *apaugasma*, translated "radiance," was used to show that in seeing the Son one was seeing God. Tying together the observable brilliance of God with the Hebrew notion of God's glory, the author stated the Son is the one who presents the invisible God in a way humans can perceive. "For the Hebrew people the glory of God was a visible and outward expression of the majestic presence of God. . . . Now, says the author of this letter, in these last days this same glory has been seen in the person of Christ who reflects or is 'the radiance of God's glory.'"[118]

---

116. Mitchell, *Hebrews*, 38.
117. Bruce, *Epistle to the Hebrews*, 16.
118. Brown, *Message of Hebrews*, 30.

Systematic theologian Augustus Strong makes the point more directly: "the radiance of the sun is as old as the sun itself, and without it the sun would not be sun. So Christ is coequal and coeternal with the Father."[119]

The second word, *charaktēr*, is translated "exact representation," and carries the meaning of the result of a die or stamp used to produce coins.[120] The Son is a precise counterpart of who God is, just as a coin is a precise image of the die used to make it. Why did the author choose to use this word to argue the Son is God? Strong offers an answer: "The word 'Image' suggests the perfect equality with God which the title 'Son' might at first seem to deny."[121] So the author, in yet another way, was ensuring the readers did not view the title "Son" as suggesting any diminution compared with "God."

It is noteworthy the author added a qualification to the concept of the Son being an imprint of God. That qualification is translated "of his being," and carries the meaning of the essence of God's nature. Whereas the sense of the word used to demonstrate that the Son reflects God's glory included the undertone of something observable, the qualification is intended to convey the opposite: "As the qualifying words 'of his being' indicate, it is not the physical image that is in view, but rather, the being or essence of God."[122] The author is showing that the core of what God is—God's nature, essence, attributes, and character—is what the Son also is. "He bears the eternal image of God . . . as one who partakes in the full divine nature."[123]

Later in chapter 1, the author makes one more argument that the Son is God. The immutability of God is one divine characteristic that is at the heart of who God is. In short, God—and only God—does not change. In 1:11–12 the author quotes from Psalm 102 to distinguish the Son from creation. Twice in the quotation the immutability of God is credited to the Son. One commentator sees "The original setting of the psalm refers to God's immutable nature. Hebrews applies this directly to the Son, making the connection between the two inescapable. From such an application one may infer the divine nature of the Son."[124] Toward the end of the letter, during the final exhortations to the readers, the author emphasized again this core attribute of God so it will not be forgotten: "the same yesterday and today and forever."[125]

---

119. Strong, *Systematic Theology*, 336.
120. See Hagner, *Encountering the Book of Hebrews*, 43.
121. Strong, *Systematic Theology*, 336.
122. Hagner, *Encountering the Book of Hebrews*, 43.
123. Bertolet, "Knowing Jesus," para. 5.
124. Mitchell, *Hebrews*, 54.
125. See Heb 13:8.

Having made the case for the divinity of the Son, the author's complex and multifaceted portrait of the Son is now complete. The readers have a picture of the living Son, the one they currently worship and serve, in addition to the human Jesus they understood from verbal accounts and eyewitness testimonies. The exalted, superior, eternal, divine Son is the one the readers are not only to worship and serve, but to seek as their guide, standard, and example. It is he who is to be their focus in their attempts to live as faithful, mature Christians in the moral realm. The readers now know who the living Son is, but what is the Son doing? If the readers truly seek the Son of which the author wrote, what will they discover? The answer lies in the author's presentation of Jesus the High Priest.

JESUS THE HIGH PRIEST

If we observe the way the author of Hebrews chose to present Jesus the Son and compare it with the presentation of Jesus the High Priest, we immediately notice two strikingly different approaches. The Son is presented boldly and occupied the author's earliest remarks, dominating the first chapter. Included are several key notions[126] that the author will later ascribe to Jesus the High Priest, but in the first chapter they are descriptive only of the Son, and no hint of Jesus as high priest is found. The theme of Son then subsides quickly and significantly, although it continues throughout much of the letter. The presentation of high priest, however, is introduced subtly, but not until the end of the second chapter and the beginning of the third, and then only in the context of Jesus the human, who suffered on behalf of the rest of humanity. At the end of chapter 4, Jesus as the high priest appears again, but still as the empathetic one who endured the trials of temptation. This gentle introduction of Jesus as high priest continues a bit in the fifth chapter and at the very end of the sixth. This approach may seem odd in light of the fact that many theologians and commentators assert that the central theme of Hebrews is Jesus the High Priest.[127]

---

126. In the first chapter, the Son is described as one who is superior to all others, a king who rules with righteousness, and one who has no end. The author later will use these same qualities to describe Jesus the High Priest.

127. See, for example, the statements from Demarest ("the so-called 'epistle' to the Hebrews systematically develops as its central motif the theme of Christ as high priest" [*History of Interpretation*, 1–2]), Bruce ("The special aspect of the person and ministry of Christ which is emphasized in this epistle is His priesthood. . . . our author stresses repeatedly Jesus' qualifications to be His people's effective high priest" [*Epistle to the Hebrews*, lii–liii]), or Harvill ("Nowhere else in the New Testament is Jesus called our High Priest. This, however, is the distinctive feature of Hebrews and the main point of the book" [*Focus on Jesus*, para. 5]).

It is not until chapter 7 when the author's full-orbed depiction of Jesus as the high priest is presented, and then only after a significant effort is expended to explain the priesthood of another—Melchizedek—who lived at the time of Abram. The picture of Jesus the High Priest is intermixed with a significant amount of material about the Aaronic priesthood through the ensuing chapters, and then declines precipitously, with only one more reference to the high priesthood of Jesus occurring in chapter 13.

The reason the author chose to present the Son and high priest with such radically different approaches lies with the author's assumption regarding how the readers would receive the notion that Jesus was their high priest: they certainly would be confused, and may even recoil in shock and disgust. There are two reasons for the author's assumption. First, as Jews they had at least some understanding of what the priests had been historically within Judaism, but their personal experience as first-century Jews was quite different. When their understanding was augmented by the testimonies of the eyewitnesses of Jesus' life and the oral records of his ministry,[128] these readers would have understood the priests to be individuals characterized foremost by political collusion and compromise for the sake of building and retaining power, with the high priest being the most corrupt of all. In addition, many Jews living at the time of Jesus suffered under the coercive hand of the Jewish religious leaders, including the priests, who wielded the threat of social ostracism in order to quell any challenge to their authority. The collusion between the priests and Pharisees,[129] for example, was so tight that they worked as one to intimidate and dominate the populace.[130]

Second, the readers would have recoiled at the suggestion Jesus was their high priest because of their understanding of how the priests plotted against Jesus. Their plans resulted in direct efforts to accuse, trap, and ultimately kill Jesus, the one who the readers had affirmed as their lord.[131] How could it be, then, that the author would use the concept of the priests as a descriptor of the exalted Jesus?

Faced with the very negative impression the readers had of the high priest, the author elected to introduce gradually the notion of Jesus as high

---

128. The readers of Hebrews did not have the written accounts of Jesus' life; the oral accounts and eyewitness testimonies which they had received ultimately would be written as the Gospels we have in our Bible.

129. See texts such as Matt 21:45–46; John 7:32; 11:45–57.

130. See, for example, the incident in John 9 in which the Pharisees sought to stop Jesus' ministry by confronting the citizens with threats, intimidation, insults, and ultimately social and religious ostracism.

131. See texts such as Matt 26:3–4, 47; Mark 11:18, 27–28; 14:53–55; 15:1–15; Luke 20:19–26; and John 19:6.

priest, and offered the first step of a corrective to the readers' thinking by including an extensive description of the ideal Aaronic high priest. Yet the author simultaneously had to show that Jesus was not like—and was superior to—the Aaronic high priests, and so painted a dramatically different picture of Jesus' high priesthood by emphatically linking it to the high priestly order of Melchizedek.[132]

Jesus and Melchizedek

Melchizedek appears only once in the Old Testament, and is mentioned only twice. It is these two brief passages[133] to which the author appealed when describing Melchizedek and likening Jesus' high priesthood to the order of Melchizedek. Arguments have continued for centuries concerning the identity of Melchizedek,[134] with no resolution. Fortunately for our purposes, determining who Melchizedek was historically is not important; what is important is determining what he was like and what he did. If the high priestly ministry of Jesus is characterized as being in the Melchizedekian order, then what characterized Melchizedek?

In the only account of Melchizedek in the Old Testament, he suddenly appears to a victorious Abram returning from a battle against four aligned kings who had previously carried off Abram's nephew Lot, Lot's family, other residents of Sodom and Gomorrah, and all the towns' goods and food. Abram had mustered 318 of his servants to engage the battle and bring back the people and provisions that the four kings had carried off. Melchizedek, who was king of Salem,[135] as a first act upon meeting Abram, "brings bread and wine from Salem 'to supply the exhausted warriors with food and drink,

---

132. The author emphasized Jesus' Melchizedekian priesthood by referencing it six times: 5:6; 5:10; 6:20; 7:11; 7:17; and 7:21.

133. See Gen 14:18–20 and Ps 110:4.

134. See, for example, the study by Bruce Demarest focused on interpretation of Heb 7:1–10 from the Protestant reformation into the second half of the twentieth century. (*History of Interpretation*).

135. For the identity of Salem, see Keil and Delitzsch: "the *Salem* of Melchizedek cannot have been the Salem near to which John baptized (John iii.23), or Ænon, which was eight Roman miles south of Scythopolis, as a march of about forty hours for the purpose of meeting Abraham, if not romantic, would at least be at variance with the text of Scripture, . . . It must be Jerusalem, therefore, which is called by the old name Salem in Ps. lxxvi. 2, out of which the name Jerusalem (founding of peace or possession of peace) was formed" (*Commentary on the Old Testament*, 1:206–7; italics original).

but more especially as a mark of gratitude to Abram, who had conquered for them peace, freedom, and prosperity."[136]

Subsequently Melchizedek, who is called "priest of God Most High" (Gen 14:18) blessed Abram "by God Most High, Creator of heaven and earth" (Gen 14:19). This blessing likely was a verbal expression of gratitude, just as the provision of bread and wine had been a physical expression. Immediately following the blessing of Abram, Melchizedek performs his third action, the praising of "God Most High, who delivered your enemies into your hand" (Gen 14:20). Notice the dual elements of this third action: a praise of God, and a message to Abram that it was God who had given him victory over his enemies.

Abram responded to the priestly actions of Melchizedek by giving him 10 percent of what was recovered from the four kings. "Giving the tenth was a practical acknowledgment of the divine priesthood of Melchizedek; for the tenth was, according to the general custom, the offering presented to the Deity."[137] Not only that, but Abram's receiving from Melchizedek both the bread and wine, and also the blessing, was "a sign that he acknowledged this king as a priest of the living God, and submitted to his royal priesthood."[138] Upon the presentation of Abram's gift, Melchizedek disappears from the narrative. Abram's response to the priest, however, continued through his interaction with the king of Sodom. By refusing to retain any of the battle bounty, Abram was affirming the praise uttered by Melchizedek: it was God, not Abram's efforts, that had secured the victory over the four kings. As such, Abram was attesting to the fact that God was the victor, and thus Abram had no claim to the battle's spoils.

Melchizedek is mentioned only one more time in the Old Testament, in Psalm 110:4. The psalm has long been regarded as messianic, in which David envisioned a victorious king in Zion.[139] The king, however, engages with enemies: "having come into the midst of the sphere . . . of his enemies, shall he reign, forcing them into submission and holding them down. . . .

---

136. Keil and Delitzsch, *Commentary on the Old Testament*, 1:207.

137. Keil and Delitzsch, *Commentary on the Old Testament*, 1:207.

138. Keil and Delitzsch, *Commentary on the Old Testament*, 1:208.

139. See Keil and Delitzsch, in which the authors reference the thought of Johann Christian Konrad von Hofmann characterizing the psalm: "This is a picture of a king on Zion who still looks forward to that which in Ps. lxxii. 8 sqq. has already taken place,—of a victorious, mighty king, who however is still ruling in the midst of foes,—therefore a king such as Jesus now is, to whom God has given the victory over heathen Rome, and to whom He will subdue all his enemies when he shall again reveal himself in the world; meanwhile he is the kingly priest and the priestly king of the people of God" (*Commentary on the Old Testament*, vol. 5:184).

In order that he may rule thus victoriously, it is necessary that there should be a people and an army."[140] That army's attire is key to understanding the purpose of the verse in which Melchizedek is later mentioned. In verse 3, we read the troops are "arrayed in holy splendor." In the opinion of nineteenth-century English author and preacher Charles Spurgeon, that phrase "is a frequent phrase for the sacerdotal garments, the holy festal attire of the priests of the Lord. . . . The soldiers are gathered in the day of the muster . . . but they are clad not in mail, but in priestly robes; like those who wait before the altar rather than like those who plunge into the fight."[141] More than just priestly attire, the garments the army is wearing are the same as those worn by Aaron when he entered the Most Holy Place on the Day of Atonement. They are "expressly called *garments of holiness*, Lev. xvi. 4. . . . which then means that the people, when they make this solemn offering of themselves to God, appear clothed in sacerdotal vestments, as the servants of a priestly king . . . and themselves a 'kingdom of priests' (Ex. xix.6)."[142] Thus the king engages his enemies with an army of priests.

In verse 4, squarely in the middle of a text about a king who uses priests to rule over and dominate his enemies, the Lord swore the king himself was a priest, but in the order of Melchizedek. The "order" is a reference to the nature of Melchizedek's priesthood; its class, its arrangement, its pattern, and its way of appointment. The Melchizedekian distinction may include many things, but chief among them are two: first, the priesthood is eternal, without end or successor; second, the priesthood is intertwined with the monarchy, thus making for a priest-king. "The priesthood is to be united with the kingship in him who rules out of Zion, just as it was in Melchizedek, king of Salem, and that for ever."[143] Recall, however, that the followers are all priests, and so their leader must be something distinct from them; thus the designation of the king as also a priest "comprehends whatever appertained to the office of the High Priest, as the head and representative of all the rest."[144]

It is this understanding of Psalm 110 that the author of Hebrews had in mind when appealing repeatedly to verse 4 to designate Jesus as a priest in the order of Melchizedek. Aligning with literary convention, the author was calling to mind the entire imagery and message of the psalm, not simply a single verse, and pictured what David pictured when the psalm was initially written: "David here hears that the king of the future exalted at the right hand

---

140. Keil and Delitzsch, *Commentary on the Old Testament*, 5:190.
141. Spurgeon, *Treasury of David*, 5:197.
142. Alexander, *Psalms*, 3:105; italics original.
143. Keil and Delitzsch, *Commentary on the Old Testament*, 5:193.
144. Alexander, *Psalms*, 3:107.

of God, and whom he calls his Lord, is at the same time an eternal priest. And because he is both these his battle itself is a priestly royal work, and just on this account his people fighting with him also wear priestly garments."[145] The readers of Hebrews would have understood that in designating Jesus as an eternal priest in the order of Melchizedek the author was calling them to be priestly followers of Jesus, and partners in his priestly work.

With this background of Melchizedek in the Old Testament, we turn to the portrait of Jesus the High Priest as painted by the author of Hebrews. The primary question is: How is Jesus like Melchizedek?

Jesus Like Melchizedek

The author of Hebrews knew the readers were aware of Melchizedek, but faced the challenge of how to paint a picture of the high priesthood of Jesus— something the readers could not readily observe. To meet the challenge, the author chose to draw a comparison between Melchizedek's priesthood and that of Jesus, aligning the two. The goal was not to suggest Jesus' priesthood copied Melchizedek's, but rather to show that the nature of Melchizedek's priesthood, which was known, was patterned after that of Jesus, which was unknown. F. F. Bruce captured this key concept thusly: "it is not the type that determines the antitype, but the antitype that determines the type; Jesus is not portrayed after the pattern of Melchizedek, but Melchizedek is 'made like unto the Son of God.'"[146] The author's reasoning was if something is true of Melchizedek it also is true of Jesus, for Jesus' priesthood was the die from which Melchizedek's was cast. This is a crucial point, since it explains why the author focused so intently on building a picture of Melchizedek the priest; in describing Melchizedek, the author actually was describing the high priesthood of Jesus.

Having referenced Melchizedek three times in chapters 5 and 6 by appealing to Psalm 110:4, the author of Hebrews at last gave a description of Melchizedek in the first ten verses of chapter 7. Much of the description follows the details of Melchizedek's one appearance recorded in Genesis 14, and expands upon them. However, the author failed to mention the first thing Melchizedek did upon encountering Abram: provide food and drink to Abram's servants. He also failed to note both the content of the blessing of Abram, mentioning only that Melchizedek blessed Abram, and also Melchizedek's praise of God. Why is it that the author chose to ignore significant elements of the very short account of the encounter, but also

---

145. Keil and Delitzsch, *Commentary on the Old Testament*, 5:194.
146. Bruce, *Epistle to the Hebrews*, 138.

expanded greatly beyond the Genesis account when describing Melchizedek in later verses?

The author was dealing with a specific burden: to show that Melchizedek was superior to the Aaronic priests and to convince the readers Jesus was a superior high priest like Melchizedek. There were certain elements of the Melchizedek account that suited his or her purpose in this regard. Also, the author's philosophical training is revealed in the approach taken to leverage the Genesis account of the Melchizedek-Abram encounter. Nearly a century ago, Scottish theologian James Moffatt commented, "it is Philo's method of interpretation which gives the clue to our writer's use of the story.... His interest in Melchizedek lies in the parallel to Christ.... like Philo, he sees immense significance not only in what scripture says, but in what it does not say, about this mysterious figure."[147] The author, then, in certain places chose to employ select elements of the Genesis account while omitting others, and in other places enhanced the account with detail that the account itself does not include.

The author initially rehearsed some of the facts of the story: Melchizedek's title as king of Salem, his function as priest of God Most High, the encounter with Abram (whom the author referred to as Abraham) upon his defeat of the four kings, Melchizedek's blessing of Abram, and Abram's gift to Melchizedek of a tenth of the spoils of the battle.[148] That recital is followed by an expansion not found in the Genesis account—an expansion by which the author created the image of Melchizedek that served his purpose in painting the picture of Jesus as the ideal high priest, superior to the Aaronic priests.

The expansion initially mentions the meaning of Melchizedek's name and title, simply indicating they refer to king of righteousness and king of peace. The notion of peace is rare in Hebrews. It is not used directly in reference to Jesus, and recurs only three times in later chapters.[149] The lack of association with Jesus, however, does not render peace insignificant to Jesus' high priestly function. The fact that Melchizedek is the type of which Jesus is

---

147. Moffatt, *Critical and Exegetical Commentary*, 91–92. See also Demarest ("the silence of Scripture was frought with significance, was a commonplace interpretive device in the hermeneutical schema of Alexandrian Judaism" [*History of Interpretation*, 133]) and Mitchell ("In a way, the author of Hebrews has 're-scriptured' the story of Melchizedek for his own purpose by taking advantage of the omission of Melchizedek's genealogy and familial ties as well as the lack of detail about his life and death" [*Hebrews*, 143]).

148. See Bruce, *Epistle to the Hebrews: First Apology*, 248.

149. Peace occurs in 11:31 describing Rachel's treatment of the spies, in 12:14 as an encouragement to faithfulness, and in 13:20 as part of the author's benediction.

the antitype is clear indication that the peace associated with Melchizedek's kingship is modeled after that inherent in the kingship of Jesus.

In 1:9, the Son was described in his kingship as the one who loves righteousness. The author, in pointing out that Melchizedek's name means king of righteousness, was establishing the first link between the Son as king and Melchizedek as king. The author's major burden of showing Jesus is a high priest like Melchizedek was approached by emphasizing the unending nature of Melchizedek's priesthood, a quality that does not occur in the Genesis account, but only in Psalm 110. For this purpose the author referenced Psalm 110 many times, both before and after the description in chapter 7. Bruce Demarest comments, "The importance of Psa 110:4 to the writer effectively ensures that the principal features of the argument focus about the idea of the timelessness of the new priestly order. . . . Hence the motif of the *eternity* of Melchizedek and of the priesthood he exercises constitutes the prominent theme of the text before us."[150]

In order to establish the eternality of Melchizedek's priesthood, and thus of Jesus' priesthood, the author resorts to a mechanism that seems odd to those of Western thinking, and perhaps even abusive of the Scripture. However, it was a standard practice within Judaism, and also was used in Alexandrian philosophical thought. Thus, it would have been known by the author and readily accepted by the readers.[151] Notice the author, in 7:3, indicated Melchizedek had no father or mother or genealogy, and had no beginning or end. This assertion, however, is not in the Genesis account. Why, then, did the author make such a claim? Thomas Long points out,

> The ancient rabbis had a principle of biblical interpretation that asserted that all truth was in the Scripture. So, as they said, "What is not in the Torah is not in the world." Now, the Scripture does not anywhere mention Melchizedek's parents, and, according to this rabbinical principle of interpretation, this is not merely an omission but an indication that Melchizedek never had any parents; they were not in the Torah so they must not have been in the world. Once that piece of logic falls, only a few more dominoes have to topple before we can say that Melchizedek was a timeless, eternal character.[152]

---

150. Demarest, *History of Interpretation*, 8; italics original.

151. See Moffatt: "Reading the record in the light of Ps 110:4, and on the Alexandrian principle that the very silence of scripture is charged with meaning, the writer divines in Melchizedek a priest who is permanent. This method of interpretation had been popularized by Philo" (*Critical and Exegetical Commentary*, 92).

152. Long, *Hebrews*, 85.

Having employed the rabbinical hermeneutical convention to suggest Melchizedek was eternal, the author solidified the assertion by stating he resembled the Son of God, and concluded his priesthood was forever. Recall that in developing the picture of the Son the author carefully constructed the element of the Son's eternality. This was not done haphazardly, but with the intent of forming the basis for what the author was to establish in chapter 7—that Melchizedek is like the Son in that he is eternal.

The author specified Melchizedek's lack of parentage and genealogy to establish two characteristics of the Melchizedekian priesthood in contradistinction to the Aaronic, ultimately for the purpose of showing both its absolute unique character and its superiority. First, the fact that the Melchizedekian priesthood was characterized by no parentage or genealogy was a direct challenge by the author to the inviolable requirement of the Aaronic priesthood that Levitical parentage in the line of Aaron be demonstrated by every potential priest. Demarest writes, "Evidence from the OT and rabbinic Judaism suggests that Melchizedek was designated thus because he failed to satisfy the prescribed requirements for accession to Levitical priesthood.... aspirants unable to demonstrate Aaronic descent from the genealogical registers were rejected as unfit for service in the sanctuary."[153] He strengthens his assertion when concluding, "The paramount reason why Melchizedek was described in such terms was to emphasize his complete disassociation from the legal priestly regime. The eminent priest-king who blessed the patriarch and who collected tithes from the progenitor of Aaron, had no link with the disenfranchised tribe of Levi."[154]

Second, the author characterized Melchizedek as having no parents or genealogy in order to show that the Melchizedekian priesthood, unlike that of Aaron's descendants, was not passed from one generation of priests to the next. There were no predecessors or successors, and thus the priesthood was eternal. "Melchizedek's priestly service was neither taken up from a predecessor nor was it handed on to a successor. The silence of the record invests Melchizedek with an intransmissible and hence continuous priesthood which symbolically portrays the unbounded perpetuity of the priesthood of Christ."[155]

In short the author, having initially highlighted the righteousness and peace that characterized the Melchizedekian priesthood, continued by placing great emphasis on the priesthood's eternality,[156] then proceeded in the

---

153. Demarest, *History of Interpretation*, 101.
154. Demarest, *History of Interpretation*, 134.
155. Demarest, *History of Interpretation*, 136.
156. See Long: "the main point of all this is not really about Melchizedek *per se* but

next verses to argue for the superiority of the Melchizedekian priesthood over that of the Aaronic one. The picture the author painted was of the patriarch Abraham voluntarily giving a tenth of the battle's spoils upon encountering the priest-king Melchizedek. In return, Melchizedek blessed Abraham.

Abraham's act of giving to Melchizedek was a clear acknowledgment of the latter's superiority. There was no law that required such payment or entitled Melchizedek to it. "The gift on the patriarch's part was entirely spontaneous. And just because it was so, it was, in the view of our author, unmistakable evidence of Melchisedec's personal greatness."[157] Abraham's payment of it was recognition that the priesthood of Melchizedek was superior to his own position.

The author went on to claim Abraham was not the only one who was acknowledging the superiority of Melchizedek through the giving of the tithe, and through this means compared the Melchizedekian priesthood with the Aaronic one. All Aaronic priests were descendants of Levi, one of Abraham's great-grandsons. F. F. Bruce writes, "an ancestor is regarded in biblical thought as containing within himself all his descendants. That Levi may be thought of thus as paying tithes to Melchizedek is an afterthought to what has already been said about the significance of this particular payment of tithes."[158] The author, in using this mechanism of linking the Aaronic priests to the action of Abraham, was arguing Melchizedek's priesthood is superior to the Aaronic one, since the descendants of Levi participated in Abraham's acknowledgment of Melchizedek's superiority by means of the tithe. Furthermore, the Aaronic priests were simply following the law when they collected tithes, and thus their act of collection was morally inferior to the spontaneous and voluntary giving and receiving by Abraham and Melchizedek, respectively.

The author commented on Melchizedek's response to Abraham's gift, observing that Melchizedek blessed Abraham even though Abraham was the one who had received God's promises. This observation is followed with the conclusion in 7:7 that "without doubt the lesser is blessed by the greater," a direct assertion of the superiority of Melchizedek over both Abraham and his priestly descendants.

Finally, the eternality of Melchizedek's priesthood compared with the Aaronic one in which priests are subject to death was presented as an argument for Melchizedek's superiority. No Aaronic priest was permanent, but

---

rather how the qualities seen in him—righteousness, peace, and timelessness—point forward to the nature of Jesus, the true and perpetual great high priest" (*Hebrews*, 85; italics original).

157. Bruce, *Epistle to the Hebrews: First Apology*, 257.
158. Bruce, *Epistle to the Hebrews*, 142.

rather received the office from predecessors and passed it on to successors. An Aaronic priest was transitory, and thus inferior, to the priest Melchizedek, who lives forever.

The author, then, created an image of the Melchizedekian priesthood that is superior to the Aaronic one. This was achieved by showing that both Abraham and his descendants, the Aaronic priests, tithed to acknowledge Melchizedek's superiority; upon receipt of the tithe, Melchizedek, as the superior, blessed the inferior Abraham; and Melchizedek the permanent priest is superior to all Aaronic priests who occupy their positons for a short while and then die. Coupled with the earlier picture of Melchizedek as kingly, priestly, righteous, peaceful, and eternal, the argument for Melchizedek's superiority completed the author's portrait of Melchizedek. Recall, however, that the author was not painting Melchizedek at all, but rather using the Melchizedek from the Old Testament account, with which the readers were familiar, as a means to paint Jesus as high priest.

Jesus Unlike Melchizedek

The author of Hebrews omitted from the characterization of Melchizedek the most essential function of priests: they offer sacrifices. Jesus, however, did perform this vital priestly function, as the author emphasized throughout the letter. The first suggestion of Jesus sacrificing himself for others is found in 2:9, in which it is said Jesus tasted death for everyone. Soon thereafter the idea of Jesus making atonement for the sins of the people is found in 2:17. His self-sacrifice for the sins of others is made explicit in 7:27, and the imagery of the high priest offering a blood sacrifice in the Most Holy Place is applied to the sacrifice of Jesus' blood in 9:11–15. This is followed by the imagery of the sacrifice of his body in 10:5–14. Since the author emphasized Jesus' self-sacrifice for others so extensively, why is the concept of sacrifice completely missing from the author's description of Melchizedek's priesthood (which actually is a literary device by which the author was describing the priesthood of Jesus)? The omission certainly would have stood out as glaring to the readers, as observed by nineteenth-century theologian Alexander Bruce: "To the Hebrew Christians it would probably appear a grave defect, rather than a merit, in the Priest after the order of Melchisedec, that He was not constantly occupied in offering sacrifices like the priests after the order of Aaron."[159]

The author did not make a mistake in failing to mention sacrifices when describing Melchizedek's priesthood. Recall the Jewish and Alexandrian interpretive principle that if something is not mentioned in the Scripture it

---

159. Bruce, *Epistle to the Hebrews: First Apology*, 282.

does not exist. In the early part of chapter 7 the author explicitly employed this principle to argue for Melchizedek's eternality, and on the subject of sacrifices used it in a silent manner to omit any suggestion Melchizedek offered them. Nothing of sacrifices is mentioned in the Genesis account of Melchizedek, so the author, by silence, was teaching that the order of Melchizedek did not include sacrifices.

Changing the minds of the readers to conceive of a high priest who did not offer sacrifices was a significant challenge for the author. To the readers, a priest who did not offer sacrifices was not a priest, irrespective of other activities in which he may be engaged. To meet the challenge the author argued sacrifice indeed was part of Jesus' ministry, but only during his earthly sojourn and only once. This idea was repeated no less than eight times as a means to reinforce what to the readers' understanding was a nonsensical notion. The mention in 7:27 that Jesus' self-sacrifice was for the sins of others also indicated it was "once for all when he offered himself." Using the slightly different imagery of the Day of Atonement, the author's reference to Jesus' blood being offered in the Most Holy Place also argued that Jesus "entered the Most Holy Place once for all by his own blood." Similar phrases were used elsewhere in chapters 9 and 10, all with the intent to establish that Jesus indeed had sacrificed himself, but only in the past during his time on earth, and only once for all time.

Why was it that the Aaronic priests had to offer sacrifices continually, but Jesus as high priest did not? Bruce explains, "The infirmity of the priest made it necessary that he should offer repeated sacrifices for himself, and because for himself, therefore for the people; for the priestly offices of sinful officials could not avail to remove the people's sins for ever, if indeed at all."[160] Jesus, however, did not suffer from the same infirmity. He did not approach the priestly function as a sinful person like the Aaronic priests, nor was he imperfect in any other way. Nor did he approach it as a temporary priest who would be replaced and thus whose work had to be taken up and repeated by another. Rather, his priesthood was ideal, and his self-sacrifice on behalf of others was not deficient in any way. It was perfect and complete, and thus never had to be repeated.

The fact that Jesus' self-sacrifice was emphasized and reiterated throughout Hebrews served one main purpose: to convince the readers that whereas sacrifice indeed was necessary, it no longer had to be offered, and thus was not a part of the high priestly ministry of the ascended, exalted Son. Jesus' self-sacrifice was completed in the past, with effects that continue through eternity. The high priest whom the readers knew, the Son

---

160. Bruce, *Epistle to the Hebrews: First Apology*, 282–83.

seated at the right hand of the Father ruling in righteousness and peace, was engaged in other priestly activities. His priestly function was, indeed, characterized accurately by the author's depiction of Melchizedek, who offered no sacrifices. Yet the priesthood of the exalted Son was crucial for the readers of Hebrews, just as it remains crucial for all today who would be faithful disciples and mature followers of their Lord.

Jesus and the Priesthood

In Hebrews 3:1, the author encouraged the readers to consider, or to reflect upon, Jesus, who is both their apostle[161] and high priest. The immediate context, in which Jesus is compared with Moses, suggests Moses was sent by God to save God's people from slavery in Egypt and establish a community of God's faithful, thus fulfilling the role of God's apostle; in the same way, Jesus as God's apostle was sent to provide people eternal salvation from sin and establish them as God's faithful community. The ensuing verses demonstrate how Jesus was true to his apostolic calling in a way that was superior to the faithfulness of Moses, and verse 6 in particular indicates that as Son he administers God's "house," which is identified as the collective of God's faithful.

The author also called upon the readers to consider how Jesus now administers and serves God's faithful community as high priest, then proceeded to lead the readers through that consideration starting at the end of chapter 4 and the beginning of chapter 5. The reflection on Jesus as high priest continues through much of chapters 7 through 9, and ends at the middle of chapter 10. There is a common thread that runs through the author's reasoning, being mentioned at times explicitly and at other times implicitly: the high priesthood of Jesus is better than that of the Aaronic high priests. It is not completely different from that of the Aaronic priests, but also it is superior to theirs in many and significant ways.

Jesus Like the Aaronic Priests

Recall that the concept of Jesus being high priest was not one the readers would have welcomed readily due to their impression that priests were corrupt, with the high priest being the worst offender. The author selected to develop the picture of Jesus as high priest initially by showing how Jesus was similar to the *ideal* Aaronic high priest, and did not reject the notion of priesthood outright. Later the author would emphasize how Jesus was

---

161. This is the only instance in the New Testament in which Jesus is referred to as "apostle."

distinct from the Aaronic priests. Barry P. Smith writes, "the author describes the high priesthood as set out in the Torah; his goal is to procure agreement from his readers in order to be able to move from that agreement to a conclusion about Jesus as a greater High Priest."[162] There were five ways in which the author showed the similarity between Jesus the high priest and the Aaronic high priests.

Both Are Human

The human limitations of priests certainly had benefits, as seen in 5:2 in which the Aaronic priest is said to deal gently with others because he himself is a weak person. The weakness of priests is a fundamental element of who they are, extending back even to Aaron: "Aaron himself, whose feeble yielding to the people's demand for a visible symbol of deity is matched only by the ineptitude of his excuse to Moses."[163] Yet it was Aaron who was chosen to be Israel's first and model high priest. The idea of the human weakness of high priests was reiterated in 7:28, solidifying the author's point that priests, above all, are human.

Earlier in this chapter we saw how Jesus fully participated in humanity in every way except submission to temptation. Indeed, his human suffering was a prerequisite for his complete high priestly service (2:17), and his experience of suffering through human temptation enabled him to help others who are tempted (2:18). Hugh Montefiore observes, "Jesus' sufferings were, presumably, those which are caused by human weakness; that is, by human fear, human grief, and human pain caused through the infliction of physical injury."[164] His human experience was complete, and his suffering under temptation was more severe than any other person, since he never succumbed. This is why the author was able to assert Jesus is a high priest who can empathize with human weaknesses, since he himself is human (4:15).

Both Are Selected and Appointed

The author began chapter 5 by stating, "Every high priest is selected from among the people and is appointed to represent the people," and followed in verse 4 with "no one takes this honor on himself, but he receives it when called by God, just as Aaron was." Recall the author was describing the

---

162. Smith, "Jesus as High Priest," 6.
163. Bruce, *Epistle to the Hebrews*, 92.
164. Montefiore, *Commentary on the Epistle to the Hebrews*, 68.

Aaronic high priest as originally conceived, and in doing so was seeking to correct the readers' experientially based understanding of high priests. Montefiore supports this idea when he writes, "Our author is again showing a splendid indifference to the actual circumstances of his day under which high priests were elected to their office."[165] He then expands, "After the Exile . . . the civil power soon assumed the right in selecting the high priest, and the office ceased to be for a life tenure. The appointment was often made in disgraceful circumstances."[166] The author, then, had to explain that Aaron and his descendants were actually called by God to their priestly office, rather than appointed by civil authorities. The focus then turned to Jesus' high priesthood, with the assertion that he too was called, just like Aaron, and he did not take on himself the glory of becoming a high priest.

Jesus' divine calling as high priest was further explained through the use of two quotes in 5:5 and 5:6, from Psalm 2 and Psalm 110, respectively. The quote from Psalm 110 appears to affirm God's calling to the priesthood, but Psalm 2 seems out of place. Yet, by choosing those two passages the author was explaining that the Jesus presented earlier—the divine Son of chapter 1 who reigns as king—*also* fills the office and function of high priest, for he was called to do so. The concept of a king who also served as a priest would have been foreign to the readers, for the Mosaic Law required the two offices be separate. The author had to clarify that in appointing Jesus to be priest God was not negating his status as Son.

BOTH REPRESENT THE PEOPLE

The selection and appointment of high priests was done for one main purpose: representation of the people before God. This representation took many forms, but fundamental to them all was the priest's role of standing between the people and God, pleading the people's case before the Almighty. In describing this role the author again was faced with the readers' impression of high priests, compared with that set forth in the Mosaic Law, and so in 5:1 the intercessory role of the priest was explicitly stated. This likely was surprising to the readers, given their experience of high priests, and so the author felt the need to describe the high priest "solely in terms of his biblical functions, to represent man to God in worship. The contemporary secular role of the high priest as President of the Sanhedrin or as Primate of the Jewish nation is ignored."[167]

165. Montefiore, *Commentary on the Epistle to the Hebrews*, 94–95.
166. Montefiore, *Commentary on the Epistle to the Hebrews*, 95.
167. Montefiore, *Commentary on the Epistle to the Hebrews*, 93.

Just as the Aaronic high priest's primary role was intercessor, so the author ascribed to Jesus the same function. Hebrews 7:25 speaks of those who come to God through Jesus "because he always lives to intercede for them." Prayer on behalf of the people was an historic responsibility of the priesthood, and so Jesus, as the new high priest, was described as one who prays for the people. Montefiore summarizes the point the author was making in describing the intercessory element of Jesus' high priestly ministry: "In our author's view the whole mission of the Son of God . . . was not primarily undertaken to express God's nature but to achieve a specific object; to bring men to God. His eternal session in heaven, since his ascension, results in the ceaseless maintenance of this priestly ministry."[168]

Both Offer Sacrifices

Another common but essential function of the Aaronic high priests was the offering of sacrifices, the most important of which occurred annually on the Day of Atonement. The sacrifices had to be offered precisely as prescribed in the Mosaic Law in order to be accepted. F. F. Bruce explains: "The Israelites who watched their high priest enter the sanctuary for them waited expectantly for his reappearance; that was a welcome sign that he and the sacrifice which he presented had been accepted by God."[169] Using this custom as background the author asserted about Jesus that "it was necessary for this one also to have something to offer (8:3)." Jesus as high priest entered the Most Holy Place to make a sacrifice, just like the Aaronic high priests, but what he offered was his own blood in order to obtain redemption for those who would come to God through him (9:11–12). Since Jesus fulfilled his obligation as a high priest to have something to offer, the author concluded, "so Christ was sacrificed once to take away the sins of many (9:28)."

Both Serve in the Tabernacle

The author of Hebrews clearly used the imagery of the tabernacle to describe the location of the high priests' activity. At the time of the writing of Hebrews the tabernacle had not been in use for about 1,000 years. The readers of Hebrews would have had no experience of the tabernacle. It is curious, then, that the author chose to use the tabernacle imagery, rather than that of the temple with which the readers were familiar.

168. Montefiore, *Commentary on the Epistle to the Hebrews*, 129.
169. Bruce, *Epistle to the Hebrews*, 223.

The author, in describing the high priest, was attempting to correct the readers' understanding of the high priesthood, and thus consistently described not the high priests with which the readers were familiar but rather the calling and duties of Aaron, the first high priest at the time of Moses, as well as Aaron's successors who ministered in the tabernacle. It was the picture of the ideal Aaronic high priest the author initially was attempting to establish in the minds of the readers prior to replacing it with the picture of Jesus the High Priest. For this reason the tabernacle imagery was an essential element of the author's description.

In 8:5, we find the high priests served at the tabernacle, which was understood to be an earthly type of the antitype in heaven. Throughout the history of Israel's priesthood the location of priestly activities, not just their protocols, was crucial. Those who attempted to conduct such activities in places other than that specifically designated by God rendered themselves disobedient. In like manner, the author showed the location of Jesus' high priestly activities was crucial. Recall in chapter 1 the Son was described as exalted to the right hand of the Majesty in heaven. This imagery is repeated in 8:1. It is there where he serves as high priest, and the angels serve as his emissaries to those who will inherit salvation (1:7, 14). The location where Jesus serves is described in the language of the tabernacle in 8:2. Alan Mitchell expresses this notion when he writes, "This first section, 8:1–6, begins by drawing on the exaltation theme of 1:5–14, thus placing Christ, the High Priest, in the heavenly realm, the sphere of his cultic activity."[170] Bruce adds the language of tabernacle to describe the location of Jesus' high priestly function: "the great high priest whom Christians have is one who is enthroned at the right hand of God, who discharges his ministry in no earthly shrine but in the heavenly dwelling-place of God, a tabernacle pitched by no human hands."[171]

The author intentionally used the language of tabernacle to describe the locus of the ministry of both the Aaronic high priests and Jesus the High Priest, even though their respective tabernacles were in different locations, being type and antitype. The intent was to convince the readers that Jesus actually was a high priest. The other parallels served the same purpose. Yet through the development of the picture of Jesus as high priest the readers would have noticed the significant ways in which Jesus' high priesthood was clearly distinct from that of the Aaronic high priests. To that distinction we now turn.

---

170. Mitchell, *Hebrews*, 163.
171. Bruce, *Epistle to the Hebrews*, 163.

Jesus Unlike the Aaronic Priests

When introducing the concept of Jesus and the priesthood, it was mentioned that a common thread runs through the author's reasoning: the high priesthood of Jesus is better than that of the Aaronic high priests. This notion of superiority forms the majority of the portrait of Jesus as high priest, and was the author's major burden through the letter. As the author developed the high priestly picture of Jesus, four strands of thought were woven together to establish the superiority of Jesus' high priesthood.

THE BETTER SACRIFICE

The Aaronic high priests had a fundamental task they had to repeat often: the offering of sacrifices. Certain sacrifices were offered only annually, but they too had to be offered repeatedly—every year. In contrast, the author pointed out many times that the self-sacrifice of Jesus was offered only once, and will never be offered again. There are three ways in which the author argued the one-time sacrifice of Jesus the High Priest is better than the repeated sacrifices of the Aaronic high priests.

First, Jesus' self-sacrifice is better because it was effectual, whereas the sacrifices of the Aaronic high priests were not. Verse 7:27 shows this superiority of Jesus: "Unlike other high priests he does not need to offer sacrifices day after day. He sacrificed . . . once for all when he offered himself." Alan Mitchell suggests the priesthoods were not only different, but that Jesus' was better: "The repeated nature of the sacrifices of the old covenant is seen as a negative thing (9:6) which Hebrews contrasts with Christ's 'once for all' sacrifice."[172] Verse 10:11 indicates an Aaronic priest performs his religious duties repeatedly, and "offers the same sacrifices which can never take away sins." F. F. Bruce writes, "The Aaronic priests never sat down in the sanctuary; they remained standing throughout the whole performance of their sacred duties. In this our author sees a token of the fact that their sacred duties were never done, that their sacrifices had always to be repeated."[173] The work of the Aaronic high priests was, in effect, ineffectual. It was a futile one, for it could not accomplish the goal for which sacrifices were offered: forgiveness. The author contrasted this futility with the result of Jesus' one-time sacrifice for sins and subsequent seating at God's right hand. Jesus' sacrifice did what the sacrifices offered by other high priests could not: it did away with sin (9:26).

---

172. Mitchell, *Hebrews*, 194.
173. Bruce, *Epistle to the Hebrews*, 238.

Second, the self-sacrifice of Jesus is better because it actually was the means to forgiveness of the peoples' sins. In chapter 10, the author made it clear the sacrifices offered by other priests were only a reminder of sins and cannot assuage guilt (10:2–3), nor can they take away sins (10:4). Raymond Brown comments, "Whenever the sacrifices were offered, man realized his spiritual need. Although these animal offerings could not fully meet such need, they pointed *inward* by exposing man's sin, and *forward* to a time when adequate provision would be made for man's pardon and reconciliation."[174] In 10:5–7, the author explained God was not pleased with sacrifices, burnt offerings, sin offerings, and other offerings, but rather was seeking Jesus' obedience to God's will. This idea would have been shocking for the readers, for whom sacrifices were a paramount and essential element of fidelity to God. Yet in Jesus God was looking for a different kind of sacrifice. Bruce explains, "the sacrifices in which God is said to take no pleasure are the sacrifices prescribed by the ancient cultic law of Israel; now that cultic law is to be superseded by a new order, inaugurated by Christ's perfect obedience to the will of God."[175] In the subsequent verses the author indicated it is Jesus' obedience to God's will that forms the basis for forgiveness of sins: "'Here I am, I have come to do your will.' . . . And by that will, we have been made holy through the sacrifice of the body of Jesus Christ once for all." Thus Jesus' self-sacrifice is better than the sacrifices of the other priests because by it the sins of the people truly are forgiven.

Third, the superior effect of Jesus' self-sacrifice renders that sacrifice better than those of the Aaronic high priests. In 10:1, the author wrote the sacrifices offered under the Mosaic Law can never "make perfect those who draw near to worship." The reason is the law is only "a shadow of the good things that are coming." Verses 7:11 and 18 argued that a priesthood separate and different from the Levitical one was required since perfection was beyond the capability of the Aaronic priests, and the law that established their priesthood was weak, useless, and unable to make anything perfect. However, the sacrifice of Jesus rendered a wholly different result. In 10:14, the author spoke of the work of Jesus, indicating "by one sacrifice he has made perfect forever those who are being made holy." Bruce writes that the author "could bid farewell to the sacrificial cultus the more cheerfully because he knew of a sacrifice, presented on quite another plane, which effectively dealt with sin as the old cultus could not."[176] And Brown adds, "our great high priest has offered *the sacrifice of himself*. This *once* for *all* sacrifice of Christ needs no

---

174. Brown, *Message of Hebrews*, 171; italics original.
175. Bruce, *Epistle to the Hebrews*, 235.
176. Bruce, *Epistle to the Hebrews*, 231.

repetition because it is so completely effective; it produces spiritual results of a kind impossible through the offering of animal sacrifices."[177]

The high priesthood of Jesus, then, is better than that of the Aaronic high priests since the sacrifice of Jesus is superior to the sacrifices under the Mosaic Law. Jesus' sacrifice only needed to be offered once for all time, it resulted in a means for sin to be forgiven, and it made perfect those seeking to be God's faithful followers.

The Better Foundation

The foundation upon which the Aaronic priesthood stood was the law of Moses, which both established it and dictated how its activities were to be conducted. Similarly, the high priesthood of Jesus was built upon a foundation. The author of Hebrews argued throughout chapter 7 that the foundation upon which Jesus' high priesthood was built was better than the foundation of the Aaronic priesthood, and thus Jesus' high priesthood itself was better than that of Aaron and his descendants. As was the case with Jesus' better sacrifice, the author developed three elements of Jesus' better foundation.

In chapter 5, the author suggested Jesus was better positioned to be high priest than were the Aaronic high priests. Verses 8 and 9 mention that Jesus learned obedience through suffering, after which he was made perfect. The learning was not intellectual, but rather experiential. By enduring physical and emotional suffering Jesus acquired an experiential understanding of obedience, which completed—or perfected, to use the author's term—Jesus' humanity and qualified him to be a fully functioning high priest. It was this element of perfection that formed the basis for God's designation of Jesus as a high priest, one who could empathize with others because he was a complete human. In addition to being complete like no other, Jesus is better positioned to be high priest because he is morally pure like no other. In 7:26, we see that as exalted high priest Jesus is "holy, blameless, pure, set apart from sinners," a claim none of the Aaronic high priests could make regarding their moral character and experience.

In contrast to the position of Jesus, the position of the Aaronic high priests fell far short. The author made the contrast clear in 7:11 by a simple statement: "If perfection could have been attained through the Levitical priesthood . . . why was there still need for another priest to come, one in the order of Melchizedek, not in the order of Aaron?" Thomas Long explained the author's reasoning when stating, "the only reason the psalmist would talk about a priesthood of the 'order of Melchizedek' is if there were

---

177. Brown, *Message of Hebrews*, 172; italics original.

something lacking in the regular order of priests, the Levitical priests."[178] He continued, "What was wrong with the Levitical priesthood? One could not attain 'perfection' through it . . . The Preacher has already told us that Jesus was 'made perfect' . . . and he will soon tell the congregation that they, too, have become 'perfected' through Jesus' priestly work."[179] The Aaronic priests, being far from perfect, simply were not positioned to be effective high priests, for their priesthood was built upon a weak foundation.

In addition to being better positioned than the Aaronic priesthood, the foundation of Jesus' priesthood included a better basis. In the middle of 7:11, the author indicated the Aaronic priesthood was based upon the law of Moses, and expanded in verse 16 that the specific law in question was that of Aaronic succession. Every potential priest had to demonstrate he was a direct descendant from Aaron as the basis for becoming a priest. Long explains, "The old priests acquired their office through connections, because they had the law on their side and they were born into the right family."[180] Jesus' high priesthood, however, was different. He was not a descendant of Aaron. Yet the basis for his priesthood was not genealogy but rather his indestructible life. The author explained further in 7:23–24 that whereas there were many Aaronic priests due to their mortality, Jesus was an eternal priest since the basis of his priesthood was the fact that he lives forever. Aaronic priesthood was based upon a temporal rule, but Jesus' priesthood was superior because it was based upon a life that had no end. Unending in his life, Jesus was able to intercede for others eternally, and provide them complete salvation.

Finally, the foundation of Jesus' priesthood was superior to that of the Aaronic priests because it included a better declaration. God gave Moses the law by which Israel was to conduct itself as God's chosen people, including rules for their conduct in worship, and ordered Moses to set aside Aaron and his sons as priests.[181] Yet the author demonstrated in chapter 6 that when God declared an oath it was not for the establishment of the Aaronic priesthood, but occurred centuries earlier when he promised Abraham divine blessings and many descendants. In 7:20–21, the author showed how God swore an oath again when establishing the priesthood of Jesus. The oath itself was a better declaration than the order to Moses, and resulted in a priesthood superior to that of Aaron and his descendants. Lane writes, "the new priest was established in his office by the oath of God. . . . His priesthood reflects God's unchangeable purpose. This cannot be said with

---

178. Long, *Hebrews*, 86.

179. Long, *Hebrews*, 87.

180. Long, *Hebrews*, 87.

181. See Ex 28:1 for God's order to Moses designating Aaron and his sons priests.

reference to the priests of the old Levitical order."[182] Just as the oath to Abraham constituted an unchanging validation of God's promises, so the oath establishing Jesus' priesthood formed the priesthood's unchanging foundation, unlike the Aaronic priesthood based upon genealogy. For emphasis, in 7:28, the author again used the language of divine oath regarding Jesus' priesthood and compared it with the law whereby Aaron and his descendants were appointed priests. The oath's superior nature resulted in the Son's perfect, eternal high priesthood, whereas the law focused on high priests in their weakness. Hugh Montefiore concludes, "The oath . . . supersedes the Law, just as the frailty of the levitical high priesthood is superseded by the eternal priesthood of the perfected Son."[183]

In three ways, then, the author of Hebrews showed the foundation of Jesus' priesthood is better than that of the Aaronic priests. Jesus is better positioned to perform priestly functions, his priesthood is established on the better base of his indestructible life, and the declaration upon which Jesus became a priest was the better oath of God compared with the law of genealogy upon which the Aaronic priesthood was established.

THE BETTER LOCUS

Throughout the author's argument concerning the superiority of Jesus' priesthood to that of Aaron's descendants we find mentioned the locus of their respective activities as priests. After its building, the tabernacle was the center of the common life of Israel, particularly the sacred activities such as the offering of sacrifices, and thus it was also the center of the Aaronic priesthood.

For the author the earthly tabernacle was only a copy of the heavenly tabernacle (8:5). In making this comparison the author not only was leveraging the incident in which Moses was told to build the tabernacle according to the pattern God had shown him, but also was leveraging his or her philosophical training to establish the superiority of the place where Jesus serves as high priest. Alan Mitchell observes, regarding 9:24, "The noun for 'copy' here, however, is *antitypos*, a term drawn from Platonic philosophy to refer to the earthly representation of what exists in the ideal world."[184] In 8:2, the author made the point that Jesus, at the right hand of the throne of the Majesty in heaven, actually is serving as high priest in the antitypical tabernacle made by God, not the earthly copy made by humans. Continuing

---

182. Lane, *Hebrews*, 110.
183. Montefiore, *Commentary on the Epistle to the Hebrews*, 131.
184. Mitchell, *Hebrews*, 194.

the reasoning in 9:11, the author argued not just that Jesus served in the tabernacle antitype in heaven, but additionally noted the antitype is a "greater and more perfect tabernacle that is not made with human hands." Mitchell notes, "A humanly constructed sanctuary is a negative description in Hebrews."[185] Thus, the locus of the priesthood of Jesus, being the antitype made by God, is better than that of the humanly formed copy in which the Aaronic priests ministered.

It may be asked, how does the better location of Jesus' priesthood make his priesthood itself better? Key to understanding the answer is to realize the difference in the nature of the ministry of the two priesthoods. The Aaronic priests brought animal blood sacrifices to the humanly made mercy seat in the earthly tabernacle. Jesus, however, ministers directly before God, and does not present a blood sacrifice.[186] In commenting on verse 9:24 Montefiore writes, "For the first time the heavenly sanctuary is identified with heaven itself, a key point for understanding our author's argument. The object of Christ's heavenly ministry is to appear in God's presence on our behalf. . . . To plead on our behalf is Christ's present work as heavenly high priest."[187] The comparison, then, is between the earthly work of the Aaronic high priests in which they offer ineffectual animal blood sacrifices in a tent made by humans, and the heavenly work of Jesus in which he appears in the presence of God on behalf of God's faithful, pleading for them. Jesus' high priestly ministry is better because the locus of his ministry is the very presence of God, in which Jesus is the advocate for God's faithful.

The Better Covenant

Building upon the divine oath that declared the priesthood of Jesus, the author argued in 7:22, "Because of this oath Jesus has become the guarantor of a better covenant." Going further, the author taught in 8:13 that the new covenant rendered the old covenant of the Aaronic priests obsolete and outdated, soon to disappear. It was Jesus' sacrificial death that launched his priesthood, by which the new covenant took effect (9:14–15).

The notion of a new covenant was not original with the author; rather, it was borrowed from the prophet Jeremiah,[188] who predated the author by six centuries. Lane writes, "The fact that God spoke to Jeremiah of a

---

185. Mitchell, *Hebrews*, 194.
186. See Long, *Hebrews*, 96.
187. Montefiore, *Commentary on the Epistle to the Hebrews*, 160–61.
188. See Heb 8:8–12, in which the author quoted from Jeremiah's recording of God's declaration of a new covenant in Jer 31:31–34.

covenant that was *new* indicates that the *old* covenant was imperfect and provisional."[189] The author used the new covenant concept to argue for the superiority of the high priesthood of Jesus. It was necessary to have a new covenant simply because the one under which the Aaronic priests functioned was "weak and useless" (7:18). The author developed two closely related ways in which the high priesthood of Jesus as mediator of the new covenant is better than that of the Aaronic high priests working under the old covenant.

Under the old covenant given to Moses, the Israelites enjoyed certain promises, particularly the blessings of God if they obeyed God's law. Throughout their history they repeatedly failed to do so, and as a result were in need of the benefits of the work of the Aaronic priesthood. The best benefits that could be had, however, were that the sacrifices resulted in a temporary delay of God's response to disobedience, and served only to remind the people of their sins (10:3). They could not make people perfect, assuage their guilt, or take away their sins (10:1-4), and they only applied to sins committed in ignorance, rather than willful sins (9:7). In short, according to A. B. Bruce, "God promised to His people temporary forgiveness of sins of ignorance and infirmity, on condition of their offering certain specified sacrifices."[190] The new covenant, however, comes with better promises than the old, and renders Jesus' high priestly ministry better than the Aaronic one (8:6). Among those promises is an eternal inheritance for those who follow Christ (9:15). Others are found in the quote from Jeremiah: God's law written on the hearts and minds of his faithful, rather than on tablets of stone; knowing God in relationship; and forgiveness of all sin, including all wickedness (8:10-12). The partial requote of Jeremiah's prophecy in 10:16-17 made the promise of forgiveness emphatic, "expressing the strongest possible negative: 'I will remember their sins and their lawless deeds no more' (v. 17)."[191] F. F. Bruce summarized the superiority of the benefits of the promises under the new covenant as follows:

> The first covenant provided a measure of atonement and remission for sins committed under it, but it was incapable of providing 'eternal redemption'; this was a blessing which had to await the inauguration of the new covenant, which embodies God's promise to His people: 'I will forgive their iniquity, and their sin will I remember no more' (Jer. 31:34).[192]

189. Lane, *Hebrews*, 117; italics original.
190. Bruce, *Epistle to the Hebrews: First Apology*, 299.
191. Hagner, *Encountering the Book of Hebrews*, 132.
192. Bruce, *Epistle to the Hebrews*, 208-9.

The promises of the new covenant are better than those of the old, then, because they yield better results for God's faithful.

The Israelites experienced severe restrictions under the old covenant. Chief among them was they could not approach God; their access to him was blocked. In chapter 9, the author rehearsed the layout of the tabernacle, including several rooms. The inner room—the Most Holy Place—contained the ark of the covenant, which represented the presence of God. Only priests could enter the anteroom to the Most Holy Place; others could not enter. Furthermore, only the high priest could enter the Most Holy Place, and then only once per year and only with animal blood sacrifices. For the average Israelite the laws governing worship and the Aaronic priesthood completely restricted access to the presence of God. Lane comments regarding worship under the old covenant, "*the severe restriction of access to God indicated that the arrangement was provisional*,"[193] and the author concluded, "The Holy Spirit was showing by this that the way into the Most Holy Place had not yet been disclosed as long as the first tabernacle was still functioning (9:8)."

The sacrifice of Jesus, however, cleansed the consciences of God's faithful, and allowed them not only access to God, but also the opportunity to serve him (9:14). His self-sacrifice, according to the author, is the reason why Christ mediates a new covenant that gives eternal benefits to the faithful, and frees them from the shackles of the old covenant (9:15). The provision of the new covenant, mediated by Jesus, whereby God's law is so implanted within the faithful that they know him, renders the new covenant better than the old. A. B. Bruce writes of the author, "the very aim of his whole work is to show that Christ for the first time deals effectually with the defilement of sin, so that we can indeed draw near to God."[194] The old covenant prevented access to God because there was no effective way of dealing with the peoples' sinful and willful disobedience, whereas the new promotes access because the mediator of the covenant dealt with human sin once for all by sacrificing himself. Now he ministers as the peoples' high priest, removing the barrier to God and granting them eternal benefits as they serve him. Just how God's faithful are to serve him is the focus of the next chapter.

---

193. Lane, *Hebrews*, 119; italics original.
194. Bruce, *Epistle to the Hebrews: First Apology*, 298.

6

Toward Maturity and Faithfulness

AT THE OUTSET OF this study we saw the author of Hebrews arguing convincingly that Christian maturity and faithfulness occur in the moral realm of human experience. The author's intent in this regard was to call the audience to pursue moral uprightness. Guiding readers into that maturity—the ability to distinguish moral good from moral evil—was at the core of the author's intent. Pursuing it entailed following Jesus the pioneer, not through simple imitation but through adherence to his way.

Entering into the author's argument we see the path to maturity leading through the discipline of training for the acquisition of skills that enable the faithful one to function in the moral realm. One matures as a faithful Christian through the conditioning of the senses via fostering of habits focused on development of the ability to distinguish good from evil. Consistent employment of thus-sensitized faculties in the moral realm was the author's vision of the mature believer.

The resulting sound moral judgment does not occur through rote adherence to some sort of code or list, perhaps learned in childhood or imposed by an employer or the government or even a religious body. Such an immature approach is insufficient to render mature moral judgment in the vast array of ethical situations the believer will encounter. Indeed, such an approach often results in abdication of moral responsibility. Only the consistent leveraging of a set of honed and sensitized skills and faculties, employed with moral courage and creativity, can result in a level of maturity that can be termed "faithfulness."

CHRISTIAN MATURATION AND THE MORAL REALM

We learn from Paul's letter to the Romans that the life Jesus now lives "he lives to God," and that his faithful followers are to regard themselves in the same way.[1] How are the mature to do this? What is to typify their living conduct, character, and response? Those who currently live in a mature and faithful way in the moral realm are destined to become a kingdom of priests who serve God and reign on earth sometime in the eschatological future.[2] Should such a destiny somehow influence God's faithful followers today?

Subsequent to his resurrection, but while still on earth, Jesus encountered some of his followers in a manner that challenged them to transition their commitment from a focus on the precrucifixion Jesus they had followed to the living one who was soon to be exalted. Their ultimate destiny was in the foggy future, and their experience living with the earthly Jesus was in the past. How were they to be mature and faithful in between, particularly in light of the fact that Jesus' own involvement in the moral realm ranged from telling parables, to interpretation and augmentation of Old Testament law, to specific engagements with members of the general populace, to certain habits of conduct, to instilling a virtue or element of character, and beyond?

On resurrection day, Jesus met Mary Magdalene outside the empty tomb. She wanted to cling to him as the one she had known prior to the crucifixion—the earthly Jesus who we now know and understand through the Gospel accounts. Jesus had to redirect her focus from who he had been to who he was going to be after the ascension and exaltation with the Father. Later that same day, the two on the road to Emmaus still expressed hope that Jesus would be a political liberator, and that for their benefit. Jesus had to alter their focus, directing them to a true understanding of the full picture of Jesus rather than simply an earthly one. Several weeks later, when asking Peter "Do you love me?," Peter became distracted by asking about the future of one of the other disciples. Jesus had to offer Peter a corrective by reminding him his obligation was to follow the resurrected Jesus, rather than concern himself with how Jesus would work with others. I suggest these correctives, as well as others seen in the human experience of Jesus, are the

---

1. See Rom 6:10–11.
2. See Rev 5:9–10; 20:6.

beginning of an understanding of what it means to be mature and faithful in the moral realm between the ascension and the eschaton.

In the second verse of the Epistle to the Hebrews, the author emphatically asserted God has spoken to us finally and completely in the Son. Toward the end of the letter, in 12:25, we find an encouragement and warning not to "refuse him who speaks." The verse's immediate context makes it clear the one who speaks this superior word is the exalted Jesus, the mediator of the new covenant. These two verses serve as bookends between which we find at least a substantial portion of that final word of God which the living Jesus speaks to us. As such, our understanding of what it means to be mature and faithful believers must include an appropriate response of commitment, engendered by the word Jesus speaks.

The Jesus we find in Hebrews is the one on whom we are to "fix our thoughts,"[3] a concept that includes not only observation but also meditation. Such meditation is the start of the task of developing skills which, when exercised to the point of habituality, will yield the ability to distinguish good from evil. Seeing the Jesus of Hebrews should lead us to efforts aimed at perception, understanding, and appreciation, all of which should culminate in an appropriate ethic of response by those who seek to be faithful and mature followers of the one who speaks.

In this final chapter, an ethic for the mature will be developed, first by describing its constituent elements, then picturing them as an integrated whole. Those seeking the prescriptive details of such an ethic may find themselves frustrated. However, it is now clear maturity in the moral realm entails the repeated employment of skills developed over time to distinguish good from evil; it does not entail rigid adherence to the minutiae of a prescribed regimen, be it compliance with commands or comportment with a pattern. The previous chapters of this book constitute a suite of tools the mature should employ to hone the necessary skills to function faithfully in the moral realm; the ethic articulated in the rest of this chapter is an attempt to demonstrate how fidelity to the suite can yield a consistent vision of Christian maturity.

EMBRACING THE COMPLETE JESUS

Much of the Jesus-based ethics we encounter suffers from a common shortcoming: it does not embrace, nor is it derivative from, the complete Jesus. In Scripture we find the Jesus story, and specifically in the Epistle to the Hebrews we find pictured the present, living, exalted Jesus between his life on earth and his ultimate triumph in the eschaton. Yet book after book

3. See Heb 3:1.

on Christian ethics appeals almost exclusively to the Jesus of the Gospels prior to the resurrection—and perhaps also the Jesus foreseen in the Old Testament or referenced in the Pauline corpus—as the sole substantiation of a Jesus ethic for God's faithful who live today, subsequent to Jesus' earthly life. The living and active Jesus whom his followers worship each Sunday and with whom they continually walk is summarily ignored when seeking to formulate a comprehensive ethic for the mature. Consider the number of references to Hebrews in the scriptural indexes of many Christian ethics books compared with the number from the Gospels or even the Pauline Epistles. The list of Hebrews references is glaringly short, and the references that are listed do not include the Jesus as pictured in Hebrews but rather the author's instructions to the readers. Why is this? Why is the living Jesus of today not embraced as at least a partial basis for a comprehensive Jesus ethic?

The Need for a Complete Jesus Ethic

In Jesus' life on earth we find the most fundamental example we are to follow in the moral realm, both in what he did and what he taught. Jesus, however, lived within the context of the old covenant of obedience, and so we would expect his teachings to be expressed in the language of obedience and his conduct to be understood as a life of obedience. This, in fact, is what we find. However, Jesus changed the common understanding of obedience, and thus expanded the expectations of what it means to be faithful and mature. Particularly in the Sermon on the Mount we see the external obedience required by the Mosaic covenant is expanded to include internal obedience concerning thoughts and attitudes, not simply external conduct. Yet even this internalization was contextualized to the language and notion of obedience. Thus we see Jesus taught whoever obeys the law will be called great in the kingdom; anger against a brother or sister is a form of violation of the command not to murder; God's followers, as the light of the world, are told to let their light shine before others; enemies are to be loved, and prayer is to be offered for one's abusers; and adultery is not limited to the physical act, but includes attitudes and intentions of the heart. These and much more are all couched in the expectation of obedience.

In our lifetimes we can never exhaust what it means to be obedient, nor can we ever emulate Jesus fully. We can never get to the point where we can legitimately assert we have fulfilled the requirement to obey Jesus and live like he lived. Thus, we can never say we have moved beyond the need to be obedient and to live like Jesus. Obedience and emulation, however, are not the complete Jesus ethic, but only a part of it. Obeying and emulating the Jesus of the Gospels does not embrace the Jesus subsequent to the time of the Gospels—the exalted Jesus living today whom we find pictured in Hebrews. Nor can obedience and emulation fulfill the expectation of maturity outlined in Hebrews 5: the ability to distinguish good from evil. A complete Jesus ethic entails much more than obedience and emulation of Jesus' earthly life lived under the old covenant. It includes living to God in light of the exalted Jesus as Son and High Priest, under the new covenant established when he sacrificed himself on behalf of humanity.

The Complete Jesus Picture

A complete understanding of Jesus is essential to the development of a comprehensive Jesus ethic if the resultant ethic is to have the scope and potential to enable the faithful to lead lives of maturity in the moral realm. It is the *total* Jesus picture, as well as the living Jesus *of* the picture, that will yield a comprehensive Jesus-based ethic for today. Employing a truncated picture of Jesus to form an ethic will yield a truncated ethic, as we would expect. Yet that is precisely the mistake made by the vast majority of Christian moral proponents, prescriptivists, activists, and agitators.

All one needs to do to substantiate this claim is to compare the Jesus pictured in the Gospels with that of Hebrews. They are not identical pictures, but neither are they in conflict. Each contains part of the total Jesus picture that must inform development of a Jesus ethic. Hebrews contains elements of overlap with the Jesus pictured in the Gospels, and even enhances our understanding of Jesus' temptation, suffering, and self-sacrifice. The majority of Hebrews, however, presents a picture of the living, exalted Jesus that is not found in the Gospels.

In contrast, the Jesus pictured in the Gospels, particularly the vast majority of the picture that is painted prior to the resurrection, primarily reveals a very human Jesus. Although he retained his preincarnate divinity throughout his earthly sojourn, he was severely limited by virtue of his humanity and submission to the overall context in which he found himself. His physical context was limited to first-century Palestine. Others' lack of faith truncated his ability to perform many miracles. In his interactions with those he encountered he was limited by the sequential nature of events through the passage of time. Whereas Jesus' teaching and conduct during his days on earth provide a valuable—even limitless—source of moral guidance, they occurred in a social and mental milieu of the old covenant, with its expectation that moral uprightness consisted primarily in obedience to commands. It is only when the picture of Jesus is expanded to include the

Jesus subsequent to the resurrection and ascension—the Jesus pictured in Hebrews—that we understand not only the moral significance of Jesus' humanity (for example the purpose of his struggle with temptation) but also the moral call of the exalted Jesus who serves as our moral authority.

The Focus of the Complete Jesus

If the complete Jesus picture is fundamental to a comprehensive ethic for today, what is the associated bedrock reality that underpins all of what Jesus was and is, from eternity to eternity—the continuous, unending, consistent, unalterable focus without which any ethic finds itself adrift? In short, the bedrock reality that captured Jesus' complete focus is the kingdom of God—the intervention of God on behalf of his people that Jesus announced at the outset of his public ministry. It includes deliverance of God's people, the establishment and administration of justice throughout creation, the development of God's people into a community of the mature, and the gift of life given to all who seek to be God's faithful. These elements of the kingdom were seen in our review of Jesus in the Gospels, but they also are found in different and heightened ways in Hebrews: ways in which it could be said demonstrate the kingdom of God in greater fullness, not constrained by the limits under which Jesus lived during his humanity.[4]

In addition to the *establishment* of the kingdom among God's people, the *values* of the kingdom are also expressed both in the Gospels and in Hebrews. We saw how the Sermon on the Mount is the clearest expression of those values; in general it is the internalization of the virtues God expects his faithful ones to embrace wholeheartedly. Simply living according to them, in a kind of imitation of Jesus, is insufficient; what is required is an actual alignment and identification with the way of Jesus in the moral realm, up to and including the ultimate expression of the kingdom of God in the life of Jesus: the cross.

---

4. For examples of these kingdom elements expressed by the exalted, present Jesus, see the following: Heb 4:14–16 and 8:10–12, where Jesus the High Priest delivers his people from the guilt associated with yielding to temptation, the fear of approaching God's presence, and the debilitation associated with unforgiven sin; Heb 1:8–13, in which the Son as King rules all with a scepter of justice; Heb 3:1–6, where Jesus the Apostle and High Priest builds and oversees God's house, consisting of both Jesus and the community of the faithful (Heb 2:11); and Heb 9:14–15, in which the sacrifice of the High Priest Jesus inaugurated a new covenant that frees the faithful from their past life that yielded death and replaced it with an eternal inheritance by which they are enabled to serve the living God. This list is not exhaustive; it merely represents a small sampling of the presence of the kingdom of God expressed through the post-ascension, living Jesus.

In Hebrews we find the kingdom values are given expression in a way not limited by the external obedience culture in which Jesus was constrained when presenting the Sermon on the Mount (due to his listeners' limited understanding of moral maturity). So, for example, in Hebrews we see divine communication came in its ultimate form through the exalted Son, and demands a response.[5] Solidarity with, and sharing in, the weakness, limitations, and suffering of others is a key way Jesus expressed himself.[6] Not only in his humanity but also in his exaltation Jesus was humble before God.[7] Self-sacrifice to the point of death was central to the values demonstrated by Jesus the High Priest.[8] Ongoing service on behalf of others is a value Jesus the High Priest expresses eternally for the benefit of God's faithful.[9] These values demonstrate the kingdom of God is still very much the focus of Jesus, even while in his exalted state he serves as the king of justice and the perfect high priest for his faithful followers.

Mary's Magnificat gives us a vision of the kingdom's *effects* subsequent to its establishment on earth and inculcation of its values in the people of the kingdom. Those effects are not limited to the time of Jesus' earthly sojourn, but extend throughout the generations, even to the time when Jesus will be given the throne of David and will reign forever—an image captured just prior to the Magnificat and repeated in the first chapter of Hebrews. What we find in the Magnificat is not the result of the spiritualized, sanitized, or socially altered Jesus endorsed by many of orthodox faith today, but rather the wake of a radical social change agent establishing a new vision of the moral realm. In this vision the proud cease to exist. Political leaders experience their downfall. The humble are exalted, the hungry are no longer hungry, and those with means are rejected. Indeed, historical social conventions are significantly altered in the Magnificat's vision of the moral realm when the kingdom of God prevails. It is this image of the kingdom of God that underlies the comprehensive ethic we discover when the complete picture of Jesus is thoroughly embraced.

---

5. See Heb 1:2; 12:25.
6. See Heb 2:14, 17–18; 4:15.
7. See Heb 5:5–8; 10:5–7, 9.
8. See Heb 7:27b; 9:11–12; 10:10, 12, 14, 19–22.
9. See Heb 6:19–20; 7:22, 25; 9:15, 24.

COVENANT TRANSITION AND MORAL VELOCITY

The author of Hebrews made it unmistakably clear that in the resurrected Jesus a new covenant was established.[10] A transition has taken place in which the Mosaic covenant, in effect from the time it was initiated through the earthly life of Jesus prior to his self-sacrifice, was supplanted by a new covenant subsequent to that sacrifice. That supplantation rendered the old covenant obsolete and disappearing.[11] We have seen that much of the daily outworking of the old covenant entailed the obligation to obey—clearly conduct within the moral realm. Obedience was the means by which God's faithful remained the community God wanted.[12] Yet when the old was replaced with the new, did something change in the ethics sphere? Is our understanding of the moral milieu subsequent to the resurrection, ascension, and exaltation of Jesus the same as it was prior, or has the new covenant brought with it a new understanding of maturity and faithfulness?

Covenant Transition

In Hebrews 8, the author argued there was something wrong with the old covenant God made with Israel at the time of Moses, and that the new covenant of which Jesus is the mediator is superior to the old since it is based upon better promises. It was the old covenant's insufficiencies that not only allowed for the new, but necessitated it. What was it about the old covenant that rendered it deficient, and how is the new covenant superior? The key lies with understanding the new covenant's better promises.

Toward the end of Hebrews 8 we read of the better promises of the new covenant: God's law would be written on the hearts and minds of the faithful, rather than on tablets of stone; God would be known in relationship; God would forgive all sin, including all wickedness (not just the sins committed in ignorance or weakness covered by the sacrifices of the Levitical priests); and God would forget all sins. These better promises, however, suggest covenantal transition. The old covenant was largely external, including laws written on stone and priestly activities that did not render forgiveness

---

10. See Heb 7:22, in which one result of the oath that established Jesus' eternal priesthood is the establishment of a superior covenant, of which Jesus is the guarantor. In addition, see Heb 9:15 and 12:24, in which Jesus is declared to be the mediator of a new covenant.

11. See Heb 8:13.

12. See Jer 11:1–8, in which God explained to Jeremiah the terms of the old covenant and the consequences of failure to obey its stipulations.

but served only to remind sinners of their sin.[13] The new covenant, however, is largely internal, and requires of both the individual and the faithful community something much broader than mere obedience.

Recall the incident of the rich ruler inquiring of Jesus what he had to do to inherit eternal life. Jesus began by appealing to life under the old covenant requiring obedience to the Decalogue. Such was the ruler's mindset, and the moral milieu in which he lived. Jesus knew simple obedience was not sufficient, however, and so began to transition the ruler from the ethics of the old covenant to that of the new. He directed the ruler to divest himself of his possessions, give to the poor, and become a Jesus-follower. The ruler responded negatively, for the ethics of the new covenant required more of the ruler, including internalization of the new covenant's moral scope. The old was not jettisoned, but was rendered insufficient by virtue of Jesus' introduction of the new.

What we see in this incident is the beginning of covenantal transition—the migration away from the old covenant and toward the new, which had not yet been established at the time of the rich ruler incident but was being introduced in a nascent form throughout Jesus' life. Jesus was calling God's faithful to greater moral maturity through internalization of the requirements of the kingdom of God and adoption of his character.

Anticipation of covenantal transition did not begin with Jesus. In Hebrews 8, we saw the terms of the new covenant outlined, but this delineation entailed a quote from Jeremiah's vision of the new covenant some six centuries prior to the life of Jesus. Even though the old covenant was in effect and still would be for hundreds of years, the old covenant's insufficiencies were understood and the superior covenant was envisioned. In addition, some of the benefits of life lived under the new covenant were anticipated by Isaiah eight centuries prior to the time when Jesus would introduce it during his sojourn on earth. Results of the new covenant in its fullness included the administration of righteousness and justice on behalf of the poor, the destruction of the wicked, harmony within nature, and ubiquitous knowledge of God.[14]

In the first chapter of Hebrews we saw the picture of the exalted Son as king in the time of the new covenant, ruling with justice while loving righteousness. This picture, however, was envisioned centuries earlier by Isaiah during the time of the old covenant when he wrote, "In love a throne will be established; in faithfulness a man will sit on it—one from

---

13. See Heb 10:3–4.
14. See Isa 11:1–11.

the house of David—one who in judging seeks justice and speeds the cause of righteousness."[15]

In order to appreciate what it means to live maturely in the moral realm and faithfully to God it is critical to understand and affirm one thing: the notion of covenantal transition in the timespan subsequent to Jesus' resurrection and prior to the eschaton. That is the timeframe described by the author of Hebrews, where covenantal transition is not only a fundamental teaching, but also an inexpressible gift to those who live under the benefits of the new covenant anticipated by great prophets centuries before Jesus' time on earth.

Moral Velocity

The concept of velocity fundamentally entails motion in a particular direction. In the moral realm, moral velocity refers to the ongoing change in moral understanding as time continues to pass. We see this sort of moral movement within the Bible in parallel with progressive revelation. Seeking to remain true to the Bible's moral requirements, we may initially sense an urge to affirm the Bible is morally static, reflecting our commitment to the immutability of God. Yet, whereas God is immutable, his disclosure of what maturity and faithfulness entail develops. As God discloses more and more of his truth, our moral understanding changes and expands. Earlier we saw perhaps the clearest example of moral velocity is Jesus' teaching in the Sermon on the Mount, where he employed various forms of the phrase, "You have heard it said . . . But I say to you" (Matt 5:21–48). The initial element of each of those six examples of moral velocity was taken from the Pentateuch, and represented the common understanding of what moral uprightness entailed as presented by the religious leaders of the day. The corrective and alternate form of the moral standard presented by Jesus demonstrated a migration in moral thinking from outward conduct to an internalization and subsequent demonstration of the values, attitudes, virtues, intentions, and commitments that were to characterize God's faithful.

We see moral velocity not just during the ministry of Jesus, but throughout the Scriptures; the moral standards of one generation do not necessarily extend to subsequent generations. Whereas Abraham's faith was credited to him as righteousness and continued as something of a moral standard, "one would be . . . hard-pressed to make the narratives of David normative for how we ought to live without a considerable amount of

---

15. Isa 16:5.

moral editing."[16] For example, would his practice of polygamy be condoned today as morally upright? We observe moral velocity from the time when polygamy was not only accepted and encouraged, to later generations in which monogamy was a requirement of those who aspired to be leaders of God's faithful.[17]

In the days of Moses, cursing a parent was a capital offense,[18] as was blasphemy.[19] Envisioning Israel's entry into the land of Canaan, Moses ordered the total destruction, without mercy, of the people in the promised land, and Joshua carried out the order.[20] Yet, in the life of Jesus we see a different view of the value of life, whether it be the life of enemies or those who utter things they should not.

Phineas was the grandson of Israel's first high priest, Aaron. In his zeal for God's honor he ran a spear through an Israelite man and the Midianite girlfriend he had brought into his tent. For such an act God commended Phineas by making a covenant of peace with him and his descendants, establishing their lasting priesthood. In Psalm 106:31, we read that Phineas' conduct "was credited to him as righteousness for endless generations to come." Immediately following the incident God commanded Moses to "Treat the Midianites as enemies and kill them."[21] Whereas one might argue such conduct was justified based upon the need to maintain Israel's purity, simple observation of Phineas' response to sexual misconduct compared with the response of Jesus to the Pharisees' condemnation of the woman taken in adultery[22] yields vastly different understandings of God's standard for his faithful who encounter such situations. Moral velocity indeed is evident between the time of the exodus and the earthly life of Jesus.

Change over time in the way God's faithful live in the moral realm did not begin with Moses or end with the life of Jesus, but continued on after Jesus' exaltation, even to the present day. For centuries the common human response to God was one of fear. Subsequent to the fall, Adam heard God walking in the garden, and hid because he was afraid. After Moses encountered God in the burning bush, he hid his face due to his fear. When the Israelites observed the thunder, lightning, a trumpet sound, and smoke as God descended on Mount Sinai, they trembled with fear and asked Moses to

16. Gustafson, *Moral Discernment*, 202.
17. See 1 Tim 3:2.
18. See Lev 20:9.
19. See Lev 24:10–16.
20. See Deut 7:2 and Josh 6:21.
21. See Num 25:6–18.
22. See John 7:53—8:11.

be their intermediary with God so they would not die. King David, the man after God's own heart, while moving the ark of God to Jerusalem, became both angry at God's wrath and afraid of God, after God killed an attendant who touched the ark to prevent it from falling off of its cart. Upon seeing the Lord Almighty, Isaiah cried, "Woe is me! . . . I am ruined" (Isa 6:5)! Daniel, upon seeing a divine vision, turned deathly pale, trembled, bowed to the ground, became speechless and weak, was overcome with anguish, and lost his breath. When Jesus' disciples saw him walking on the water they cried out in fear and were terrified, and at the transfiguration their terrified response was repeated.[23] Whereas comfort or reassurance was offered in at least some of these instances, the common experience of encounter with God resulted in an immediate fear response. Paul captured this reality in Galatians 5:4, when he described the sense of alienation from God that occurs when one attempts to live according to the old covenant of obedience rather than the new covenant of grace.

All of those included in the foregoing examples had not experienced any form of moral velocity. Even so it existed, even prior to the earthly life of Jesus, and internalization of God's law associated with transition from the old covenant to the new had begun to happen hundreds of years prior to the incarnation. Transition from mere obedience to increasing sensitivity to the internal working of God had started even for David: "Sacrifice and offering you did not desire—but my ears you have opened . . . I desire to do your will, my God; your law is within my heart."[24] In Proverbs 21, we see the good is defined by what is in the heart, not just outward obedience to the law,[25] and the prophet Amos, in the eighth century BC, recorded God's disdain at outward religious expressions, preferring instead the expression of justice and righteousness on an ongoing basis.[26]

Subsequent to Jesus' resurrection and exaltation we find an invitation to a very different kind of response from that seen prior. The invitation is to draw near to God with confidence and sincerity, even entering the most holy place of his presence,[27] rather than respond with fear as did God's people of old. When doing so, the focus is to be in the moral realm, where encouragement of others to love and good deeds in the context of the gathered

---

23. See Gen 3:8–10; Exod 3:1–6; 20:18–21; 2 Sam 6:1–10; Isa 6:1–5; Dan 10:1–17; Matt 14:25–26; and 17:1–6.

24. Ps 40: 6–8.

25. See Prov 21:2–3: "A person may think their own ways are right, but the Lord weighs the heart. To do what is right and just is more acceptable to the Lord than sacrifice."

26. See Amos 5:21–24.

27. See Heb 4:16; 10:19–22.

community of the faithful is the expectation.[28] We see the understanding of what is included in maturity has changed, being augmented from obedience in fear, to tangible heart expressions of justice and righteousness, to internalization of the values and attitudes of Jesus, to a response of confidently approaching God while simultaneously working to help others mature in the moral realm. Indeed, moral velocity is a fundamental outworking of the progressive revelation of God in Scripture.

CHRISTIAN MATURATION AND THE BROADER JESUS ETHIC

Articulating the scope of moral velocity may at first seem elusive, and the notion of moral velocity itself may appear confusing or nebulous. However, for purposes of formulating a broader Jesus ethic, one that accommodates the entire picture of Jesus rather than a truncated one, moral velocity's scope can be captured through a suite of four sequential elements. The process of maturation is not as simple as progressing from one element to the next; rather, the mature follower of Jesus embraces all elements to different degrees in various circumstances while living in the moral realm. The degree, however, to which an element is consistently missing from the habitual exercise of one's moral skills—those skills that enable one to distinguish good from evil—is approximately proportional to the level of immaturity of the believer, although it is folly to seek precision in this arena. Maturity varies between individuals and even between local believing communities, so the notion of developing metrics in the area of Christian maturity is a misguided one. Nevertheless, it certainly is possible to be descriptive of the four elements to a significant degree. This suite of elements, expressed in a moral understanding that includes the kingdom of God as primary focus, the reality of the new covenant as the moral milieu in which the mature believer lives, and a realization that there is moral velocity within the ethical standards found in the Bible, completes the constituent parts of a broad Jesus ethic that is driven by the complete Jesus picture up to the eschaton.

There are two characteristics of the elements that should be pointed out. First, the lines of demarcation between the four elements are not clear and distinct. Rather, there is a fuzziness among them that results in overlap. Consistent with the understanding that ethics cannot be reduced simply to a list, the definitional imprecision amongst the elements should not come as a surprise.

---

28. See Heb 10:24–25.

Second, as one moves logically from the first element—obedience—to the fourth—response—it becomes more difficult to articulate the nature and scope of a particular element. This challenge reflects the migration from infancy in the moral realm to maturity. As there is progression from outward comportment to habitual use of skills that allow one to determine good from evil, the clarity of scope of each of the elements reflects the maturation process itself.

Obedience

The notion of obedience to the command of God is introduced very early in the biblical narrative, in the second chapter of Genesis. God commanded Adam not to eat the fruit of the tree of the knowledge of good and evil. Obedience was the earliest form of expected conduct in the moral realm. However, it was the disobedience of the first two people that actually brought an end to their innocence, and triggered their knowing good from evil. This distinction is the fundamental notion the author of Hebrews leveraged at the end of chapter 5 when describing "the mature, who by constant use have trained themselves to distinguish good from evil" (Heb 5:14). Throughout the rest of the Bible we see this theme of obedience repeated scores of times, in a multitude of situations, with differing consequences for those who obey compared with those who do not. Whereas obedience may include the attitude of the heart,[29] at its core the idea concerns outward conduct that comports with that which was commanded. The intent to comport without the commensurate conduct is not obedience at all.

The most striking early example of obedience is the incident in which Abraham was commanded by God to kill his son, Isaac. In short, Abraham did what he was commanded, and the result was God's promise, "all nations on earth will be blessed, because you have obeyed me."[30] We see in this episode the concept of moral consequences linked to human decisions and conduct. The nations of the earth would enjoy God's favor only after, and as a result of, Abraham's decision to act in accord with God's command, and his actual conduct in doing so.

---

29. Consider, for example, Jesus' rebuke of the religious leaders for focusing their conduct on external activities without a commensurate focus on the internal (Matt 23:25–28).

30. See Gen 22. The fact that God intervened the moment prior to Isaac's death does not change the moral reality that Abraham obeyed the command of God, and the result was God's goodness granted to all nations on earth.

At the time of the exodus the notion of obedience to God was paramount to Israel being and remaining God's faithful people.[31] The most fundamental obligations of Israel were capsulized and conveyed by God in codified form in the Decalogue. This revealed morality has continued to form the faithful's most basic moral understanding for millennia. Notice that numbers 1, 5, and 10 involve at least an element of inward attitude and intention. In this we see an example of what was mentioned at the end of the previous section—an overlap between various elements of moral velocity—in this case an overlap between obedience and formation. By the time of Joshua the notion of obedience spanned the entire law of Moses.[32]

God's expectations for obedience became more clear and nuanced at the time of the establishment of Israel's kingship. Not only did the Mosaic law have to be obeyed, but so did everything else that God commanded. It could be argued mere obedience to the ritual law, though required conduct, was of less importance than obedience to these other divine directives. For example, when King Saul did not fully obey God's command regarding the Amalekites, Samuel confronted him by indicating obeying God is better than sacrificing to him, and disobedience is tantamount to rejecting the word of God.[33]

Obedience was a significant element of Jesus' experience during his time on earth, even to the point of submitting to death.[34] The author of Hebrews expanded on this idea when indicating obedience is something Jesus learned through suffering, and led to completion of Jesus' human experience.[35] Obedience in suffering also was a precursor to Jesus becoming the source of salvation for all who emulate him in obedience. Here we see yet another example of the blurring of the demarcation lines between the elements of moral velocity: this time between obedience to Jesus and emulation of him.

In the earthly life of Jesus we also observe another change in the understanding of obedience. When asked about the law's greatest commandment, Jesus gave a dual response: complete love of God, and loving neighbor as self. According to Jesus, "All the Law and the Prophets hang on these two

---

31. See, for example, Jer 7:22–23: "For when I brought your ancestors out of Egypt and spoke to them, I did not just give them commands about burnt offerings and sacrifices, but I gave them this command: Obey me, and I will be your God and you will be my people. Walk in obedience to all I command you, that it may go well with you."

32. See Josh 1:7–8.

33. See 1 Sam 15:22–23.

34. See Phil 2:8.

35. See Heb 5:8–9.

commandments."[36] Repeating this meshing of love and obedience, Jesus told his followers to keep his commandments in order to remain in his love, and that his command is to love each other in emulation of his love for them.[37] We see, then, within the life of Jesus as through Israel's history, not only the fundamental expectation of obedience, but change and development in the understanding of what obedience entails. There is no question, however, the most fundamental understanding of what it means to be faithful and to be mature in the moral realm is to obey.

Emulation

Emulating is not the same as rote copying. To be a clone of Jesus would entail living under the old covenant in a moral milieu prior to the crucifixion, resurrection, ascension, and exaltation. It would mean knowing only the emptied, human Jesus of his earthly sojourn, and it would include a personal mission of giving one's life as an atonement for the sin of the world. Not only is that not possible for any sinful human being, it is not what faithfulness to God and Christian maturity entail. Rather, to emulate Jesus is to follow in his way.

Presenting a comprehensive picture of what it means to follow in the Jesus way is not possible in a few pages. However, there are some distinctives that characterize this element of the moral velocity suite. A short description of each of them should suffice to convey the element's scope and nature. One distinctive, which may at first seem obvious, is to embrace the complete Jesus. This was addressed earlier in the chapter, but warrants a brief mention here as a distinctive of emulation. Recall how Søren Kierkegaard pointed out Jesus does not desire admirers or adherents, but rather followers. Jesus is the pattern for them to follow, just as one walks in the footsteps left by another. We learned from the apostle John that following in Jesus' footsteps means "as he is so are we in this world."[38] In reading both the Gospel accounts of Jesus' earthly life and the Hebrews account of the current, living, and exalted Jesus, we recognize the full picture of the Jesus who serves as our pattern, and as his faithful ones we embrace not only the picture but the living Jesus of the picture. When the entire Jesus is embraced it becomes clear walking in his footsteps means our conduct is patterned after his, including a basic commitment to implementing justice and righteousness in the society (as we see in the exalted king of Heb 1), as well as a fundamental predisposition

---

36. See Matt 22:34–40.
37. See John 15:9–14.
38. 1 John 4:17 RSV.

toward the poor, outcasts, foreigners, women, children, the powerless, the despised, the contagious, the sinful, the oppressed, and the accused. This was the stance Jesus adopted following the prophetic tradition in which he lived, and the stance he expects of those who fully embrace him.

Another distinctive of emulation is drawn from the bedrock reality of all Jesus was and is: establishment of the kingdom of God. In emulating Jesus the mature apply themselves to the establishment of the kingdom, as did Jesus. That, we learned from John Howard Yoder, entails the promulgation of a new regime in the context in which the faithful find themselves. Unlike that which is typical in secular society, the kingdom regime is effectuated through peaceful means rather than violent, and concentrates on the restructuring of relationships, the changing of societal norms in alignment with the values of the Sermon on the Mount, elevation of the oppressed poor and needy while seeing the demise of the oppressive rich and powerful, and transformation of the dominant mentality to reflect the divine character. For the faithful to emulate Jesus in the establishment of the kingdom means conduct in solidarity with the suffering, as well as continual service of, others. Such is the example left by Jesus as we find it in Hebrews.

Only in Hebrews do we see Jesus in his priestly role. Yet, to qualify experientially for his priesthood Jesus first had to endure the fullness of humanity. It is in his human experience of suffering that Jesus became the pioneer for others; in this we see a third distinctive of emulation as a moral velocity element. During his life much of Jesus' suffering involved resisting temptation, and that to an extent not experienced by any other human. Jesus never succumbed to temptation while all others have, and thus his temptation-related suffering was greater than theirs. It is Jesus' resistance to temptation that the mature are to emulate, and it is the priestly work for which the resistance qualified him that the faithful are to view as their pattern of conduct. The mature align themselves with those who suffer temptation, as did Jesus.

As the priest who is exalted, Jesus administers and serves God's faithful community. This priestly function is something the author of Hebrews called upon the readers to consider,[39] indicating they are to spend their time reflecting on the nature and extent of Jesus' high priesthood. When they do, they realize the parts of that priesthood the faithful are to emulate. Chief among those is Jesus continues to empathize with others in their weakness, just as in his humanity he aligned himself with those who are tempted. His mature followers are to imitate him in empathizing with fellow believers in times of weakness, suffering, and failure. In doing so, they position themselves to function as representatives of others before God while remaining

---

39. See Heb 3:1.

present with them, just as Jesus represents them continually while seated at the right hand of the Majesty in heaven.

The fourth distinctive associated with emulation of Jesus has to do with the making of disciples. This was one of Jesus' fundamental and ongoing tasks during his three-year earthly ministry, and is one of the fundamental responsibilities of the mature. The Twelve (or perhaps Eleven, if Judas Iscariot is discounted), plus many others who accompanied or engaged with Jesus while he was on earth, experienced Jesus' teaching and conduct as a call to become his disciples, which many of them did. Toward the end of his ministry, however—after the resurrection—Jesus' expectation of the mature changed. No longer did he call them to be his disciples; rather he called them to emulate him by becoming disciple-makers. During his last appearance to his followers on resurrection day he gave them a commission: "As the Father has sent me, I am sending you,"[40] and prior to his ascension he reiterated the commission in different words: "All authority in heaven and on earth has been given to me. Therefore go and make disciples of all nations . . ."[41] In Hebrews, we see the exalted Jesus actually functioning in this regard in a way different from his actions on earth: he serves as his followers' priestly advocate, thus helping them in their quest to become and remain disciples. The author, as a result of this conduct of Jesus, encouraged them to faithfulness as they approach God with confidence. Those who are mature emulate Jesus' example of encouraging and helping others to faithfulness.

The last distinctive of those who emulate Jesus—those who follow in the Jesus way—is they follow the way of the cross. Jesus' self-sacrifice was a demonstration of how the mature are to conduct themselves. In Hebrews 12 we find this notion explained in some detail. Jesus, the pioneer and perfecter of faith, committed himself to enduring opposition, shame, and crucifixion, and his faithful followers are to emulate him in that commitment. As was the case with the extreme resistance to temptation Jesus demonstrated, so is the way of the cross to which the mature are called—the most extreme, reviled, and disgraceful humiliation and suffering known in the culture in which Jesus lived. To endurance of this level of disgrace the mature are summoned, in emulation of their Lord.[42] Even if the means to resist such humiliation is available, following in the Jesus way means not employing such means since Jesus did not do so when he had the opportunity.[43]

40. John 20:21.
41. Matt 28:18b–19a.
42. See Heb 13:13.
43. See Matt 26:50b–54, in which Jesus refused both the use of violence by his followers in defending him during his arrest, and employment of the celestial forces that were at his immediate disposal. This conduct was in complete alignment with his

A complete Jesus ethic entails more than emulation, even when coupled with obedience. Those two elements of the suite in which we observe moral velocity cannot alone enable one to develop the skills necessary to distinguish good from evil, although they are essential to such development. Maturity entails living to God as the exalted Jesus now does. That requires the remaining elements of the suite.

Formation

The formation of character is a fundamental enabler of the ability to distinguish good from evil. When considering this element one soon realizes inherent to it is a greater ambiguity and imprecision than occurred with either obedience or emulation. Attempting to answer the question "Which biblical examples or paradigms are to be viewed as authoritative for the formation of character?" is frought with challenges and conflicts, creating a sense of frustration among those seeking clear and precise answers to such questions. Nevertheless, since the complete Jesus picture is foundational to development of a broader Jesus ethic, referring to that picture will reveal solid character content.

Often character is formed within the context of a community—one's social surroundings and the values of the context in which one lives—and thus unless an individual determines to develop a particular sort of character, one's character normally is an outgrowth of the immediate milieu in which one exists. Such does not have to remain the case, however. Character can be altered, for it entails the adoption and habitual enacting of particular values, attitudes, intentions, virtues, commitments, priorities, and the like. This is the intention of the author of Hebrews 5 when describing maturity as the habitual use of developed abilities in order to determine good from evil, and when encouraging the readers to engage actively in the development of such abilities.

Why is character formation so crucial to Christian maturity? The simple answer is most moral choices and actions are driven by character. Rarely is a moral choice the result of fresh consideration of data and the independent application of rational thought to arrive at a decision. Rather, moral choice normally is derived from engrained character, even if one engages in reflection prior to making a moral determination.

In the fourth century BC, Aristotle wrote a structured approach to ethics in the West. In his presentation of character he focused on virtue,

---

teaching in the Sermon on the Mount regarding how enemies are to be treated.

"the state of character which makes a man[44] good and which makes him do his own work well."[45] Critical for Aristotle was the notion that desirable virtues reflect an intermediate commitment between two extremes.[46] Specific virtues of character, then, included courage, between fear and confidence; temperance, between pleasure and pain; liberality, between prodigality and meanness; proper pride, between empty vanity and undue humility; and good temper, between irascibility and inirascibility.[47]

What we find in Aristotle is what we might expect: a tempered mediation that results in a type of character generally condoned by the dominant secular society. Whereas we may endorse at least some of his virtues, the mediating nature of them is something we do not find in the character of Jesus. His character components tend to be anything but reflective of the greater society's values, and his expectation of his faithful followers is they will identify not with their surrounding social context, but with God's community: the kingdom of God.

The primacy of the Sermon on the Mount for moral maturity was something we considered earlier, with the specific understanding that the expectations contained therein are anything but theoretical; rather, they are the way God desires the members of his faithful community to conduct themselves. The Sermon also contains at least some of the character components that are to drive the conduct of the mature. Included in those components are a spiritual attitude of poverty and mournfulness, an intent to be merciful toward others, and a disposition that pursues peace in everything. Yet there also is a prickly component of the character of the mature, one that goads those of the broader society to acknowledge God and render him his due. The internalization of certain parts of the law are included in character formation, such as a gracious attitude toward those with whom one can be justifiably angry, a sense of awe when engaging with God, and seeking the best for one's enemies and abusers. An attitude of generosity—particularly toward those most in need of it—is to be cultivated, the natural tendency to hoard is to be replaced by a desire to be faithful, focusing on the kingdom of God is to be maximized, and a sober assessment of one's self should supplant the urge to criticize others. These are but a few of the character components found in the

---

44. Once again we encounter the use of exclusively male language to describe human beings. Whereas this certainly is unfortunate, perhaps the reader will be gracious enough to disregard the exclusivity and understand the reference is to humanity.

45. Albert et al., *Great Traditions in Ethics*, 50.

46. See Albert et al.: ". . . a master of any art avoids excess and defect, but seeks the intermediate . . . " and "Virtue, then, is a state of character concerned with choice, lying in a mean" (*Great Traditions in Ethics*, 51).

47. Albert et al., *Great Traditions in Ethics*, 52–53.

sermon. Together, they form a picture of one whose values, intentions, attitudes, commitments, and virtues not only are in contradistinction to those of the secular context, but are extreme. As such, they reflect God's radically different regime that characterizes the kingdom of God.

When we come to the picture of Jesus presented in Hebrews we find additional character components the mature are expected to cultivate in order to determine good from evil. These components are seen not only in the humanity of Jesus, but also in the living, exalted Jesus who is the focus of our loyalty and adoration. As such, they hold a place of primacy among the mature.

In the human Jesus of Hebrews we see a number of character components that warrant inculcation by the mature. Chief among them is Jesus' priority of complete identification, oneness, alignment, and solidarity with sinful humanity, to the extent of viewing other humans as part of his family. Those who are made holy and the one who makes them such are co-family members. Jesus' attitude toward sinners-made-holy was to endorse them as his siblings.[48]

We also see in the Hebrews depiction of the human Jesus his intention to sacrifice himself for others, and to suffer more than any other human in order to secure the salvation of humanity. Jesus' self-sacrifice and suffering were not experiences he sought to avoid, even though in the garden he struggled with the temptation to seek an alternative; rather, they were an outgrowth of his character—the intention to give himself for the benefit of others.

In looking at the human Jesus of Hebrews we see a number of other character elements, including the virtue of endurance to the point of suffering intensely, valuing the freeing of others from that which makes them most fearful, and prioritizing the glorification of many of his "sons and daughters."[49]

When viewing the exalted Son pictured in Hebrews, particularly as depicted in the first chapter, we immediately observe an attitude of mutual dependency between the Father and the Son. Each needs the other: the Son for appointment as heir of all things, his calling as high priest, the resurrection, and his exaltation; the Father for conveying his final and supreme revelation to humankind and creating the universe. Independence is not found in the Godhead, but rather mutuality. Such should characterize not only mature individuals, but also the mature community of God's faithful.

At the end of the first chapter of Hebrews we find God's will for the eternally enthroned Son regarding his attitude toward enemies. This attitude both complements and reinforces what was seen in the Sermon on

48. See Heb 2:11–13.
49. See Heb 2:10.

the Mount regarding how enemies are to be treated: loving them and seeking them best. The exalted, enthroned Son is to be passive toward enemies. Rather than take any action against them, he simply is to wait until the Father deals with them. This pacifistic call to the Son, even though he has the ability and right to conduct himself otherwise, is consistent with Jesus' call to his followers at his betrayal not to use force or violence, but to entrust enemies to the Father. That expectation of Jesus' teaching, his example, and the call of the Father to the enthroned One remains an undebatable expectation of the mature who seek to be faithful to God. To the extent that an individual's or community's character fails to internalize this value, it fails to reflect faithfulness to God.

Toward the end of Hebrews, in chapter 12, the author encouraged the readers to fix their eyes on Jesus, then described Jesus' focus on the joy set before him. In his character Jesus had a commitment to joy because of the nature of his future, particularly his future as exalted and seated at the right hand of God's throne. To an extent joy enabled him to endure all the forms of suffering he experienced during his human sojourn, including his torturous death for the benefit of others. Such joy is to be internalized by the mature, following their moral authority—Jesus—for as was the case with Jesus it will enable them to endure the challenges they will face by virtue of living lives of faithfulness.

The priesthood of Jesus in Hebrews yields a number of character elements that should typify the mature. Two, however, stand out. First, in Jesus as our high priest we see a commitment always to live to intercede for others. This is the fundamental priestly commitment of Jesus: he will continue to be an advocate for others for their benefit. This is how he spends his exalted life as priest,[50] and should be a fundamental element of the mature believer's character. We should commit ourselves to living our lives as intercessors and advocates for others.

Second, Jesus as high priest takes on the attitude of a servant, being God's conduit. Similar to being the one through whom God conveyed his final word to humanity, Jesus seeks to be the Father's channel for conveyance of God's desires to his faithful community. As humanity's intercessor and advocate, Jesus, if you will, faces the Father and argues humanity's case; as God's conduit, Jesus faces humanity and presents the Father's desires for the mature and faithful, transmitting without distortion the will of God. In this regard he adopts the stance of the eternal moral authority, standing between the source of morality and individual or corporate moral agents, and is the one through whom the source's expectations are conveyed to the agents. As

---

50. See Heb 7:25; 9:24.

mature followers of Jesus we are to adopt the same attitude as Jesus, seeking to convey to the less mature—without distorting God's final revelation in Jesus or co-opting their freedom as moral agents—God's desires for them.

Response

The final element of the suite through which we observe moral velocity entails encounter with God and the associated moral response. Its focus is on those portions of the Jesus picture that do not lend themselves to the other elements of the suite: obedience, emulation, or formation of character. Recall that as one's thinking progresses through the elements, ambiguity and imprecision increase to the point that articulating the appropriate response of the mature can only be approached through examples or suggestions. An understanding of appropriate responses or standards for response will vary among moral agents, and often is given definition not by the individual but by faith communities, each of whose identity is driven by a common understanding of what it means to respond to encounter with God. Whereas a particular community's internal response may be observed through that community's piety and worship, the challenge we face is to explore how the community—or the individuals that make up the community—should respond as they engage the broader society in which it and they exist.

Throughout Hebrews we see in the author's development of the picture of Jesus many aspects that cannot be aligned with the other elements of the moral velocity suite. When engaging with the human Jesus, for example, we encounter him as the pioneer and forerunner of salvation; God's unique apostle; and the one who made purification for sins by tasting death for all other humans, thus becoming the source of eternal salvation. In none of these aspects can we do what Jesus did or be what he was. However, they should engender from the faithful some type of response, and they most certainly should not be ignored simply because we cannot be like Jesus in these aspects.

Similarly, in Hebrews' picture of the postresurrected, exalted Jesus we find many aspects that are beyond our attainment as sinful humans. Upon encountering them we can only seek to perceive them, then respond in faithfulness. In this regard, for example, Jesus is God's final spoken word which must not be ignored; the heir of all things; the one who is the object of worship; the holy, pure, and blameless one who is set apart from sinners; the one who is faithful over God's entire house, the church; the radiance of God's glory and the exact representation of his being; the administrator who guarantees and mediates the new covenant; and the one seated at the

Father's right hand—the place from where justice and mercy are administered—advocating for the faithful and conveying to them God's desires for their lives. To these aspects of Jesus we can only respond.

There are two other pieces of the Jesus picture that can serve as examples to which appropriate response can perhaps be suggested: Jesus as creator and sustainer of all, and Jesus as the exalted one. These two aspects do not lend themselves to the first three elements of the moral velocity suite, but they are appropriate for the fourth. For these two, then, what may constitute correct moral response by the mature and faithful as they engage in the broader society in which they find themselves?

When we encounter the Exalted Son as the Creator of the universe, a proper response may be first to realize and affirm creation does not simply exist as something into which Jesus entered for a period of time and over which he now reigns. Rather, creation is fundamental to the divine expression, and was enacted by the preincarnate Second Person of the Trinity. Creation was one of God's demonstrations of his moral goodness, and it retains its moral element. Recall during the creation process each successive created element was pronounced "good" by God. The created order, though destined ultimately to perish, is part of the current expression of God's kingdom in the moral realm, and is a declaration of the goodness of God. As such, the created order does not exist for our exploitation or consumption, but rather demands preservation and cultivation by the mature.

In addition to being the universe's creator, the Son also is active sustaining all things. The word translated "sustaining" (*pheron*) includes a basic sense of bearing a burden, or carrying something along. Whereas we can in no way sustain all things—or ultimately anything—we can respond in faithfulness to the sustaining Son by adopting and exercising a sustaining attitude and intention toward all of our engagements in the society, realizing that such action will come at a cost. It will entail a burden that must be borne, just as the exalted Son continues to bear the burden of sustaining all things.

In the second example we encounter the Son as the exalted one. He is the priest-king pictured by Melchizedek, who was simultaneously king of righteousness and king of peace. Administration of righteousness and peace are the two means by which the enthroned Son reigns in justice, which is the scepter of his kingdom. Without them there is no kingdom administration. As Melchizedekian priest—the superior priest over all—he blesses those who come to him, just as Melchizedek blessed Abram, and as the enthroned high priest seated at the right hand of the Majesty he spends himself advocating on their behalf.

We as sinful and extremely limited humans cannot be exalted like the Son, be it king or high priest. Yet we can respond to him by engaging in our society with the same means he uses: righteousness and peace in all of our conduct. Righteousness and peace are not only the ends we seek to achieve when working for the same justice that is the scepter of the Son's reign. They are that, indeed, but they also are the means to be employed. Thus, in responding to the exalted Son we are constrained never to engage either in unrighteous conduct or force and violence. The king of justice demands we respond only with the means he employs—righteousness and peace—thus taking a lesson from the earthly Melchizedek.

Finally, we can respond to the High Priest seated at the Majesty's right hand by adopting a stance of blessing all with whom we come in contact. As an earthly exemplification of the Eternal High Priest, Melchizedek responded by blessing even the greatest he encountered: Abram. We would do well to respond in the same way.

INTEGRATED BROADER JESUS ETHIC

The components of the broader Jesus ethic have been described as individual elements. However, their functioning as a dynamic working ethic—by which we distinguish good from evil and thus live as God's mature and faithful people—exists as an integrated whole. Following is a visual depiction of the integrated broader Jesus ethic.

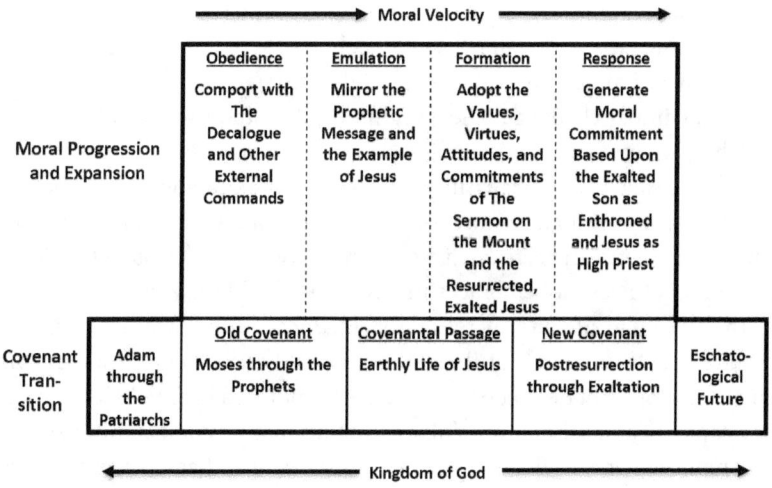

7

Conclusion

EARLY IN HIS REIGN King Solomon recognized God had been kind to his father David, whom he believed to be faithful, righteous, and upright in heart. Solomon, however, viewed himself as immature—even childish—when compared with his father, and bemoaned his inability to follow David in faithfulness. When given the opportunity to receive from God anything he wanted, Solomon chose a discerning heart and the ability to distinguish between right and wrong. In his wisdom he perceived sound moral judgment was fundamental to moving from immaturity to maturity, and essential to living faithful to God's calling. For his choice Solomon received what he requested and much more, including God's commendation.

Our initial challenge when beginning this study was similar to that which Solomon faced: to determine how to move from our current state to one where we become increasingly faithful to God's calling to us as believers. We are not without resources to help in that quest. Early in our investigation we learned the path to that determination travels through the moral realm and of necessity embraces the living, exalted Jesus. Ongoing growth in the Christian life and increasing yieldedness to the lordship of Christ require the daily pursuit of the ability to distinguish good from evil, and entail development of a set of skills that are employed habitually. Successful development and use of those skills—and thus maturity and faithfulness—is accomplished only by living as the living Jesus. Doing that, however, is a significant challenge for each of us. Although none of us will ever completely achieve the goal of Christian maturity, it certainly is possible to make significant progress toward that goal.

Throughout the biblical records of Jesus' earthly life we find repeatedly the simple notion of following Jesus. In reviewing various incidents in Jesus' life—particularly those in which he encouraged others to join with him—his consistent call was "follow me." We see that following in the Jesus way entailed such concrete commitments as denial of self, selling possessions and giving to the poor, listening to the voice of Jesus, adopting an attitude of service, and taking up one's cross daily. All of these are actions that take place in the moral realm of human experience.

The challenge we face is how to respond daily to the call to follow Jesus. We have seen the set of tools outlined in the preceding chapters will help greatly in the quest to acquire and habitually use the skills necessary to distinguish good from evil—a fundamental element of faithfulness to Jesus' call. A broader Jesus ethic, one driven not only by the Gospel accounts of Jesus' earthly life but also the picture of the current, living, exalted Jesus of Hebrews, was formulated as a model of how the skills, when appropriately applied, result in maturity for both the believer and the believing community. Essential to that model is a fundamental commitment to the kingdom of God and its values, realization that we live in the milieu of the new covenant administered by the exalted Jesus rather than the insufficient and receding old covenant that it replaced, an understanding of moral velocity that parallels God's progressive revelation, and maturation through a suite of various forms of ethical expression.

What remains to be done is to highlight some practical learnings that will give us guidance for following in the Jesus way in our time and culture. The first learning may appear obvious, but it bears repeating. Whereas the Gospel picture of Jesus should never be diminished, circumvented, or dismissed, in no way also should it serve as our exclusive understanding of what the Jesus pattern is. As Western Christians we have been socialized to limit our understanding of what it means to follow in the Jesus way to the pattern of Jesus found in the Gospel recordings of his earthly life. Instead, we constantly need to be asking ourselves what the entire Jesus picture looks like, and how it should shape and drive our engagement in the world as Jesus followers. Failure to do so is failure to live as mature followers of our Lord. Our study has focused chiefly upon augmenting the Gospels' depiction of Jesus with that found in the Epistle to the Hebrews, and rightfully so, for in Hebrews we find Jesus pictured in a way significantly different from that found in the Gospels. Whereas in Hebrews we see elements of the humanity of Jesus, the primary picture of Jesus in Hebrews is that of the exalted, living Jesus who reigns and intercedes on our behalf. In Hebrews we find the Eternal One, the Creator and Sustainer of all, and the Enthroned One who rules in perfect justice. We dare not ignore this Jesus if we seek to be his faithful followers.

There are elements of the Jesus picture included in the Pauline corpus, as well as other New Testament letters and Acts, which should be investigated for whatever possible additions they can make to an understanding of the complete Jesus picture. Those have been out of scope of the present study, but warrant investigation. Additionally, the possible inclusion of the Jesus picture in Revelation should be investigated for whatever contributions it can make to a complete understanding of Jesus. Although the focus of Revelation is a period when the temporal is ultimately supplanted by the eternal in the eschaton, and thus also is out of scope of this study, we can all benefit greatly in our time by understanding better the Jesus of the future. The primary learning we must not forget, however, is the complete picture of Jesus is to be fundamental in our thinking.

Second, those who walk in the Jesus way display a strong commitment to—even a predisposition toward—the needy of society. We have learned from the Jesus we studied that the faithful and mature have shifted their attention away from their own interests toward those who are much needier. In Jesus' earthly life he consistently displayed a predisposition toward the weak, the abused, the disenfranchised, those without resources, the rejected, etc. All the poor—both the poor in spirit and the poor in society—were beneficiaries of the special care of Jesus for alleviation of their suffering; conversely those who were the established of society, the powerful, the influential, and the well-connected normally found themselves at odds with Jesus' way and opposing what he did. In Hebrews we see the same predisposition in the current and ongoing ministry of Jesus the Great High Priest. He gave himself for others, he sympathizes with those who are weak and suffering, and he invests himself advocating before the Father for fallen humanity. The conduct, attitude, values, priorities, and responses of those who follow Jesus are to reflect their alignment with the Jesus committed to the needy.

The third learning is the way of Jesus is in conflict with society's way, even while remaining juxtaposed to it. Jesus' way is not an addition to the way of the dominant society, nor is it intended to supplant it any time prior to the eschaton. It is only for those who are God's faithful people. The Jesus way is distinct, yet exists within the society rather than being withdrawn from it. In committing to the Jesus way the mature reject the way of the social environment in which they find themselves. The ethic of the kingdom of God is the ethic of a distinct regime, not one blended with that of the secular society. As such, it is not applicable, nor should any attempt be made to adopt it more broadly, to the surrounding society. The broader Jesus ethic is only for those who are part of the reign of the Exalted Son, not for those who have failed to yield to and accept the Jesus way. Any objection to the Jesus way on the grounds it will not work for all exposes a basic misunderstanding of the intended scope of the Jesus ethic. The notion that the moral expectations of Jesus are irrelevant because they cannot be met by the broad scope of normal humans living in society reflects this misunderstanding, and fails to perceive that the broader Jesus ethic is only intended for a few: God's faithful.

We have seen the great implication of this learning: the attitudes, commitments, values, responses, conduct, and such that Jesus articulated and demonstrated for those who walk in the Jesus way truly are meant to be adopted by them. They are not simply lofty ideals intended only for an ideal society. These expectations are a significant stumbling block for many Christians, yet the faithful are to distinguish themselves from the broader society by living as Jesus lived rather than aligning themselves with it. Chief among Jesus' difficult expectations is that his followers not participate in or contribute to one of society's most prevalent tools for accomplishing its ends—violence. They are not to employ or endorse it as a means to any conceivable end. Particularly when it comes to treatment of violent enemies, as Jesus so aptly modeled even as he was being arrested, enemies are to be treated with love, and prayer is to be offered for them. The commitment of Jesus' followers is to be what is in the best interest of enemies, even their physical healing (as opposed to their physical destruction). The attitude of the mature toward enemies is to emulate that of the Exalted, Reigning Son: simply waiting until the Father subdues them. This conduct, it is sometimes asserted, will not work in the broader society, and thus is rejected by many Christians. Yet, it is not intended as an expectation of any other than those who walk in the Jesus way—those who have adopted the Jesus ethic as opposed to that of their worldly environment, be it local, regional, national, or international. Not only is it intended for them; it is Jesus' nonnegotiable requirement of his followers.

The final learning is that the faithful follower of Jesus must maintain a single loyalty—to Jesus and the values of the kingdom of God—while living in a secular society to which she or he is not to pledge any loyalty. This learning is in direct conflict with a common approach to daily living adopted by many who affirm orthodoxy: living in such a way as to blend what they view as Jesus' expectations with the obligations they incur by virtue of their significant loyalty or allegiance to their secular society, often at the national level. Their effort is focused on the same subject Luther addressed with his doctrine of the two worlds, or what H. Richard Niebuhr outlined in his notion of Christ and culture in paradox. Fundamentally such thinking deals with the two realities of the spiritual world and the secular one, and seeks some sort of synergy between the two, such that the individual can create a settled overall reality in which to live. Some view the two realities as simply existing together, but administered according to two sets of rules, or moral standards. Others see that the two cannot be reconciled, so the believer lives in a constant state of tension between them. Still others adopt a syncretistic approach, seeking to blend the two into one, and in doing so obliterate the distinction of each. The learning from our study, however, is that the Jesus-follower is not permitted to pledge even a secondary loyalty. We see this concept consistently displayed when viewing the complete Jesus picture. It is capsulized in Jesus' teaching in the Sermon on the Mount that nobody can serve two masters, and in Hebrews in such admonitions as "Let us, then, go to him outside the camp, bearing the disgrace he bore" (Heb 13:13). Indeed, the core problem the author of Hebrews addressed was that the readers, who claimed to be followers of Jesus, wanted to retain their socially acceptable Judaism so they would not have to endure the consequences of aligning themselves with Jesus alone. For those who would be faithful and mature, their loyalty must be pledged to only one: the Jesus in whose way they are to follow.

The author of Hebrews went to extraordinary lengths to create a picture of the exalted Jesus as the guidepost for all who would follow faithfully in the Jesus way. That path always leads through the moral realm of human experience. Along the journey the pilgrim is called to distinguish good from evil continually—a challenge that requires constant effort to refine the skills necessary to do so. The quest to live like Jesus, both while he was on earth and as now exalted next to the Majesty in heaven, is the means to that refining work. It is a worthy quest, for in the end it yields maturity. To that end, as the author of Hebrews encouraged, "let us draw near to God with a sincere heart and with the full assurance that faith brings . . . and let us consider how we may spur one another on toward love and good deeds" (Heb 10:22, 24).

Bibliography

Adams, E. M. "The Philosophical Grounds of the Present Crisis of Authority." In *Authority: A Philosophical Analysis*, edited by R. Baine Harris, 3–24. Tuscaloosa: The University of Alabama Press, 1976.
Adelmann, Frederick J., ed. *Authority*. Boston College Studies in Philosophy III. The Hague: Nijhoff, 1974.
Albert, Ethel M., et al. *Great Traditions in Ethics*. New York: American, 1953.
Alexander, J. A. *The Psalms*. Vol. III. 3 vols. Sixth ed. New York: Charles Scribner, 1865.
"Anagogical." *Oxford Reference*. https://www.oxfordreference.com/view/10.1093/oi/authority.20110803095410408.
Bainton, Roland H. *Christendom: A Short History of Christianity and Its Impact on Western Civilization*. Vol. II. 2 vols. New York: Harper & Row, 1966.
Bateman, Herbert W. IV. *Charts on the Book of Hebrews*. Grand Rapids: Kregel, 2012.
Bauer, Walter. *A Greek-English Lexicon of the New Testament and Other Early Christian Literature*. Fourth revised and augmented edition. Translated and edited by William F. Arendt and F. Wilbur Gingrich. Chicago: The University of Chicago Press, 1974.
Beach, Waldo, and H. Richard Niebuhr, eds. *Christian Ethics: Sources of the Living Tradition*. New York: Ronald, 1955.
Berkhof, Louis. *Systematic Theology*. 4th ed. Grand Rapids: Eerdmans, 1974.
Bertolet, Tim. "Knowing Jesus: The Portrait of Jesus in Hebrews." http://www.alliancenet.org/placefortruth/column/theology-on-the-go/knowing-jesus-the-portrait-of-jesus-in-hebrews.
Birch, Bruce C. "Scripture in Ethics: Methodological Issues." In *Dictionary of Scripture and Ethics*, edited by Joel B. Green et al., 27–34. Grand Rapids: Baker Academic, 2011.
Birch, Bruce C., and Larry L. Rasmussen. *Bible and Ethics in the Christian Life*. Minneapolis: Augsburg, 1976.
Bloesch, Donald G. "The Primacy of Scripture." In *The Authoritative Word: Essays on The Nature of Scripture*, edited by Donald K. McKim, 117–53. Grand Rapids: Eerdmans, 1983.
Bonhoeffer, Dietrich. *Ethics*. Translated by Neville Horton Smith. New York: Touchstone, 1995.

Boulton, Wayne G., et al., eds. *From Christ to the World: Introductory Readings in Christian Ethics*. Grand Rapids: Eerdmans, 1994.

Bretall, Robert, ed. *A Kierkegaard Anthology*. New York: Random House, 1946.

Bretzke, James T. "Using Scripture in Ethics: Some Methodological Considerations in Light of Fundamental Values and Root Paradigms." Last update: February 16, 2016. https://www2.bc.edu/james-bretzke/UsingScriptureInEthics.pdf.

Brock, Brian, *Singing the Ethos of God: On the Place of Christian Ethics in Scripture*. Grand Rapids: Eerdmans, 2007.

Brown, Raymond. *The Message of Hebrews*. Edited by J. A. Motyer and John R. W. Stott. The Bible Speaks Today series. Downers Grove, IL: InterVarsity, 1988.

Bruce, Alexander Balmain. *The Epistle to the Hebrews: The First Apology for Christianity: An Exegetical Study*. New York: Charles Scribner's Sons, 1899.

Bruce, F. F., ed. *The Epistle to the Hebrews*. The New International Commentary on the New Testament. Grand Rapids: Eerdmans, 1964.

Carnell, Edward John. *An Introduction to Christian Apologetics*. Grand Rapids: Eerdmans, 1966.

———. "Is Drunkenness a Sin?" *United Evangelical Action* 7.2 (March 1, 1948) 6, 8.

———. *The Theology of Reinhold Niebuhr*. Revised Edition. Grand Rapids: Eerdmans, 1960.

Claiborne, Shane (@ShaneClaiborne). "BREAKING NEWS: @JerryFalwellJr has denounced Jesus: 'I don't look to the teachings of Jesus for what my political beliefs should be.' Every pro-Trump Christian has the nagging problem of Jesus to deal with." Twitter, November 6, 2018, 1:07 a.m. https://twitter.com/ShaneClaiborne/status/1059733910299435009.

Clark, Gordon H., "Ethics, History Of." In *Baker's Dictionary of Christian Ethics*, edited by Carl F. H. Henry, 220–21. Grand Rapids: Baker, 1973.

Clark, Gordon H., and T. V. Smith, eds. *Readings in Ethics*. New York: Crofts, 1931.

Cosgrove, Charles H. "Scripture in Ethics: A History." In *Dictionary of Scripture and Ethics*, edited by Joel B. Green et al., 13–25. Grand Rapids: Baker Academic, 2011.

Croatto, J. Severino. *Biblical Hermeneutics: Toward a Theory of Reading as the Production of Meaning*. Translated by Robert R. Barr. Maryknoll, NY: Orbis, 1987.

Crowe, Brandon D. "Our Great High Priest." *Credo Magazine* 6.2 (July 2016) 16–21.

Culpepper, Robert H. "The High Priesthood and Sacrifice of Christ in the Epistle to the Hebrews." *The Theological Educator* 32 (1985) 46–62.

De George, Richard T. "Authority and Morality." In *Authority*, edited by Frederick J. Adelmann, 31–49. The Hague: Nijhoff, 1974.

———. "The Nature and Function of Epistemic Authority." In *Authority: A Philosophical Analysis*, edited by R. Baine Harris, 76–93. Tuscaloosa: The University of Alabama Press, 1976.

Demarest, Bruce. *A History of Interpretation of Hebrews 7,1–10 from the Reformation to the Present*. Tübingen: Mohr, 1976.

Dods, Marcus. *The Epistle to the Hebrews*. In *The Expositor's Greek Testament*., vol. IV, edited by W. Robertson Nicoll, 219–381. 5 vols. Grand Rapids: Eerdmans, 1956.

Encyclopedia Britannica Editors. "Hermeneutics." *Britannica Academic*. https://academic-eb-com.eres.qnl.qa/levels/collegiate/article/hermeneutics/40159.

Foord, Marty. "The Real Meaning of Sola Scriptura." *The Gospel Coalition Australia Edition*, August 25, 2017. https://au.thegospelcoalition.org/article/the-real-meaning-of-sola-scriptura/.

Frankena, William K. *Ethics*. 2nd ed. Englewood Cliffs, NJ: Prentice-Hall, 1973.
Friesen, LeRoy. "Issues in Christian Ethics Methodology: A Bibliographic Essay." *Direction* 9.2 (April 1980) 32–37.
Gansky, Alton. *40 Days: Encountering Jesus Between the Resurrection and Ascension*. Nashville: B&H, 2007.
Graham, Chris. *Mind the 40-Day Gap of the Resurrection*. San Bernardino, CA: CreateSpace, 2014.
Green, Joel B. "Introduction." In *Dictionary of Scripture and Ethics*, edited by Joel B. Green et al., 1–3. Grand Rapids: Baker Academic, 2011.
Grenz, Stanley J. *The Moral Quest: Foundations of Christian Ethics*. Downers Grove, IL: InterVarsity, 1997.
Gustafson, James M. *Christ and the Moral Life*. New York: Harper & Row, 1968.
———. *Moral Discernment in the Christian Life: Essays in Theological Ethics*. Edited by Theo A. Boer and Paul E. Capetz. Louisville: Westminster John Knox, 2007.
———. "The Place of Scripture in Christian Ethics: A Methodological Study." In *Theology and Christian Ethics*, by James M. Gustafson, 121–45. Philadelphia: United Church, 1974.
———. *Theology and Christian Ethics*. Philadelphia: United Church, 1974.
Hagner, Donald A. *Encountering the Book of Hebrews*. Edited by Walter A. Elwell and Eugene H. Merrill. Encountering Biblical Studies. Grand Rapids: Baker Academic, 2002.
Harvill, Jerry. "Focus on Jesus: The Letter to the Hebrews." http://www.domcentral.org/library/spir2day/853745harvill.html.
Hays, Richard B. *The Moral Vision of the New Testament: Community, Cross, New Creation: A Contemporary Introduction to New Testament Ethics*. New York: Harper Collins, 1996.
Higgins, Angus J. B. "Priest and Messiah." *Vetus Testamentum* 3.4 (Oct. 1953) 321–36.
Houlden, James L. *Ethics and the New Testament*. New York: Oxford University Press, 1977.
Jenkins, Iredell. "Authority: Its Nature and Locus." In *Authority: A Philosophical Analysis*, edited by R. Baine Harris, 25–44. Tuscaloosa: The University of Alabama Press, 1976.
Johnstone, Robert. *Lectures Exegetical and Practical on the Epistle of James*. New York: Randolph, 1871.
Keil, Carl F. and Franz Delitzsch. *Commentary on the Old Testament*. 10 vols. Translated by Francis Bolton et al. Grand Rapids: Eerdmans, 1975.
Kierkegaard, Søren. *Attack upon Christendom*. Translated by Walter Lowrie. Princeton: Princeton University Press, 1946.
———. *Concluding Unscientific Postscript*. Translated by David F. Swenson. Princeton: Princeton University Press, 1974.
———. *For Self-Examination and Judge for Yourselves! And Three Discourses 1851*. Translated by Walter Lowrie. Princeton: Princeton University Press, 1968.
———. *Training in Christianity*. Translated by Walter Lowrie. New York: Vintage, 2004.
King, Martin Luther, Jr. "The Humanity and Divinity of Jesus." https://kinginstitute.stanford.edu/king-papers/documents/humanity-and-divinity-jesus.
———. "The Theology of Reinhold Niebuhr." https://kinginstitute.stanford.edu/king-papers/documents/theology-reinhold-niebuhr-0.

Lane, William L. *Hebrews: A Call to Commitment*. Vancouver: Regent College Press, 2004.

Long, Thomas G. *Hebrews*. Louisville: John Knox, 1997.

Lünemann, Göttlieb. "Commentary on the Epistle to the Hebrews." In *Critical and Exegetical Hand-Book to the Epistles to Timothy and Titus, and to the Epistle to the Hebrews*, vol. 9 of *Meyer's Critical and Exegetical Handbook to the New Testament*, translated from the fourth edition of the German by Maurice J. Evans, 327–748. 11 vols. New York: Funk & Wagnals, 1885.

MacIntyre, Alasdair. *A Short History of Ethics*. New York: Macmillan, 1976.

Maclaren, Alexander. *After the Resurrection*. Grand Rapids: Kregel, 1992.

Mackintosh, Hugh R. *The Doctrine of the Person of Jesus Christ*. Edinburgh: T. & T. Clark, 1913.

Magnuson, Norris. *Salvation in the Slums: Evangelical Social Work, 1865–1920*. Metuchen, NJ: Scarecrow, 1977.

Manetsch, Scott M. "John Calvin's Doctrine of the Christian Life." *Journal of the Evangelical Theological Society* 61.2 (2018) 259–73.

Mathison, Keith A. *The Shape of Sola Scriptura*. Moscow: Canon, 2001.

McClendon, James Wm., Jr. *Ethics: Systematic Theology, Vol. 1*. 3 vols. Nashville: Abingdon, 1991.

McKenny, Gerald. "The Rich Young Ruler and Christian Ethics: A Proposal." *Journal of the Society of Christian Ethics* 40.1 (Spring/Summer 2020) 59–76.

McKim, Donald K., ed. *The Authoritative Word: Essays on The Nature of Scripture*. Grand Rapids: Eerdmans, 1983.

McMahon, C. Matthew. "The Doctrine of Sola Scriptura in a Nutshell." http://www.apuritansmind.com/creeds-and-confessions/the-doctrine-of-sola-scriptura-in-a-nutshell-by-dr-c-matthew-mcmahon/.

Mealand, David. "The Christology of the Epistle to the Hebrews." *The Modern Churchman* 22 (1979) 184.

Meeks, Wayne A. *The Moral World of the First Christians*. Philadelphia: Westminster, 1986.

Mickelsen, A. Berkeley. *Interpreting the Bible*. Grand Rapids: Eerdmans, 1963.

Mitchell, Alan C. *Hebrews*. Sacra Pagina Series 13. Collegeville: Liturgical, 2009.

Mitchell, Elizabeth. "The Sequence of Christ's Post-Resurrection Appearances." *Answering Genesis*, March 21, 2012. https://answersingenesis.org/jesus-christ/resurrection/the-sequence-of-christs-post-resurrection-appearances/.

Moffatt, James. *A Critical and Exegetical Commentary on the Epistle to the Hebrews: The International Critical Commentary*. Edited by Charles Augustus Briggs et al. Edinburgh: T. & T. Clark, 1968.

Montefiore, Hugh. *A Commentary on the Epistle to the Hebrews*. New York: Harper & Row, 1964.

Moore, T. V. *The Last Days of Jesus; or, The Appearances of Our Lord During the Forty Days Between the Resurrection and Ascension*. Philadelphia: Presbyterian Board of Publication, 1858.

Mott, Stephen Charles. *Biblical Ethics and Social Change*. New York: Oxford University Press, 1982.

Mouw, Richard J. *The God Who Commands*. Notre Dame: University of Notre Dame Press, 1990.

Niebuhr, H. Richard. *Christ and Culture*. New York: Harper & Row, 1951.

Niebuhr, Reinhold. *An Interpretation of Christian Ethics*. New York: Harper & Brothers, 1935.

———. "Interpretation of Christian Ethics." https://spiritual-minds.com/religion/philosophy/Niebuhr,%20Reinhold%20-%20Interpretation%20Of%20Christian%20Ethics%20(Philosophy,%20Theology)%20(Christian%20Library).pdf.

Nygren, Anders. "Luther's Doctrine of the Two Kingdoms." *Journal of Lutheran Ethics* 2.8 (August 1, 2002). https://www.elca.org/jle/articles/931.

O'Neil, Michael, "On Hermeneutics and Ethics." *Theology and Church*, March 17, 2017. https://theologyandchurch.com/2017/03/17/on-hermeneutics-and-ethics/.

Parsons, Mikeal C. "Son and High Priest: A Study in the Christology of Hebrews." *Evangelical Quarterly* 60 (1988) 195–216.

Ramm, Bernard. *Protestant Biblical Interpretation: A Textbook of Hermeneutics*. Third Revised Edition. Grand Rapids: Baker, 1970.

Sanders, Jack T. *Ethics in the New Testament*. Philadelphia: Fortress, 1975.

Siker, Jeffrey S. *Scripture and Ethics: Twentieth-Century Portraits*. New York: Oxford University Press, 1997.

Smith, Barry D. "Jesus as High Priest in the Letter to the Hebrews." *Religious Studies 1023: The New Testament and its Context*. Atlantic Baptist University, October 24, 2011.

Smith, Timothy L. *Revivalism and Social Reform*. New York: Harper & Row, 1965.

Spencer, Bonnell. *They Saw the Lord*. New York: Morehouse-Gorham, 1947.

Spurgeon, Charles Haddon. *Sermons of the Rev. C. H. Spurgeon, of London*. New York: Sheldon, Blakeman, 1857.

———. *The Treasury of David*. Vol. 5. 7 vols. New York: Funk & Wagnals, 1882.

Stassen, Glen H. *A Thicker Jesus: Incarnational Discipleship in a Secular Age*. Louisville: Westminster John Knox, 2012.

Stassen, Glen H., and David P. Gushee. *Kingdom Ethics: Following Jesus in Contemporary Context*. Downers Grove, IL: InterVarsity, 2003.

Strong, Augustus Hopkins. *Systematic Theology*. Valley Forge, PA: Judson, 1974.

Surburg, Raymond F. "The Presuppositions of the Historical-Grammatical Method as Employed by Historic Lutheranism." *The Springfielder* 38.4 (October 1974) 278–88.

Talmage, T. DeWitt. *Social Dynamite; or The Wickedness of Modern Society*. Chicago: Standard, 1888.

Tambasco, Anthony J. *The Bible for Ethics*. Washington, DC: University Press of America, 1981.

Telford, William. *The Theology of the Gospel of Mark*. Cambridge: Cambridge University Press, 1999.

Terry, Milton S. *Biblical Hermeneutics: A Treatise on the Interpretation of the Old and New Testaments*. New York: Eaton and Mains, 1890.

Theological Dictionary of the New Testament. 10 vols. Edited by Gerhard Kittle and Gerhard Friedrich. Translated by Geoffrey W. Bromiley. Grand Rapids: Eerdmans, 1964–76.

Theology of Work Project. "The Character Approach." https://www.theologyofwork.org/key-topics/ethics/systematic-presentation-of-ethics/different-approaches-to-ethics/the-character-approach.

Thiessen, Henry Clarence. *Introductory Lectures in Systematic Theology*. Grand Rapids: Eerdmans, 1975.

Trench, Richard C. *Synonyms of the New Testament*. 9th ed. Grand Rapids: Eerdmans, 1975.

Tufts, J. H. "Authority in Ethics." Review of *History of Ethics Within Organized Christianity*, by Thomas Cuming Hall. *The American Journal of Theology* 15 (Jan. 1911) 148–51.

Velasquez, Manuel, et al. "What Is Ethics?" *Markkula Center for Applied Ethics at Santa Clara University*. Jan. 1, 2010. https://www.scu.edu/ethics/ethics-resources/ethical-decision-making/what-is-ethics/.

Verhey, Allen. *Remembering Jesus: Christian Community, Scripture, and the Moral Life*. Grand Rapids: Eerdmans, 2002.

Wild, John. "Authority." In *Authority*, edited by Frederick J. Adelmann, 7–23. The Hague, Netherlands: Martinus Nijhoff, 1974.

Wilson, Andrew. "All God's Laws Are Equal. Are Some More Equal Than Others?" *Christianity Today*, November 22, 2019. https://christianitytoday.com/ct/2019/december/greatest-commandment-gods-laws-equal-jesus.html.

Wilson-Hartgrove, Jonathan (@wilsonhartgrove). "So, about these Religious Right spokesmen who claim to speak for Christians every election. They seem bothered by Jesus & the Bible. Here's Jerry Falwell, Jr., speaking to the @nytimes. 'I don't look to the teachings of Jesus for what my political beliefs should be.'" Twitter, November 5, 2018, 5:40 p.m. https://twitter.com/wilsonhartgrove/status/1059621636079566848.

Wogaman, J. Philip. *Christian Ethics: A Historical Introduction*. Louisville: Westminster/John Knox, 1993.

Yoder, John Howard. *The Politics of Jesus*. Grand Rapids: Eerdmans, 1972.

———. *The Priestly Kingdom*. Notre Dame: University of Notre Dame Press, 1984.

www.ingramcontent.com/pod-product-compliance
Lightning Source LLC
Chambersburg PA
CBHW070317230426
43663CB00011B/2168